VIETNAM:
A MARINE'S CHRONICLE
OF CHANGE

A Marine's Challenges From Boot
Camp to "In Country" Leadership of a
Combined Action Platoon.

Byron A. Mezick

This book is dedicated to Marines
who died, to wounded Marines,
and to those Marines who fought battles
recorded and unrecorded by history.

CONTENTS

PREFACE

This series of narratives from the 1960s provides a personal and dynamic description detailing experiences that were catalysts for change. Living a Marine's life from boot camp to combat, I discover the fundamental concepts of fear, courage, violence, compassion, sex, and death. My belief in a creator brings me to the edge of my comprehension, where knowledge stops and faith begins as I face my imminent death. These stories expose the hardwired evolutionary survival instinct: "Better him than me," and how uncomfortable that reality is. The components of combat leadership will emerge as each story unfolds.

These experiences happened many years ago, but quite frankly, when they surface, it's as though they occurred yesterday or just moments ago. No, you don't forget transitional events seared into your brain. Inevitably these stories surface, and sometimes, I have shared them. For most of my life after Vietnam, I would be embarrassed to reveal such intimate details. The stories I told were true; however, the raw reality they exposed often caused others to see me as someone different, not normal. Now, I need to share my experiences with everyone. Let the judgment of my actions, failures, and successes fall where it may!

I set the ground rules by declaring that these vignettes of change are not fiction; they are, without embellishment, accurate to the author's memory. Most of the names used for people in the stories are not their proper names. The experiences that created lifelong change within a young Marine in combat are at times harsh and politically incorrect by today's standards of appropriate language and conduct. However, the words selected were not chosen to amplify, only to reveal the unfiltered experience. "Vietnam. A Marine's Chronicle of Change" is unedited by those who desire to rewrite history.

With that caution, let us begin.

INTRODUCTION

Located on Tam Hai Island, off the coast of Chu Lai, Vietnam, is the command post for Bravo Company, First Battalion Fourth Marines[1]. Sitting at a desk within a squad-size tent, Captain Wentworth, the company commander, addresses two Marines standing at attention facing him. One is a corporal, E-4, that would be me. The other, a lance corporal, E-3. We are both asked to chronicle a series of events that happened during a night ambush. Throughout the entire inquiry, each of our statements contradicts the other. That's right, the two recollections of the same event are vastly different. The lance corporal standing next to me is dismissed before Captain Wentworth, looking at me with an expression of disgust and anger, begins to speak. "After reviewing the entire situation, I conclude that you are a liar, that you are immature and incompetent. I will not allow you to kill my Marines with your obvious lack of leadership ability. The legal limits of punishment I have as your company commander are insufficient. I am referring you to the battalion commander requesting that the colonel recommend you court-martial proceedings. There under the Uniform Code of Military Justice's decree, lies the legal authority to punish you properly by reducing your rank and confining you in a brig; because that's where you belong, not here leading my Marines. You disgust me, leave, move, get out of my sight. I can't stand to look at you any longer."

After being verbally assaulted and humiliated by Bravo Company's captain, I walk out of the command post extremely dejected. Realizing that I am in

---

[1] **Bravo Company, First Battalion, Fourth Marines translates to**: B Company of the First Battalion of the Fourth Marine Regiment.

U.S Marine unit organization 1966: Fire team = 3 Marines + fire team leader = 4 Marines, **Squad** = 3 fire teams + squad leader = 13 Marines, **Platoon** = 3 squads + platoon leadership = 42 Marines + one Navy Corpsman = 43 total, **Company** = 3 platoons = 126 Marines + 3 Navy Corpsman + weapons attachments = on average 150 members, **Battalion** = 3 companies + attachments = on average 730 Marines and Corpsman, **Regiment** = 3 Battalions + attachments on average 2,187 Marines and Corpsman, **Division** = 3 regiments + attachments = on average 6,561 Marines and Corpsman.

severe trouble and the penalty I am soon to receive will negatively affect my wife, who expects to deliver our first child in February. I realize that I am on the path of failure, a man not deserving to be a husband, father, or hold corporal rank in the U.S. Marine Corps. Leaving the company headquarters, I feel ashamed and discouraged. I don't grow up at that moment. I am "jerked up" into the reality of who I am. Oddly, there is another strong emotion, one of self-esteem. I am proud of my decision to stick to my lies and not incriminate the other Marines who have all agreed to the same lies.

When you step on your character, you are going down a slippery slope of internal ruin. I stood up for the untruthful description of the events that we as a group had agreed to provide as our collective statement of the incident under investigation. I am not declaring we made a correct decision by deciding to lie. However, I am defending my personal decision to stick with the lies. I took it on the chin. After Captain Wentworth's investigation, I alone am held responsible for everyone's conduct, the only Marine to receive official punishment. Why, because I was in charge. The Marine Corps is exceptionally critical of leaders who don't lead, and I am guilty of that charge.

Adding to my difficulties, I am alone, without friends; I had just arrived. I enjoyed lasting friendships while previously stationed at Camp Lejeune, North Carolina, with men I served with in the Caribbean, Europe, and later in our first combat in the Dominican Republic. We were like a family sharing a bond. Not now. I am totally by myself under investigation in a combat zone. I had been declared disgraceful by the company commander. The Marine Corps has a word for those of us who are in limbo between levels of military judicial proceedings. The expression is "Shit Bird." A shit bird is not to be tolerated, respected, or accepted. A shit bird is just that, a shit bird. He won't be here long; leave him alone.

Since June of 1965, at the age of nineteen, I was thrust into a series of events that would forever change my life. I had gotten my girlfriend pregnant, necessitating an immediate marriage. Diana's mother and father were acutely dissatisfied with her choice of me as a husband, realizing that I would be the father of their first grandchild. Their daughter was marrying a Marine, which was disappointing to them, even more so when they discovered that I didn't have a college education. Returning to my duty station in North Carolina, I am presented with transfer orders to Vietnam. My orders assign me to a combat seasoned line company stationed on an island off the coast of Chu Lai, Vietnam. Within the first two weeks of my arrival, I led an ambush so poorly that my company commander recommended me for a court-martial.

VIETNAM: A MARINE'S CHRONICLE OF CHANGE

CHAPTER ONE

BOOT CAMP

"Hey Man, Pass Me the Bread"

August 25, 1963, midafternoon, a passenger train gently pulls away from the Philadelphia train station. Young men fill one of its carriage cars with their noses pressed against the windows, taking a brief last look at parents and girlfriends before departing for Marine Corps Recruit Depot Parris Island, South Carolina. My girlfriend and one of my sisters are slowly waving goodbye, visually saddened by my departure. A middle-aged woman stands next to them, vigorously waving with an unmistakable expression of delight. Someone asked, "Whose mom is that"? I answer the stranger's question, "That's my mom." He jokingly replies, "Man, you must be an asshole."

If it weren't for my mother and her influence, I never would have graduated from high school. The woman with the big smile vigorously waving me goodbye has accomplished a mission. She has climbed a mountain. Somehow, she has gotten me to graduate from Eddystone High School even after being suspended four times in my senior year. One month after my eighteenth birthday, I am on my way to Parris Island to become a United States Marine. She hopes the Corps will bring me under control because no one else can.

At this point in my life, I am arrogant, resentful of authority, and without direction. Once, in the summer before I left for the Marine Corps, I was gone for three days returning home with a black eye and one shoe. I didn't remember who hit me or where my shoe was. After I left the neighborhood to attend boot camp at Parris Island, South Carolina, the group I had been partying with crashed a car, resulting in the death of three girls.

So, how did I decide to join the Marine Corps? Can I claim that I was a patriotic young man desiring to defend his country in time of war?

Bullshit, I never read the paper or listened to the news. I'm sure I heard of the Vietnam War, but I didn't concern myself with it. I didn't care about anything other than the immediate moment, a "Space Cadet." At the age of seventeen, I was living a high-risk lifestyle.

After discovering that a friend of mine, who was going steady with my girlfriend's sister, had enlisted in the Marine Corps, I joined. Everyone thought he was "The man"; they were proud of him. I went to the recruiter's office in Chester, Pennsylvania, and told the Marine who seemed to be in charge that I wanted to join the Marine Corps. He replied, "We have a six-month reserve, a two-year reserve, and a three and a four-year regular enlistment. Which would you prefer"? I asked, "What did Frank signup for"? He said, "Frank is a four-year regular." I immediately responded, "Give me one of those like Frank has."

That's how I made one of the most important decisions of my entire life. No research, no special requests, nothing except, "Give me one of those like Frank has." When I told my parents of my decision to join the Marine Corps, my stepfather spoke first, "Boy, you need to think this over because you are going to a place that will have total power over you. Are you sure you understand what you are doing"? Eventually, my mother signed the documents that allowed her underage son to join the Marine Corps.

The enlistment program I selected allowed me to join the Corps one hundred and twenty days before leaving for boot camp. I did volunteer but wasn't motivated by anything other than the need to do something. College was never a consideration. However, I did like the idea that maybe I could become a machine gunner; how cool would that be? During the hundred and twenty days, before I would leave town, I got into one problem after another with the local police and then with a judge in Chester, Pennsylvania, who intended to put me in jail. Trust me; I had no idea what I had gotten myself into by joining the Marine Corps. A collision between my irresponsible lifestyle and the rigid discipline I was about to experience soon thrust me into a whirlwind of transition.

Just before our group of recruits leaves Philadelphia Naval Station, one of us, a tall, slender, black fellow, is put in charge of our entire group.

Our only travel restrictions are not to enter the ladies' room or the club car. The man in charge is to report all violations of these rules. Three of us, Hank, Sonny, and I, who all have joined the Marine Corps on the Buddy Program[2], go to our assigned sleeping berths and put away our travel bags before heading straight to the club car.

We are on our second beer when in comes the fellow who is in charge. He walks directly to our table and says, "You guys got any room"? After grinning from ear to ear, I answer, "Hell yeah, sit down." We immediately buy him a beer and ask, "Dude, aren't you in charge of proper conduct"? He says, "No, man, I am not in charge. I was supposed to be out of Philly two weeks ago, but they gave me a checkup and discovered that I had the clap when I reported. So, after two weeks of antibiotics, I'm all fixed up, clean as a whistle. They decided to play a game by saying I was in charge. I don't give a shit what you guys do."

That's when the party starts. Everyone drinks and laughs, and soon we have a beer bust attended by every recruit on the train. No one eats dinner. We order one beer after another. When Hank, Sonny, and I finally leave the club car, we stagger back to what we think are our sleeping quarters. We abruptly enter a berth occupied by three nuns. How do we know they are nuns? Their habits hang from an overhead rod, and they are quite embarrassed to be seen out of them. We profusely apologize and leave immediately. They don't make a fuss, and after finding our assigned quarters, we fall into our beds. I do remember a sense of excitement; something powerful is about to happen. I can remember feeling the train swaying back and forth and the sound of its wheels rolling on the tracks below us.

When the conductor wakes us in the morning, he suggests that we dress quickly because the next stop is ours. Twenty minutes later, the train pulls away, leaving us recruits gathered by the railroad tracks. Immediately, a Marine sergeant approaches us. He looks like a polished tree trunk in

---

[2] The **buddy program** is designed so that people who enlist in the Marine Corps together from the same area can get sent to recruit training at the same time and be in the same platoon. DVIDS - News - Buddy Program Ships Childhood Friends (dvidshub.net)

a perfectly tailored uniform with close-trimmed hair. He addresses us by saying, "There is no reason for any of you to remember me unless you don't follow my instructions."

Breakfast is provided at a small café directly across the street from the train station. The place has a charm to it and serves up perfect bacon and eggs. Finishing our meal, we board a bus that transports us to Parris Island. The sergeant shouts instructions, "Get on the bus, sit two by two, and remain silent." He goes on to say that the bus driver will report anyone who speaks or smokes. After the bus pulls away from the grumpy sergeant, everyone begins to whisper to those around them. Most of us light up cigarettes after noticing that our bus driver doesn't seem to care what we do. Unbeknown to us, that will be our last opportunity to smoke - we were all about to quit tobacco products, like it or not.

We enter Parris Island confines via a causeway leading to a checkpoint guarded by a Marine dressed in an impeccably crisp uniform. His stern expression seems to say; this is your last chance to turn around. I sit very still, hoping the driver will not report me for talking or smoking. The bus progresses deep into the Island's interior before pulling over next to a wooden building. We sit quietly as a Marine enters the bus. His presence is perfect. Not a bulge of fat protrudes anywhere from his tight-fitting meticulous uniform. However, his face has a scar that starts on his left cheek, progressing across both lips to his chin. He walks to the back of the bus like he owns it and starts shouting. "Get off, get off this God damn bus! Get off, move, get off my bus, you slimly shits, get off." Man, he gets us fired up. We are tripping over each other, trying to get away from the crazy man. That's where the loud screaming starts and continues for the next thirteen weeks.

Entering the receiving room, we sit at desks aligned in single file, the same kind we used in high school. Next, they empty our travel bags, our wallets, and our pockets. They declare ninety-nine percent of our possessions illegal before throwing our treasures into a giant garbage bag. Any medication, even an aspirin, is forbidden. They closely watch as we dump the contents of our wallets. We can only keep two photos, our driver's licenses, and our folding money. They have us empty our pockets and throw away most everything we produce. Prohibited from speaking, we sit and sit for hours. Each time they talk, they scream memorized instructions and insults. We continue to sit without any explanation of what will occur next. Eventually, it becomes apparent that we are waiting for other recruits to arrive and fill a recruit platoon's ranks.

August in South Carolina is much hotter than I expect. We are told from this moment on; we will drink, shit, and piss as a unit. Everything will be done as a team, no individual anything. I am beginning to feel the impact of forced change, and I don't care for it. What? I can't pee, I can't defecate or get a drink of water without doing it with everyone else? Oh my God, this place sucks. They feed us, but I can't remember what I ate or where I ate it. I do remember going to bed that night. After the lights go out, it is pleasant to be away from the stress of constant supervision. However, accustomed to smoking two packs of Lucky Strikes a day, I need a cigarette.

Finally, the waiting is over, and boot training is about to begin. After assembling outside the receiving center, we form four columns by standing on top of spray-painted images of feet. Three drill instructors who look like tin soldiers wearing funny hats begin screaming instructions at us. These men look physically fit, wearing starched utilities and shined boots. Starting with the recruit at the front of the first column, they tell us to "Count Off." With some coaching, we began to count. Each man shouts out a number that adds one to the number shouted by the man in front of him. One of the drill instructors asks each recruit the number he called and writes it on a small piece of paper. When asked to report my number, I tell the drill instructor, "I'm not sure, but I think it its forty-something." Oh my god, that answer pisses him off. "Forty-something, you don't know. Do you remember where your pecker is, shit for brains"? He is in my face shrieking at me. I am not enjoying this; I decide I want to leave Parris Island and go home. I feel confident they will soon ask who among us wants to leave their Island? I intend to be the very first to step forward.

They order us to "Come to attention." I have no idea how to "Come to attention." They are screaming something about turning right. I think they say, "Right face." But they don't speak the last word; they don't say face. They belt out, "Right, Augh." Whatever the Hell that means. Then they scream, "Forward Augh." When everyone moves, it becomes evident we are to start walking. While we walk, one of the drill instructors makes these funny sounds. I think he is trying to say left, right, left, right. We later learn that when they say left or, as he pronounced it, "Lelp," your left heel should be striking the ground. He doesn't give us any instructions. He sounds like a wounded animal - "Lelp, Lelp, Wight, Lelp - One Top Pre, Pre-Piddle Lelp, Lelp Wight Lelp." What the Hell. I don't understand these words. I am now beyond not having a good time.

We arrive at a building called the processing center. I think of it as a human assembly line. Here, the U.S. Marine Corps creates a sequence of events designed to remove your entire personality. First, we enter a barbershop with lots of chairs. The so-called barber asks, "Do you have any moles on the top of your head"? I reply, "Not that I know about." Within one minute, all my hair is on the floor. Next, we enter a postal room where we remove every bit of our clothes, insert them in a box, and mail them to our families. Then we march to a shower in the nude and experience a lukewarm wash, fifteen or twenty of us at a time. A doctor then thoroughly inspects our bodies, especially our armpits, testicles, and butts. Next, he instructs us to pull back on our penis as he looks for signs of venereal disease. We are then sent to another room and issued utility uniforms, white boxer shorts, and T-shirts. Each recruit receives a hat, now called a cover, and a "Chrome Dome," the inside headliner of a metal helmet. None of the clothes fit well; think baggy. The only thing they measure is our feet. They want to be sure our boots and socks fit correctly.

We all look the same after having our hair cut and dressed in our new baggy wrinkled clothes. Our identities, previously determined by hairstyle and dress, have disappeared. We are not crisp and sharp like the drill instructors; we are wrinkled. But our boots fit.

Unaccustomed to being screamed at, the boot camp experience is becoming increasingly irritating. I can't wait to tell them that I don't want to stay.

The whole Marine Corps thing is a bad idea. What arrangements will be needed to send me back to Trainer, Pennsylvania? I no longer want to be a Marine.

Leaving the processing center, they march us to a barracks where every two recruits stand in front of a pair of beds, one stacked on top of the other. The recruit on the right is to sleep in the top bunk, the one on the left the bottom bunk. After being assigned beds and footlockers[3], it is time for our evening meal. So off we go to the mess hall, trying to march in time to all those strange words. "Forward Augh, Lelp Right Lelp."

Before entering the mess hall, we are instructed not to speak under any circumstances and sit very erectly at the dinner table. What all this means is if you want a piece of bread that is too far away for you to reach, you are not allowed to ask the fellow close to it to pass it over. Now that is ridiculous. Who would put up with such restrictions to get a piece of bread? Not me, not Mr. Space Cadet, not the young man who has bucked all authority his entire life. I can tell by the man's expression sitting in front of the bread that he has had enough of this bullshit just as I have. I look his way and say, "Hey, pass me the bread." He goes, "Sure," and hands me the bread platter."

Out of nowhere, a drill instructor leaps onto the table and begins jumping up and down in my food. Yes, literally with his boots in my mashed potatoes and gravy. Every time he jumps and lands back on my platter, mashed potatoes and roast beef fly everywhere. That's my dinner, and this asshole is jumping up and down in it. Next, he pours a pitcher of pink Kool-Aid over me and bangs me in the head with the empty container. Then, screaming at the top of his lungs, he orders me to disappear. "Hide, hide, you scuzzy hog." What the Hell does he mean, hide? I look up perplexed, and he screams: "Get out, get away from me." Eventually, I figure out that I need to leave the mess hall and stand outside its screened entrance door.

---

[3] **Footlocker** - a trunk for storing personal possessions; usually kept at the foot of a bed (as in a military barracks). Webster's Unabridged Dictionary

Six of us recruits, the violators, stand outside the screen door hungry and humiliated. No drill instructors are present to prevent other recruits from taunting us as they leave the mess hall. When they pass us, they say things like, "Look at Sally with her pink shirt. Did you get in trouble, sweetheart"? I announce to the other violators that I am going coldcock the next smartass that runs his mouth. Only a moment later, another wise guy begins mocking and laughing at us. I pull back to whack him, and three drill instructors come out of hiding. One of them grabs and twists me until I am directly in front of another drill instructor who puts the brim of his hat against my forehead and begins screaming. I am turned again to face the third drill instructor, who repeats the whole sequence hat and all. He yells, "If you want to fight, you little fuck, fight me." He repeatedly challenges me to fight. "Fight, fight with me, come on, let's see what you got fuck face." I am overwhelmed. Suddenly it is not such a good idea for me to start fighting, especially when I can only see one of them at a time. I am intimidated.

All Hell breaks out when we get back to the squad bay, a long rectangle of a room with bunk beds on both sides. Everyone stands in front of the beds with both hands clasped behind them, legs spread apart to shoulder width. They call that position "Parade Rest." We, the six violators, are called to the center of the barracks and ordered to stand in front of the drill instructor's table in view of all the other recruits. The senior drill instructor explains to the rest of the platoon that we are the type of weaklings that get Marines killed in combat because we won't follow orders. Then, pointing at us, he says, "These people are scuzzy hogs lower than whale shit. Because they have fucked up, everyone else must suffer, just like in combat." Following the drill instructor's demonstration, the other recruits begin doing "Side Straddle Hops," an exercise most of the world calls "Jumping Jacks."

The drill instructor has no mercy as he punishes the platoon for what we did. The summer heat and humidity in South Carolina cause the exercising recruits to sweat profusely. They must perform the "Side Straddle Hops" precisely in step with everyone else. They are dying; they want to quit but are not allowed. The senior drill instructor declares the word quit is never to be spoken by any of us again.

The six of us must stand directly in front of each recruit, being punished to the point of physical exhaustion, and point a finger a few inches from his face screaming, "Ha, ha, ha, I made you do this." After the platoon of tired and angry recruits are ordered to stop exercising, the six of us violators are directed into a hallway and told to do "Bend and Thrust" exercises. One of the drill instructors demonstrates the movement, bending over at the hips and placing his palms on the deck as he simultaneously throws his feet out behind him. He brings his feet back to his hands from the push-up position before standing. The count goes 1, 2, 3, 4, one, 1, 2, 3, 4 two, 1, 2, 3, 4, three. Four body movements are required to complete one "Bend and Thrust" exercise. We are ordered to do 1,000 "Bend and Thrusts." No, I didn't make a mistake. We are instructed to do 1,000 "Bend and Thrusts" as a group shouting out all four counts of each exercise in step with one another. The Marine Corps functions as a team doing everything together. The drill instructor explains, "There is no advantage in arriving at a firefight early because you are the fastest runner in a platoon."

The "Bend and Thrust" exercise requires little strength; however, it does require a tremendous amount of energy. Soon we can see an imprint of our body shapes crated by sweat falling on the wooden floor below us. Somehow, we manage, with enormous effort, to perform over 300 "Bend and Thrusts" before one of us passes out. He collapses, face down, barely conscious, not able to do another exercise. Of course, we all stop as well. We are shocked that the drill instructors have pushed us so hard.

How do the three men from Hell respond to their blatant abuse of authority? They throw a bucket of water over the man on the floor and order him to get up. The exhausted recruit stands. The drill instructor bellows out, "Girls, you quit without permission. Now you must start from the beginning. Ready Exercise – One."

They know how hard they are pushing us. One thousand "Bend and Thrusts" are beyond all but a very few. They know a lot about us physically.

From the time we signed enlistment papers in our hometowns until the time we arrived at Parris Island, our vital signs are checked and rechecked. It is our mental attitudes that concern them. If we continue to be defiant, they will cut us from the recruit platoon.

After completing another thirty or so, "Bend and Thrusts," it is time for bed. Everyone else has showered. We violators collapse in our bunks after removing our sweat-drenched clothes and boots. After the drill instructors turn off all the squad bay lights, I lay in the upper bunk on my blankets. The recruit bunking below me reaches up and grabs my left thigh. He announces in a loud menacing voice, "This is one of the sons of bitches that made us do all the exercises." I smash my fist into his extended hand, driving it into the angle iron bed frame. Then, in a cautionary voice, I tell him, "Fuck off." He immediately stops his aggressive intentions, and so does everyone else. Laying in my bunk, tired and fed up with the Parris Island experience, I can only think, oh my God, I volunteered to go Hell.

Why had I not quit during the impossible exercise ordeal? It would have been the perfect time to find out if I could cancel the enlistment contract. However, something strange happened when I was exhibited and mocked as the type of weakling that gets Marines killed in combat because I can't follow orders. Being referred to as a scuzzy hog lower than whale shit does not sit well with me either. At this point, it is not about bucking authority as usual. No, I am beginning to question if I am man enough to graduate from basic training in the U.S. Marine Corps.

Marine Recruit – Lower Than Whale Shit

The most important point to share about the Parris Island experience is that physical demands are not our most difficult challenge. Most of us are between 18 and 20 years old. Young men's bodies respond quickly to daily calisthenics and never-ending running. The experience of Parris Island is exceedingly challenging mentally. Stress is the operative word. We are awakened most mornings by the sound of a baseball bat banging inside a large shiny trash can. The sound is abrupt. Hearing it is a signal to immediately jump out of your bunk and start the daily chores. Before using the bathroom, the "head," you must dress and make your bunk to strict specifications. When we hear the order, "Clear the head," we all must scream, "Clear the Head." We then have thirty seconds to be standing in front of our bunks. Our drill instructors don't suspend training on Saturdays and Sundays, nor do they stop the workday at five o'clock and let us hang out at a pub or relax in the barracks. They wake us at 0500 hours, 5:00 am to begin a regimented strenuous day, then put us to bed at 2100 hours, 9:00 at night. That is the routine for thirteen weeks, continuous stress. The daily procedures are repetitive, the schedule often changes, but the pressure does not. To put the experience of boot camp in perspective. Ninety-eight percent of the time, you can't talk with the recruit standing next to you.

On the second day of boot camp, the senior drill instructor has each of us scream out our name, race, and religion. How considerate; maybe these guys are not as insensitive as I first thought. However, after recording all our responses, they read aloud their interpretation of our answers. "We have 15 Wops, 7 kikes, 13 Micks, 12 Niggers, and 13 too fucked up to be identified. Religion: 20 harps, 7 Jews, 29 Protestants, and some far-out weird-ass Christians. "Church of Holy Christ Today," what kind of bullshit is that? You are all the same, Marine recruits, lower than whale shit on the bottom of the ocean. We do not give a damn who your father is. We do not care where your family came from, what professional credentials they hold, or how much money they have. We do not care if you or your family are the biggest losers to walk the face of the earth. None of that matters to us. That was your life before you came to our Island. Here you will be judged by how well you fight for the title of United States Marine. Your ass now belongs to the Corps. I will discover the weaklings, the non-hackers[4], the cowards among you. I will not allow quitters to contaminate my Marine Corps."

Everything the drill instructors say is preprogrammed. They have been thoroughly schooled and psychologically screened in a challenging training program before becoming drill instructors. We never see a

---

[4] **Non-hackers:** A recruit that could not or would not keep up mentally or physically with the other recruits. To call a Marine a non-hacker is an insult.

Marine Corps commissioned officer during the entire thirteen weeks of boot camp except when one occasionally conducts a special inspection and on our graduation day. Everyone who instructs us is an enlisted man. Boot camp is the only place where one enlisted man addresses another by Sir. During recruit training, the first word out of your mouth is Sir – the last word out of your mouth is Sir. You do not speak without screaming.

They have no bias or preconceived opinions about us. They don't care if we are black or white, Christian or Jew. Regarding religion, they were not atheists. In their belief system, the Marine Corps did not have time for men without God. Therefore, they often spoke of God and how it was the Marine's mission to send the enemy to God or meet him yourself.

The Marine Corps trained us to make close contact with the enemy and kill him or her. They are not particular. Take away all the distractions; Marines kill- Marines die. That is what they do.

We get no food or drink at Parris Island except what is given to us when they give it to us. No snacks, cokes, or beer. They control every aspect of our lives, diet, sleep, exercise, and motivation. If they detect the slightest abnormality with your presence or attitude, they will exploit it. We learn to accept ourselves in the image of a Marine. They bring everyone down to a common level, clearing the way to progress to a predetermined degree of physical excellence and mental confidence. Those that can't make the transition will not graduate from Parris Island.

Life gets more problematic for those recruits who decide to give up their pursuit of becoming a Marine. Let us say a recruit chooses to quit Parris Island and tells the drill instructors to go to Hell. The Marine Corps has in-depth experience dealing with recruits that challenge their system. You can't say or do anything they have not seen or heard before. Drill instructors prepare for every act of defiance. All belligerent recruits are reassigned to motivation platoons designed to mold attitudes; think of Parris Island on steroids. Screamed at constantly, recruits in motivation platoons perform meaningless activities like moving a mountain of sand. The recruits load sand into buckets on a cadence count specifying when their shovels will be pushed into the sand, lifted, and emptied. Then, with a full bucket of sand in each hand, the motivation platoon recruits run in step as a unit about a mile before dumping the buckets to a cadence count. Then, on command, they run as a unit back to the enormous pile of sand, where they will fill the buckets again. Welcome to Parris Island's Motivation Platoon, nothing but extreme stress and pressure.

If you prove to be that rare type of individual who can't be regimented, you are classified as "unfit for military service." However, for ninety-nine percent of 18 years old recruits, it is immensely easier to fall into line than to buck the system. It is extremely difficult for someone to pretend that he is unfit for military service when he is not.

Physical training at Parris Island begins with a physical fitness test. Sit-ups, push-ups, pull-ups, and a run. If a recruit scores below what they consider a minimum fitness level to start basic training, a strength conditioning platoon provides the required exercises. After obtaining the minimum level of physical fitness, the underperforming recruit joins a new platoon.

A word of caution. No one who is overweight should ever show up for training at a Marine Corps Boot Camp. Fat recruits go through an extra hell. The Marine Corps detests fat. If you cannot pull your body weight plus your rifle and other combat gear over obstacles, you cannot become a Marine. They have nasty names for overweight recruits. They are called "Fat Bodies." Overweight recruits are cut from their units and assigned to "Fat Body Platoons," where they constantly exercise and eat rabbit food. The drill instructors don't determine what they eat; nutritionists do. Many of the "Fat Bodies" are not immediately recognized by their parents when they return home.

The drill instructors have a favorite expression; "We didn't ask for you - you asked for us." So, yes, we did all volunteer to join the Marine Corps. However, suppose a judge offers a young man an opportunity to join the Corps or suffer the fate of punishment for some hometown misbehavior. In that case, he may very well become a volunteer.

I did volunteer and enlisted four months before I would attend boot camp. However, I managed to get arrested several times during that period. My buddies and I thought it was a good idea to steal four tires from a parked car rather than purchase them. That idea cost me a night of incarnation in Chester, Pennsylvania. The following day, we were given one phone call and assigned a court date. I naively thought the authorities would forget my little discretion when they discovered that I was in Marine Boot Camp.

One afternoon after our platoon returns from physical training, the senior drill instructor, standing in front of his desk in the barracks' center, orders me to report. Standing at attention, I scream, "Sir, Private Mezick reporting to the senior drill instructor as ordered, Sir." Holding a letter high for all the platoon to see as they stand at "Parade Rest" in front of their bunks, the sergeant begins speaking, "A judge in Chester, Pennsylvania, wants to verify that you are here, with me, in Platoon 166. He says that you are a certified asshole and wants to put you in jail. So, how should I respond? Oh, I know. Unfortunately, Private Mezick is here in my platoon, but I think he would better serve his country in jail because, as you declare, he is a certified asshole. What do you think of that dick head? You want to start a career-locked up with a bunch of idiots that think you are beautiful?"

Parris Island is straightforward. You achieve a standard established by the Corps, or you will not become a Marine. The bar is high and never lowered to let in non-hackers. The drill instructors are in total fear of letting even one individual into their beloved Marine Corps who can't cut it, that is not hardcore, who is not totally into their program.

Parris Island stands on a foundation of thought reform called brainwashing. If you want to get a young man to run into Hell, commit organized suicide, kill on command, you need to control his mind. At that task, the U.S. Marine Corps is very proficient. If ordered to shoot the U.S. Army, we will do it. All the extreme mental pressure at Parris Island and their demand that we obtain physical excellence defined by their standards doesn't make any sense until ordered into combat. Only after experiencing the brutal reality of war will we comprehend why we recruits are subjected to a world of extreme stress and harshness.

Port Arms Instruction

Marines march well; it's a beautiful sight to behold. You become part of a unique community when you march and move your rifle precisely to cadence called by a drill instructor. Every detail of where you touch your rifle is trained. The rifle position of "Port Arms" has many precise requirements. Your left hand grips the forearm of the rifle while the fingers of your right hand clasp around the small of the stock with the rifle muzzle bisecting a 45-degree angle between your head and shoulders. Standing in the "Port Arms" position, your rifle is held six inches to the front of your chest with your elbows positioned close to your sides.

With every two men standing in front of their bunks, the exact details of the "Port Arms" rifle position are instructed. We can't be dependent on anyone to help us if we don't understand the drill instructor's detailed instructions because we are forbidden to speak or look at the recruits standing next to us. We train to place our hands, fingers, arms, head, feet, and rifles so the entire platoon looks the same.

Observing the recruit directly across from me on the other side of the barracks, I see how sharp he looks and position my rifle as is his. I am then copying the rifle position of a man facing me from across the room. His left is my right. His rifle is correctly pointing to his left; my rifle is incorrectly pointing to the right. Just imagine the entire line of Marines on my side of the squad bay with their rifles all pointing to the left except mine, pointing to the right. The drill instructor personally inspects every recruit as we stand in the port arms position. He looks for the slightest of errors as he carefully reviews each of us. When he discovers a firearm not centered six inches to the front of a recruit's chest, or his arms and fingers not positioned precisely as ordered, he explodes in a rage of insults.

I am proud of what I consider perfect alignment for a recruit standing at "Port Arms." I am sure I have complied with every detail, just like the recruit across the room. Standing directly in front of me, the drill instructor bends over and whispers into my ear, "Don't you think you are a little fucked up, sweetheart"? For the first time all morning,

I look to my left and see everyone else's rifle pointing in the opposite direction than mine. My bunkmate, a large man with a big barreled chest standing next to me, looks out the corner of his eye and notices my rifle bisecting a perfect 45-degree angle between my head and shoulder on the wrong side. He doesn't want to laugh, knowing that will draw the drill instructor's ire, but he can't control his chest from jumping around as he tries to suppress laughter. He saves me because the drill instructor immediately yells at him for laughing. I take advantage of the distraction to flip my rifle to the left side of my head. His words, "Don't you think you are a little fucked up, sweetheart," will be with me for the rest of my life.

Swimming Lesson

Early one morning, after our platoon boards a bus, the senior drill instructor announces we are on our way to the swimming pool, where we will demonstrate that we are all qualified swimmers. In a booming and menacing voice, he declares, "There are no non-swimmers in this platoon. Do you understand, girls"? All the recruits respond, "Sir, yes, Sir."

When we arrive at the combat swimming facility, they have us stand in single file formations in front of blue lines painted on the bottom of a 50-meter Olympic-sized pool. The swimming instructors direct that on their command, each recruit is to jump into the deep end of the pool and swim down and back for a total of 100-yards.

We can use any swimming stroke we know to propel ourselves. The swimming instructors don't care if we dog paddle, crawl stroke, sidestroke, whatever. The objective is to swim down and touch the wall on the other end of the pool and swim back. The United States Marine Corps declared any recruit that could traverse 100 yards of water a "Qualified Swimmer."

Everyone who successfully passes the swimming test then begins training for a series of combat swims. The most strenuous swimming I have ever attempted is when my clothes and equipment's weight causes me to sink.

Without training, the normal tendency for anyone in the water, exhausted and uncontrollably submerging, is to panic.

We are taught how to jump off an extremely high diving platform as though we are leaping off a sinking ship at sea. As we fall towards the water, we place one hand under our chin and the other between our legs to protect our bodies' critical areas from striking floating debris. The challenge of the high platform jump with both our arms positioned to defend our bodies causes us to turn sideways as we descend. Think scary.

Before we enter the water for our swimming test, each recruit stands in line, waiting for his turn to earn the title of "Qualified Swimmer." We are, for the second time, that morning, asked if there are any among us that can't swim? A young black man directly to my right, standing one person ahead of me in the adjacent line, is so frightened of the water he involuntarily urinates down his leg. Not quite as noticeable as you might think because the surrounding area is already wet. Nevertheless, one of the sergeants administering the test asks, "Private, are you sure you can swim"? The frightened young man remembering the instructions we were all given on the bus by our senior drill instructor, responds, "Sir, Yes, I can swim, Sir."

He can't swim because he comes from Mississippi in the 1960s, where black people could not enter white people's public swimming pools. If black folks in those communities didn't have access to other water, they are all non-swimmers. He has never been in swimming depth water in his entire life but is too afraid of the senior drill instructor to report otherwise. He jumps in the deep end of the pool, where he displays the best case of incompetent swimming I had ever witnessed. He has no idea how to reach the surface. He sinks like a rock. The water is crystal clear, allowing everyone to monitor his plight. The expert swimming instructors are not about to let him drown. However, they fully intend to provide him with an uninterrupted self-taught swimming lesson. They offer a rescue pole for him only after determining he is not a quick learner.

The black recruit who sank so well eventually learns to swim with additional instruction. Most of our platoon members have no idea how poorly this recruit performed during his first attempt to pass the swimming test. The scheduled time for water training ends except for a few recruits who still have not qualified. Time taken from other activities provides them additional swimming instruction and an opportunity to retake the "Qualified Swimmer Test." All recruit platoons desire a record of 100 percent achievement from every recruit in all training categories, especially marksmanship and swimming.

The time allotted to our platoon for additional swimming instruction and testing of nonqualified swimmers is about to expire, with only a last session remaining. Our platoon has just one recruit still unqualified as a swimmer. The pressure the drill instructors put him under is immense. His life has become miserable. He knows he is failing himself and the platoon.

The last day has come for the nonqualified recruit to pass the swimming test. If he fails to swim 100 yards in the allotted time, he officially becomes an unqualified swimmer. Realizing Marine's survival in combat may depend on their ability to swim. Everyone wonders if he can pull it all together when he and the senior drill instructor leave for his final test.

Late that afternoon, the platoon returns to the barracks after physical training to an incredible scene. The recruit under consideration is sitting in the senior drill instructor's chair with feet crossed on top of the white sheet covering the senior drill instructor's table. He is wearing the senior drill instructor's wide brim cover and smoking a cigar. We all stand at "Parade Rest" in front of our bunks as the senior drill instructor begins to speak. "Privat Jones has passed his swimming test. Ladies, I am here to tell you Private Jones cannot swim. However, Private Jones is now a qualified swimmer. That's correct. This young man just walked 100 yards underwater. This son of a bitch cannot swim a lick. He sank to the bottom of the pool and pushed off, advancing a foot or so. He sank again, pushed off, and advanced another foot or so. Finally, he surfaced, flopped around, fucked around like a drowning dog, and sank and pushed again and again. That's what the Marine Corps is all about, and that is what I demand from all of you, never quit, do the impossible. Earn the title of United States Marine."

PUGIL STICKS

Pugil stick fights are a mind-altering experience that will forever change your sense of fairness in applying violence. What are pugil sticks? Think of a heavily padded short pole. The fights provide an opportunity for the Corps to instill aggression by using bayonet and rifle strikes against a live opponent. Before the pugil stick fights begin, each recruit is issued a protective mask that resembles those used by baseball catchers. Our bodies are further protected below the waist with the bottom portion of a flak jacket, and our hands are covered in protective gloves.

The pugil stick fights take place within a circle about twelve feet in diameter. Our platoon is divided into two groups, positioned on each side of the fighting ring. When my turn comes to fight, my opponent and I crouch down, growling at one another. Such antics may seem humorous until you face a growling excited Marine recruit on the other side. Then, the instructors blow a whistle the fight is on. Only blows from the array of strikes we learned in bayonet class, the butt stroke, slash, and smash, are acceptable. Every other type of strike is illegal. Swinging the pugil stick like a baseball bat is expressly forbidden because that type of strike creates an unacceptable advantage to the enemy by exposing our unguarded lower bodies.

These fights are intense, ending when the instructor decides to stop them by blowing a whistle. Everyone gets hit. The recruit facing me across the circle has been motivated to tear my head off. He is fit as a fiddle. Trust me when I say many recruits report to Parris Island in top physical condition. Some naturally mature with the muscle mass that other men can only dream of. Think of a Greek statue of a male figure depicted with excellent muscle definition. Many of these outstanding physical specimens confess they have never lifted a weight in their entire lives. They are born athletes.

The growling fired-up opponent faces me from the other side of the circle and attacks when the whistle blows. I meet him in the center of the fighting ring delivering vicious blows to his head and body as he counterattacks with equal intensity. We are in a fight that demands aggression and grit as we absorb a relentless pounding from one another. The pugil stick instructor seems to enjoy our fight and lets it continue without interruption. Not all matches are acceptable to the instructor. Fighting with low aggression or swinging the pugil stick like a bat earns you a fight with the next fresh opponent in line. We all get the message; be aggressive, only strike with a butt stroke, mash, or slash. The pugil stick fights progress with much excitement and cheering.

With our platoon divided into two separate groups, each facing the other across the circle, there is no consideration for an individual's weight, height, or athletic ability. In combat, no system of fairness selects the opponents. You kill, or you will be killed by the enemy you face, not the one someone chooses for you.

Often recruits facing one another across the fighting ring are mismatched physically. The two combatants who now face off across the circle growling and ready to explode into violent aggression are at the opposite extremes of the allowable heights and weights to join the U.S. Marine Corps. One recruit is more than a foot taller and one hundred pounds heavier than the other. It is a terrible mismatch of body size, like an adult and a child about to fight with padded bags attached to a short stick. At the sound of the whistle, the large recruit advances with caution, desiring not to hurt his diminutive opponent. The smaller recruit aggressively attacks with expertly delivered strikes that would have disabled the larger recruit if he hit him with a rifle or bayonet. However, the impact of his padded pugil stick has little effect on the larger man. The close combat instructor screams at the big man to attack with aggression. He then strikes his diminutive opponent with one horizontal butt stroke that lifts him entirely off his feet. The small recruit is now on his back, looking up at the giant of a man above him. The instructor screams at the large man who stands motionless, looking down at his opponent, "Kill him – Kill him!"

The bigger man is supposed to beat the smaller recruit until ordered to stop. He refuses to strike. Angered by the larger recruit's lack of aggression, the pugil stick instructor orders the big man to his knees. At the sound of the whistle, the pugil stick war restarts. The smaller recruit realizes that he will again be at his mercy if his opponent gets off his knees. Yes, the slighter recruit is much smaller than the giant of a man now on his knees, but don't mistake him for a weak man. He displays strength and aggression as he delivers one blow after another to the larger man below him. Every time the larger man attempts to stand, he falls under a brutal attack. He gets the Hell beaten out of him as he absorbs the correctly delivered blows to the front and sides of his head. The drill instructor orders the smaller standing recruit to "Kill him – Kill him!" The big man can barely stand when the ass-kicking is over.

The instructor uses the mismatched pugil stick fight as a teaching moment. He explains, "Close contact combat is not a fair fight. Never give an enemy, man or woman, a chance to recover; kill or be killed. Should you hesitate for one second, you will most likely die or be mutilated. A close encounter fight in war lasts only seconds before someone is injured so badly; they become defenseless or die. Size does not matter; aggression does. Therefore, you must deliver the first lethal strike."

That day, we all learned the Marine Corps' philosophy of "Disciplined Aggression." It was to become our dominant approach to life.

Fist Fight Solution

The drill instructors utilize numerous methods to make us more aggressive, from pugil stick fights to obstacle courses. Hard to believe, but they figured a way to use the shower as an opportunity to instill aggressive behavior. Returning to the squad bay after a vigorous run in the heat and humidity of South Carolina, they provide us an opportunity to take a much-desired shower. The challenge is to shower in the limited time they allow before ordering us to "Clear the Head."

The shower is without partitions. A big room with maybe 15 shower heads to service sixty recruits who all desperately desire to shower. The point is you need to get wet before they give the order to "Clear the Head." If the guy under the falling water takes too long, you grab him and fling him away. When you are under the showerhead, the other recruits nearby will give you only so much time before you get jerked away. No rules, no drill instructors; they leave it up to us to figure out a schedule.

We all get grumpy and impatient, awaiting our turn to shower. You may think someone will take issue with all the pulling and jerking and start fighting. Well, a fight sometimes does break out among the recruits. However, unscheduled fighting is against the rules, a big no-no. Recruits are government property. It is illegal to destroy government property. Young men's muscle mass responds quickly to the physical training in boot camp. We are all now strong enough to do severe damage to one another. Therein lies the problem, broken recruits cannot continue training.

When two recruits do start hammering on each other, the drill instructors have a unique solution. The offenders face one another in the center of the squad bay, where the rest of the platoon can observe them. The drill instructor standing between the angry recruits provides an outlet for their anger and an opportunity to resolve their dispute. He begins by setting the ground rules, "You two morons want to fight so bad I believe you should. Now both of you stand at attention. You, on my left, with an open hand, slap his face." He does. Then he orders the other recruit, "Slap his face," he does. Then he says to the recently slapped recruit, "slap him back." That's how it goes, with the drill instructor repeating the command, "Slap him, slap him, slap him, slap him." The slap's intensity increases to the point that they both receive and deliver mighty blows to the face. The drill instructor orders them to get on the deck and start doing push-ups in sync with one another. It isn't long before they are both exhausted with stinging faces. Not just a red slapped face, think severe headaches. They have both landed hard strikes before the push-up contest. They again are ordered to stand and face one another. The drill instructor informs them, "You now have to make a choice. You can shake hands, or we can start another round of slapping. Maybe we need a winner in this conflict"? I observed that proposed solution to warring recruits twice. Both times the dispute ended after the first round, with both men enthusiastically shaking hands. The rest of us decide it is not a good idea to get in a fight at Parris Island.

Pissing On The Floor

Parris Island in the 1960s was harsh beyond acceptable practice today.

One morning the drill instructors decide that our platoon is moving too slowly after waking and performing our morning chores. They punish us by screaming the command, "Clear the Head," before most of us have used it. Only moments later, we began a mile or more run to the mess hall. After breakfast, we perform all activities without being permitted to urinate. During lunch, we still haven't emptied our bladders since the previous night. Yes, we are thirsty but hesitant to add more pressure to a full bladder.

Late that afternoon, the platoon returns to the barracks. Still, no permission to use the head; they don't allow unscheduled visits. Standing at "Parade Rest" in front of our bunks, we listen to the drill instructor delivering some sort of presentation. I can no longer concentrate; I am distracted due to the pain I endure from my extended bladder.

Several recruits at the other end of the squad bay have screwed up somehow and are ordered to mop the entire squad bay. One of them works his way towards my position by wetting the deck with the water from his bucket before mopping it up. My bunkmate standing next to me pulls out his penis and releases a bit of bladder pressure just before the mopping recruit wets the floor in front of us. He believes no one will notice a little extra wetness. I agree. Good Idea. I do the same to relieve just a bit of the unbearable pressure I am experiencing.

The recruit mopping the deck looks at us and says, "I am not cleaning that up." My partner and I plead with the highly irritated recruit to please mop up our urine before it's discovered. The drill instructor standing in the center of the squad bay blurts out, "Who the fuck is talking? You, three idiots, get up here and tell the rest of the platoon what is so God damn important that you need to discuss it at their expense."

The drill instructor has no idea at this time that two of us have pissed on his deck. Our destiny is now in the hands of the recruit that has been mopping. When no one speaks, the drill instructor repeats his question, "What were you horrible hogs talking about"? I respond first by saying, "Sir, we were talking about home, Sir." My bunkmate asked the same question replies, "Sir, we talked about home, Sir." Both of us have just lied to a drill instructor. Now it is time for the recruit, the man we had expected to mop up our urine, to answer the question. Our lives are literally in the hands of a man we had each disrespected only moments ago. He responds immediately, "Sir, we were talking about home, Sir." I could have kissed him.

I then became aware of a profound transition. Why has the recruit we expected to mop our urine lied to protect us? He has every right to rat us out. He is in just as much bladder discomfort as we are. So why did he protect two strange recruits? We don't even know his name, and neither of us has ever spoken to him.

The bond, the invisible glue that connects Marines, is forming. He didn't stand up for us; he stood up for a brotherhood. Even today, I can't explain how and when men who successfully overcome physical pain and mental challenge begin to admire and respect one another. The bond is invisible and untouchable yet sensed. I never forgot my first experience with the invisible bond. It would not be my last. A man I did not know stood up for me. He put himself in danger of punishment when he had done nothing wrong.

Our penalty for talking was minor. The drill instructor never discovered my bunkmate, and I had pissed on the deck of his squad bay.

The Solution to a Trigger Jerk

No Parris Island report will be complete without sharing the Marine Corps' extreme effort to teach all its recruits how to shoot well. Marksmanship training is more intense than any other period of our thirteen-week boot camp. Every Marine is a "Rifleman." It does not matter your "Military Occupation Specialty[5]"; you are first and foremost a "Rifleman." A vivid example of this concept is publicly provided by a Commandant of the Marine Corps testifying before Congress. They begin the proceedings by asking him his rank and job description. He reports, "Commandant, United States Marine Corps, Rifleman."

Marksmanship training begins by teaching us how to lock ourselves into stable firing positions with our rifles' slings tightly wrapped around our forward arm. Then, we learn proper sight alignment and trigger squeeze by aiming at paper targets. That phase of marksmanship training is called "Dry Firing" and lasts several days. Finally, we graduate to the 25-yard rifle range. To determine our initial sight adjustments, called dope, we first fire our M14 rifles at a target 25 yards away. The ballistics of the 7.62 mm cartridge we fire has remarkably similar flight patterns at 25 yards as it does at two hundred yards.

Each night before retiring to our bunks, we sit on the squad bay deck in a semicircle. The drill instructor individually reviews our 25-yard targets hoping to find a tight group of bullet holes indicating the shooter is aiming his rifle and squeezing its trigger correctly. From the position of a tight group, he can determine what rear sight adjustments are necessary to move the point of impact to the bullseye. If your target has bullet holes all over it without a defined group, rifle site adjustment is impossible.

The drill instructors will not tolerate a recruit who produces a target with scattered holes. That kind of random distribution of bullet strikes means the shooter is bucking or jerking his rifle. Bucking means that you push your shoulder forward just before you fire your rifle, anticipating

---

[5] **The United States Marine Corps Military Occupational Specialty (MOS)** Like the Army, the Marines break their enlisted jobs down into MOS's, or "Military Occupation Specialties." In the Marine Corps, the MOS's are FOUR digit codes used to organize and designate the variety of jobs and skills offered in the USMC. Marine Enlisted Jobs Main Menu (thebalancecareers.com)

heavy recoil. Jerking is a similar reaction to recoil. Just as you are about to fire, you jerk the trigger instead of slowly squeezing it.

Late in the evening, standing in front of our platoon as we sit in a semicircle, the drill instructor holds up a recruit's target and declares, "No one can successfully adjust the sites for a shooter who jerks the trigger of his firearm. Look at this target, no group, no consistency. I can't tell if this target was shot with a rifle or a shotgun. Which hole should I use as a reference? It is impossible to hit what you aim at if you jerk the trigger. To keep other Marines alive, I must fix "Private Jerkoff's" subconscious problem."

The offending recruit is called to the squad bay center and told to extend his trigger finger and place it on the drill instructor's table. After directing him to look away, the drill instructor takes a heavy-duty Navy coffee cup and smashes it into the recruit's fingernail. Whap, the tip of his finger instantly becomes exceedingly tender, making it extremely difficult to jerk the trigger of a rifle. The next day the young man with the sore finger fires shots that are in a group.

Letters to Nikita Khrushchev

Following our basic marksmanship training on the 25-yard range, our platoon moves to the Island's primary rifle range. We now practice shooting our M14 Rifles at targets presented at distances of 200, 300, and 500 yards. The pressure to shoot well is extreme. Each evening the drill instructors evaluate the platoon's performance at the rifle range. Some nights the drill instructors would be so disappointed with our rifle accuracy they would punish the entire platoon. On one occasion, we had to compose a letter to Nikita Khrushchev, the then presiding leader of the Communist Party of the Soviet Union. We all wrote him a personal letter stating that our platoon couldn't shoot straight. We wrote the following declaration: "Please come to the United States and rape our mothers and sisters. We can't possibly stop you because we can't shoot a rifle worth a shit. We like to jerk – we like to buck - we don't give a fuck. Have no fear of retaliation. We like to jerk - we like to buck – we don't give a fuck." We inserted our letters into envelopes, addressed to the Kremlin for delivery to Nikita.

After collecting our letters, they continue their assault on our pride and patriotism. The drill instructors spread a vast U.S. flag on the deck of the squad bay. Recruits lying on their stomachs stacked four high surround the flag with outstretched arms. With the entire platoon stacked in layers around the flag, we maul it as we sing the song of those that can't shoot; "I like to jerk – I like to buck. I don't give a fuck. I can't shoot; I can't shoot. The entire affair is not a joke; they are profoundly serious. We feel terrible.

Lose the Smile

The involuntary facial smirk that has earned me the nickname "Mr. Smart-Ass" and caused so much trouble in Eddystone High School will soon be lost.

Strong gusty winds blow across the rifle range for several days before and during the qualification shoot to determine what marksmanship badge each of us will earn. Regardless of the blustery wind, the drill instructors still expect us to shoot well. Trust me; intermittent wind gusts will affect your rifle's point of impact, especially at five hundred yards.

That evening, the platoon sits in a semicircle, each recruit waiting for the drill instructor to call his name before standing to hear a public review of his rifle range score. Usually, shooting is easy for me; however, my score on this day is low, abysmal. My stepfather taught me marksmanship at an early age. I grew up smelling "Hoppes No. 9 Bore Cleaner," we used to clean the family's rifles and shotguns. Hearing my name, I come to my feet with a broad smile. Noticing my lack of respect, the drill instructor blurts out in a booming voice, "Holy shit. You think your pathetic rifle range score is so fucking funny you need to look around my squad bay and give everyone a big grin? Report to my house."

The most feared command at Paris Island is "Report to My House." I leave the squad bay and walk down the hall to the drill instructor's quarters, where I must stand just outside the door of his private room. The lights go out; everyone else is in their bunks. The drill instructor walks past me as I stand perpendicular to his room's door called the bulkhead. He commands me to report. I scream, "Sir, Private Mezick reporting to the drill instructor as ordered, Sir." He replies, "Knock first, you idiot." I had forgotten the correct procedure for reporting to his room. First, I must cross my body with my right arm and forcibly strike the bulkhead with my hand. Repeat that striking sequence three times before reporting. I then strike his bulkhead three times and scream, "Sir, Private Mezick reporting to the drill instructor as ordered, Sir." From within the room, He shouts, "I can't hear you." I repeat the entire sequence of striking the bulkhead and screaming even louder than at first, "Sir, Private Mezick reporting to the drill instructor as ordered, Sir." He replies, "I can't hear you, sound off, you maggot." With all the force I can muster, I again strike the bulkhead three more times and scream even louder, "Sir, Private Mezick reporting to the drill instructor as ordered, Sir." He finally orders me into his room. My voice is squeaky, and the palm of my right hand is in pain.

I stand at attention as he closes the door behind me. Oh, shit, no witnesses in a little room with a pissed-off drill instructor. He stands directly to my front and orders me to report, "Sir, Private Mezick reporting to the drill instructor as ordered, Sir." He stares at me for a long time as if to look into my soul and then begins speaking, "Your rifle scores are pathetic, and you think it's funny. Do you have any idea what we are training you for? Your rifle is your life! You think your inability to shoot your weapon is so funny you have to smile at everyone in the room." He then drove his right fist into my solar plexus. Perfect strike into a bundle of nerves that forces me to double over involuntarily. He strikes me two additional times in the same sensitive spot. He keeps screaming, "Do you understand, do you understand"? I am trying to answer, "Sir, yes, Sir," but it is difficult to speak due to the acute pain just below my rib cage.

As I stand bent at the waist, he smashes the heel of his hand into my cheekbone. The hand strike should force me upright, but my solar plexus nerves continue to compel my abdominal muscles to contract. He hits me three times in the face as he screams, "There is nothing more important to a Marine than his rifle. Shoot well or die. You will become a qualified shooter. You will never laugh about your ability to shoot again, you miserable piece of shit." He then orders me to leave his room. I take one step back and scream, "Sir, Aye Aye, Sir," and do an about-face. I am so confused and discombobulated that I walk into the wall. I find my way to the door and go to bed.

The drill instructors knew how to beat recruits without hurting them. So the next day, I have no trouble running or performing any other required task. I don't have a black eye, only an intense feeling of shame.

Whatever was going on in my brain that previously caused me to smirk in the face of authority is now gone, never to return. As a result, my attitude about how well I shoot a rifle becomes much more severe. I finally realize the gravity of the life and death decision I had made when I signed a four-year contract with the United States Marine Corps. Some transitions come to a man naturally over time. Others come immediately, think of a lightning bolt.

Reference Point Shift

The day Platoon 166 will graduate from Marine Corps Recruit Depot Parris Island, South Carolina, is less than a week away. For me, the thirteen weeks of recruit training was a life-changing experience. My whole attitude changed; I became a young man who truly desired to become a U.S. Marine. Trust me when I say the Marine Corps is very proficient in training a recruit's mind and body.

Unbeknownst to us, we are about to experience a profound object lesson of how successful Marine recruit training transforms a young recruit's body and mind. I came to call this lesson "The Reference Point shift." A three-word description for the method used to reveal the extent of our ability to persevere while enduring the pain of physical and mental exhaustion.

We run wearing leather boots, the liner of a helmet, tee shirts, utility trousers, and carry a nine-pound M14 rifle at port arms. In addition to the weight of what we wear and hold, there are two more challenges. First, you are not in control of the pace of the run. The second challenge is running with sixty other men in platoon formation, consisting of four columns, fifteen men deep. Formation running is problematic due to the natural stride differences in individuals, determined mainly by leg length. For example, when the recruit in front of you picks up his left foot, you must place your left foot into that space.

The day we experience the "Reference Point Shift Lesson" seems at first like any other until it is time for our platoon to run on the quarter-mile track at the physical fitness field. For some reason, they run us further than the usual three to four miles. Following months of aerobic training, we are all well-conditioned; we can certainly run a bit further.

However, this run seems never to end. The large muscles in my legs are becoming heavy and thick due to lactic acid accumulating in them. I am close to my limit of endurance; I wanted to quit forty minutes ago. What the Hell are they doing? Why don't they end the run? Tears stream down my contorted face as I push through the pain.

Finally, the senior drill instructor breaks his silence. He shouts out, "I know there is a quitter in this platoon, and I am going to find him. One of you sons of bitches is going to quit. Who the fuck is the non-hacking cock sucker that's trying to sneak into my Marine Corps"? We then began to follow his lead in a song. "I don't know, but I've been told – Eskimo pussy is mighty cold - We going to run all day – We going to run all night – We going to run until the running done - I know a girl her name is Sue – She don't screw, but her sister do - Lift your head and hold it high – Platoon 166 is passing by."

Oh shit, this is the senior drill instructor's final exam! The only way to keep yourself running is to focus on the man's back in front of you; block everything else out. Just keep pounding with sheer determination.

Finally, we veer from the track and head back towards the barracks about a mile and a half away. Usually, when ordered to leave the quarter-mile track, they would command "Quick Time." That meant for us to stop running and begin marching. We continue to run; it becomes painfully evident they intend to run us another mile and a half. Approaching the barracks steps, we are given the command, "Quick Time - Augh," now, we can finally stop running and march. What a blessing it is to end the run! Within two minutes, we are given a command to turn around, "To the Rear- Augh, Lelp - Right- Lelp." Why are we marching away from the barracks? What's going on? Then, the unthinkable, we are ordered to begin running with the command, "Double Time – Augh." The senior drill instructor announces, "I know that there is a quitter in this platoon, and I am going to expose the worthless maggot. Which one of you will it be? Ladies, let's go for a run."

He runs us back to the track to begin a new series of laps. He is undoubtedly screwing with our heads. We run around and around, forcing our then exhausted, wobbly legs through the sand trap. Yes, their quarter-mile track has a section about twenty yards long of soft South Carolina sand. Believe me when I say the soft sand is an energy suck on our tired legs.

The senior drill instructor loves that section of the track and has unique names for it. He calls it his "Cunt Trap," his "Pussy Trap." The devil himself could not have designed a grander temptation for "Non- Hackers" to quit.

I have no idea how many miles we ran that day. I just fixed my eyes on the man's back in front of me and took the pain. Again, he ran us back to the barracks before giving the "Quick Time" command. We enter the barracks and are treated to a shower. Our most challenging run of boot camp is over. They never explained why they ran us so long and hard.

I eventually figure it out. The purpose of the never-ending run is to let us know that we are no longer the person we were when we arrived at Parris Island. We are now physically and mentally stronger. However, we are not aware of our new abilities. We need a new "Reference Point." Life is all about reference points. What is hard, what is easy, what is quick, what is slow? Life is all about establishing reference points through experience. The day of the never-ending run is a gift far beyond its intended purpose of showing us just how far we can run beyond what we had previously considered possible.

Knowing the principle of "Reference Points" is extremely valuable because it is the foundation of change. Conversely, life determined by reference points set too low is a path to mediocrity.

Parris Island Graduation

PLATOON 166

FIRST RECRUIT BATTALION
SGT. C. L. BARNES
NOV. 7th, 1963

SSGT. L. A. CULBERTSON

M.C.R.D. PARRIS ISLAND, S.C.
SGT. D. R. BOWERS
PHOTO BY J.F. MAAG

The night before we graduate from boot camp, the platoon is addressed by our senior drill instructor. He begins, "Your drill instructor team has done everything in our power to train every one of you to become a Marine, and you all have succeeded. Some of our methods were harsh and controversial in the approved procedures of proper conduct. We made you sweat and endure discomfort so you will bleed less in war. Some of you may hold personal grievances with me or the sergeants under my command. We understand and only ask that you bring any issues to me after you graduate tomorrow. You will find me behind the barracks wearing a tee-shirt, not displaying my rank. Any man among you will have the opportunity, if you so desire, to take out your anger on me. Your other option is to file an official report. During your tour in the Corps, you too may have to shoulder the responsibility of bringing change to others before they go into combat. Then, you will understand why we made the extra effort. I would be proud to go into the Hell of war with any one of you. Well done, Marines."

Looking back on that presentation, I realize it was his moment to express respect and accept each of us into the Marine Corps. Our true graduation.

No one met the senior drill Instructor behind the barracks. Trust me when I say we had men in our platoon who far exceeded his height and weight and who could have punished him in a bare-knuckle fight. The operative word is respect. We would have defended him rather than fought him or reported him. Most of us did go to war and came to realize that those hardcore drill instructors who pushed us so relentlessly did their best to prepare us.

The day I graduate from boot camp Parris Island, South Carolina, my mother and stepfather are in attendance. It is one of the proudest days of my entire life. The grand finale of graduation is when Platoon 166 marches in front of a reviewing stand staffed with commissioned officers before proudly presenting ourselves to our parents seated in bleachers. We move our rifles from one shoulder to another in perfect unison as we pass by. Everyone looks fantastic dressed in their impeccably tailored uniforms. We have pride in ourselves and each other. On this day, we graduate into a brotherhood that touched our souls. We had each earned the title of "United States Marine." We will proudly carry that achievement in our hearts for the rest of our lives.

Cry Baby

After graduation, our platoon travels by bus to Camp Geiger, North Carolina, to begin one month of infantry training. We are on our way to our next adventure. The 340-mile trip takes over five hours. No one says we can't talk; It just seems as though no one wants to. We are, for the first time in thirteen weeks, without supervision. We can do whatever we want, even smoke. I immediately lit up a Marlboro. I don't know why. I do remember it was a great release; I think it was an act of liberation. Every Marine, regardless of his military occupancy specialty, MOS, is required to take infantry training.

During the trip to Camp Geiger, I reflect on the last three months I spent in boot camp. Of all the extraordinary events that took place, there is one incident that stands out. The most incredible psychological transformation I ever witnessed. This event will horrify most folks, perhaps even more so for those trained as professional psychotherapists or psychiatrists.

This instance involves one member of Platoon 166 who suffers from an acute emotional reaction when being screamed at by a person of authority. He is superbly physically fit, acing every activity, a rock-solid performer. However, he does have one major problem, every time the drill instructors get in his face screaming at him, he will start crying. Yes, he will cry like a small child. First, you notice the muscles in his face begin to quiver, soon followed by tears and then outright sobbing. Of course, he is christened "Cry Baby" by the drill instructors. To avoid being cut from the platoon, all unacceptable conduct, performance, or appearance must be resolved. Crying under pressure is intolerable and will certainly prevent him from graduating. His crying problem is detected early but remains unresolved week after week. However, we are advancing in our training program to a point where he must stop crying or be dropped from the platoon.

The drill instructors test him periodically by ordering "Cry Baby Up." He then has to run to the squad bay center and report to the drill instructor team. The three drill instructors take turns verbally assaulting the troubled recruit. His ability to withstand the pressure is improving, but he continues to fail the cry test. You can see him slowly breaking down with a slight involuntary movement of his cheeks, that once he begins, will escalate into a total crying session.

Final judgment day comes for "Cry Baby." One last chance to control himself or be cut from the platoon. Under pressure, he fails. The senior drill instructor asks the other two drill instructors to step back. He looks into the eyes of the crying recruit and screams, "Why are you crying"? The question makes the recruit sob even harder; he is now an emotional wreck. Hearing no answer, the senior drill instructor again screams, "Tell me why you are crying." The crying recruit blurts out, "Sir, my father – my father, Sir." The senior drill instructor screams, "He beat you, didn't he"? The crying recruit shrieked out, "Sir, Yes, my father beat me, Sir!" Those words, "My Father Beat Me," are screamed with such passion it becomes evident that he has never publicly spoken them before. The senior drill instructor asks, "What did he beat you with"? The recruit shouted at the top of his lungs, "Sir, he beat me with a belt, Sir!" "Where did he beat you"? "Sir, he beat me across my back, Sir!" The senior drill instructor removes his wide shiny black belt and lets one end fall to the deck as he holds the buckle end high for everyone to see. "Was it a belt like this"? "Sir, yes, Sir."

The senior drill instructor hands the recruit the belt and orders him to wrap the buckle around his right hand. Then he turns, so his back faces the recruit and screams, "Beat me, boy." The young recruit stands uncontrollably crying as he faces the staff sergeant's back with the belt held high, ready to strike. The senior drill instructor screams, "Beat me, beat me! Of course, the recruit is reluctant to strike too vigorously, so he stricks with a light blow. The senior drill instructor screams, "Beat me, beat me harder." The young man begins to strike the drill instructor's back with great intensity. Once he starts, he brutally swings the black belt letting out years of fear and frustration. Everyone can hear the cracking sound made by the belt as it transfers its energy of motion onto the back of the senior drill instructor, who screams, "Beat me harder, beat me harder."

After absorbing several more licks from the blistering belt, he turns around with tears in his eyes and says, "You just beat me. You beat me as hard as you could. Did I fucking disappear? Do I have any broken bones? Am I bleeding? Am I dying? Hell no, because all that beating business is nothing but a black belt. You do not have to be afraid of a little bit of pain because that's all it is. So, stop being afraid of what you imagine it to be and see it for what it is, nothing but a belt."

"Turn around. I'm going to beat you with a black belt. You are going to handle it for what it is –a smack on the back, just a belt kicking your ass, nothing more, nothing less. Get that other shit out of your head. Turn around, dick head." He then struck the recruit repeatedly before he ordered him to turn and face him. The recruit is not crying. Oh, he had shed a few tears from the sting of the striking belt, but he is not the out-of-control sobbing emotional wreck he was previously. You can almost see how the fear of his father's beating has flowed from him as he stands in control of his emotions. It is as if an exorcist had expelled an evil spirit from him. "Cry Baby" never cries again.

I have no idea what would have happened if all that mutual belt beating didn't produce the desired outcome. I don't think the senior drill instructor cared. For him, it was either you fix this problem now and come with us or, I must declare you broken.

Yeah, I couldn't get that out of my mind as the bus transported us to Camp Geiger. Something else came to my mind now that the pressure is off, my girlfriend. I began to remember how soft and warm she is.

Camp Geiger

When we arrive at Camp Geiger, North Carolina, we notice the sergeants don't always scream at us. Parris Island boot camp is over. We are treated as Marines, not boot camp recruits. The effect of our thirteen weeks of regimentation takes a while to wear off. We don't feel comfortable brushing our teeth without an order.

Here, at Camp Geiger, they encourage us to make decisions as they teach us the basics of infantry tactics. Mostly, we learn fire team and squad maneuvers, map and compass navigation, and weapons training. We are taught how to load, fire, and disassemble different weapons, from 45-caliber pistols to machine guns and rocket launchers. Hand grenade training is held in a fortified pit with an instructor walking us through every step. We are taught how and when to use fragmentation, smoke, white phosphorus, and incendiary grenades. Without a doubt, the incendiary grenade is the most impressive. We practice how to survive the fallout from a nuclear explosion. We begin to feel quite comfortable in the field because that's where we spend most of our time, day and night. When it rains, we train as though it isn't raining.

For those of us with 0311 MOS[6] classification, the field training we endure at Camp Geiger is our Marine Corps experience. Infantry training at Camp Geiger is just our starting point. We will come to know the meaning of the words "The Grunts." Life in the grunts is one of working and playing hard. I would later become good, exceptionally good at both.

President Kennedy Assassinated
A Portent of War

A sergeant interrupts a map and compass class with an announcement, "President Kennedy has been assassinated." A hush falls over everyone that November afternoon as we try to comprehend his words. We all are shocked. One of us asks, "What does this mean"? The sergeant answers, "It means we are going to war." I don't understand how the president's death will start a war. Later, when President Jonson makes a famous

---

[6] **Marine Rifleman 0311** is the quintessential military occupational specialty (MOS) for the United States Marine Corps. It is the MOS that most people envision when they imagine a U.S. Marine. It is the MOS that has changed the course of history for countless wars dating back to 1775. It is the MOS designation for the Marine Corps infantryman. Marine Rifleman (MOS 0311): 2019 Career Details (Operationmilitarykids.org)

statement, it becomes more apparent, "I'm not going down in history as the first American President to lose a war." He doubles down on what he thinks was President Kennedy's commitment to a war in Vietnam. Looking back, the sergeant was prophetic. Most of us hearing his words that fateful day did go to war.

Gas Chamber

The most challenging infantry training event at Camp Geiger happens when exposed to CS gas in a small shed. The gas chamber experience is a component of nuclear, biological warfare training.

The Marine Corps' method of exposing us to the mental and physical effects of CS gas is a bit brutal. After studying gas warfare for several days in a classroom, we are transported to a small one-room, one-door gas chamber located in remote woodland. We enter the chamber in thirteen-man squads. First, you notice an ugly-looking furnace-like contraption in the center of the room. That is the device they use to dispense the CS gas. There is enough residual gas left over from the previous group to immediately cause our bodies' warm, moist parts to burn.

The instructor wearing a gas mask tells us what we must accomplish as a group before being permitted to leave the gas chamber. "I am going to put gas tablets into the oven; on my command, you are going to retrieve your gas mask from its pouch and mount it on your face as you purge the air from it. We will then have a conversation." When the instructor drops the tablets into the furnace, a white smoke cloud rises and spreads throughout the room. He shouts, "Gas, gas!" Everyone withdraws and mounts their masks as they blow into them to remove any lingering gas. The mounted and purged gas masks work well. We can breathe and see. The instructor approaches each of us and asks our name, rank, and serial number to determine if every recruit's gas mask protects him from the toxic gas. After questioning the entire squad, we progress to phase two.

The instructor's voice is distorted and unsettling as he speaks through his gas mask, "On my command, everyone will remove their gas mask and place it into its carrying pouch. After closing the pouch's three snaps, you are to put your right hand on the shoulder of the man in front of you. The gas will most likely temporarily blind you, do not panic. You will need to feel the third snap on your pouch when you can't see it. No one leaves until every man has properly completed my instructions. Have faith in the Marine in front of you to guide you to the door when and only when I order you to follow me out."

Given that horrible command, "Remove your gas masks," we all hold our breath. Yes, that is my plan. I feel sure I can hold my breath until led out of the gas chamber. I remove my mask and place it into its pouch. Snapping all three of its snaps becomes challenging because my sinuses and eyes begin to burn. The first snap, not too tricky, but by the time I work at the second snap, my vision is blurry, and I can't breathe properly. I am blind as my fingers attempt to feel their way to secure the third snap. I want to run out of the room long before I get the third snap fastened. I fumble with it forever but finally snap it into position and place my hand on the man's shoulder to my front by guessing where he is. My brain is demanding that I break ranks and run, run, run for the door. I can't breathe; I desperately need to get the Hell out of this horrible little room. After checking to see if we have replaced our gas masks correctly, the instructor finds that one of us has missed a snap. We are informed of his discovery and told to check our gas mask pouches to determine which of us is responsible for delaying our departure. Finally, I hear the beautiful sound of a snap as one of us pushes his loose fastener into position. Thank God maybe we can now get the Hell out of here.

No, we're not leaving yet. Each of us, on command, is individually instructed to scream out our name, rank, and serial number. When the last man responds, we all sing what has to be the worst ever rendition of the Marine Corps hymn's first verse. When you can't breathe, you can't sing. Our instructor is making sure we all ingest a total dose of the debilitating gas. No one can hold their breath while they are shouting or singing.

After completing our singing attempt, we follow the first man in the squad to the door by holding onto the man's shoulder in front of us. Outside we threw up, cough, gag, and endure burning skin. The next squad to enter the gas chamber looks at us with an expression of, "Oh my God, is this going to happen to us?"

In war, learning not to panic under stress is a must-know survival skill. I believe panic control was by far the most valuable lesson we learned while in the gas chamber. Trust me when I say the urge to run from a room filled with CS gas can be overwhelming.

I am pleased to report that I never experienced gas warfare in Vietnam. Others did in the Battle of Hue and Khe Sanh.

CHAPTER TWO

CAMP LEJEUNE

Life of a Grunt

After just seventeen weeks of the Marine Corps' mental and physical training programs, I now see the world differently. My neighborhood's negative influences fade away like an early morning fog yielding to the rising sun.

Upon completion of infantry training at Camp Geiger, we are off to our duty stations. The four-digit military occupancy specialty number, MOS assigned to each of us, now becomes particularly important. Your MOS determines the type of service you will perform and where you will perform it. My orders assign me to Camp Lejeune, North Carolina, just a few miles away, where I become a member of Charlie Company, First Battalion, Sixth Marine Regiment, 2nd Marine Division.

Upon arrival, the first sergeant of Charlie Company asks me to choose which holiday I would prefer to celebrate, Christmas or New Year's, during ten days of leave? I select Christmas, by far, my favorite holiday. I am given a bunk assignment and then transportation to a nearby train station.

The train ride home seems to take forever. When the other passengers begin to complain about a robust outdoor odor, I am delighted. The smell of the Trainer Refinery owned by Sinclair Oil Company was ever-present in my childhood. Arriving home after completing four months of Marine Corps training, I am immensely proud of myself; the "Space Cadet" has accomplished something. My family and neighborhood receive me well.

After spending some time with my parents, I reconnect with my girlfriend and soon discover our relationship has changed. You can never entirely go home again. Once you leave and then return, it is never the same because you have disturbed an unexplainable timeline. Everything is the same but different. Friends are still friends yet; you have changed. The girlfriend and I get along well. However, I am the only person in town who doesn't know she is enjoying the company of several other young men. I, too, eventually figure it out. Although not happy, I chose to let it slide for now. Why not? I am in a great mood and need her companionship.

After Christmas leave, I return to Camp Lejeune and make my way to the squad bay that billets Charlie Company's 2nd platoon. I begin unpacking, and of course, all my new friends, the guys I now live with, come over to help. The old salts, the ones who have been there for over a year, start going through my stuff, picking up most everything. They soon discover that my Mom has put a packet of chocolate milk into my luggage; how embarrassing for me when they find a brightly colored waxy cardboard box with an attached straw designed for children. Oh yeah, it has a series of transparent plastic circles so you can watch the chocolate milk progressing through the swirls before it reaches the adorable little bear at the top. One of my new friends picks it up and says, "How lovely, he has chocolate milk with a little bear straw." Then another guy speaks up, "Whoa, there is more, "Check out the charming rubber booties." My Mom has also packed a pair of rubber booties designed to slip over your dress shoes on rainy days. She had packed both items so her little boy could enjoy chocolate milk sucked through a kiddy straw, and his shoes would not get wet. Oh, they have great fun at my expense. Within a few weeks, nothing about me is unknown to them. We repeatedly mess with each other, and I soon learn to roll with the punches.

Stationed at Camp Lejeune with an MOS of 0311, I experience the life of an infantryman for the next two years. Infantry tactics and infantry weapons have become my specialties. Ongoing infantry training is now the dominant activity of my life. My MOS' more common name is "The GRUNTS," where the smell of sweat and recently fired weapons is routine. However, you do not spend two years at Camp Lejeune. That is where you train before being deployed to either the Caribbean or the Mediterranean. The cycle works like this; starting in January, new Marines just out of boot camp join the line companies, and the Marines that have been there for two years move on to guard outfits. Marines who receive an MOS of 0311 serve in infantry units or guard duty stations. I don't want to be a guard of any kind because Marine guard outfits have stacks of strict rules; we call them "chicken shit" rules. Marine guards must wear the uniform of the day every day. Your dress and appearance must be meticulous; I prefer the field.

We train from January to April. When I say train, I mean extensive training. Repetition of all the infantry skills we learned at Camp Geiger but much more in-depth. We spend at least three and a half days and three nights of every week playing war games in the pine forests of North Carolina.

The First Battalion, Sixth Marines deploys on a Caribbean cruise in early June of 1964. On a ship, you soon discover the connection between the Marine Corps and the Navy[7]. We live in very cramped quarters, always within a few feet of one another, sleeping on hammocks stacked one above the other six high and two abreast. We disembark from the ship by going over the side using nets to climb into landing crafts that move up and down with ocean waves' rhythm. One moment the small vessel is just under your foot; the next moment, it is several yards below the net.

One infantry company from our battalion defends the fence lines separating Guantanamo Bay Naval Base, "Gitmo," from the rest of Cuba's island. The other two companies of the battalion go to Vieques, an island owned by Puerto Rico. Vieques is primarily barren and sparsely populated. No problem for the "Green Machine – the U.S. Marine Corps," which finds it perfect for practicing everything from infantry tactics to close air support from jets dropping ordnance or strafing with machine guns. Constantly training on the island of Vieques, we all become more proficient at the skills of applied violence.

The Marine Corps does not allow its infantry Marines to become too comfortable. It is customary for us to spend most of our days and

---

[7] **Did you ever wonder why the Marine Corps is part of the Department of the Navy?** Historically, marines serve as a navy's ground troops. In fact, the word "marine" is the French word for sea, which may be why the French military historically called English troops — who all had to arrive by sea — "marines." WWW.defense.gov

nights in the field. When we are not in the field, we enjoy the luxury of sleeping on cots in Quonset huts large enough to hold an entire platoon. On the weekends, we enjoy movies at an outdoor theater. The projected picture and sound work well as we sit on railroad ties embedded into a bank. They also have a tent where you can purchase beer for ten cents a can—beer and movies; make for a big night on Vieques' island.

One evening, our outdoor movie is unexpectedly interrupted by an order to dress in full combat gear and prepare to board ships waiting off Vieques' coast. Rumor has it that there was an altercation between the Marines and Cubans guarding the fence line at "Gitmo," about 650 miles away. When we arrive, we use landing crafts to transport from the ship anchored in deep water to the dock onshore. Two-line companies immediately move to the fence line as reinforcements. It is pretty dull, hot as Hell, with nothing going on. Whatever the problem was, it went away naturally, or perhaps the Cubans have a change of heart after discovering two other Marine infantry companies in their backyard. After a couple of days of baking in the sun, we return to our transport ships. The following day, we are delighted to hear that everyone, Marines, and Sailors, will be given liberty on Guantanamo Bay Naval Base and encouraged to enjoy recreational opportunities from 1300 to 2400 hours (1:00 pm to 12:00 am).

Liberty sounds excellent, and we can't wait to get ashore. The average age of Marines and Sailors is between 18 and 20 years. We are all anticipating the services of friendly, warm prostitutes. That doesn't happen. There are no women of any kind here, nothing but love-starved young men, lots of them. Civilized types of recreation are available, bowling alleys and movie theaters are plentiful. However, most everyone goes to the enlisted man's club where women are absent, but whiskey and beer are abundant and cheap. A shot of whiskey costs twenty-five cents. The Marine behind the bar pouring whiskey doesn't want to keep refilling our drinking glasses, so we all get a double shot of Stoch or bourbon or whatever it is we are drinking for twenty-five cents. Our chosen recreational activity is to consume copious amounts of alcohol; everyone gets whiskey drunk.

Late that evening, hundreds of intoxicated Marines and Sailors waiting for landing crafts to transport them back to the ships create a dangerous situation. There is way too much testosterone in one place resulting in chaos as fights break out everywhere between Marines and Sailors.

A young Second Lieutenant jumps up on the piles at the end of the dock. From his perch, he orders everyone to attention. A drunk PFC picks him up and throws him into the ocean. The entire military structure has fallen apart; there is no order whatsoever—just too many young men whiskey stupid drunk in too small an area. Marines are fighting with Sailors, or if they can't find a Sailor, other Marines. This night the military structure goes to Hell, a total cluster fuck of men fighting for no apparent reason. The only way to get out of a fight is to get into a fight. You see, if you politely stand around waiting for the landing craft to transport you back to the ship and someone who just got their ass kicked sees you standing by yourself, they will walk up and coldcock you. The next day the investigators could not charge anyone because everyone is guilty to some extent or another. The military decides to forget the entire night of madness because no one was sober enough to tell them who, what, or why it all occurred.

For some reason, the transport ships on which we board head for Panama. We don't go ashore. We circle off the coast for a week or so, and then it's back to Vieques for more war games. We are becoming good at our jobs as infantrymen; that part of our deployment is working well. However, we are also getting claustrophobic on that small rock protruding from the Atlantic Ocean.

One afternoon the monotony of training is interrupted with a perfect example of "negotiation." Two of the largest and most powerful men in our company begin to fight. Their altercation provides the rest of us with a live demonstration of a foundational life skill, "The Art of the Deal."

One of the men fighting is Shawn Grady, a tall Marine with a large, stocky frame. He indeed carries his size well; a gifted athlete, moving his large body with rhythm and speed. He is unnaturally strong and can run like a panther.

I came to realize just what a physical threat this man is about four months before our deployment to the Caribbean one evening when six or eight of us were playing cards in the barracks at Camp Lejeune. We have our regular session of telling stories and teasing one another before entering a psychological discussion about women and oral sex. All of us, so-called worldly young men with testosterone dripping from our fingernails, are happily pontificating about our favorite subject.

The discussion becomes one of determining if all women will provide oral sex. Several members of our scholarly group proclaim that good girls will never participate in oral sex. When asked for my opinion, I report with complete confidence that all women will provide oral sex. It is natural and will occur with the right man without exception if he can light them on fire with sexual desire.

Shawn immediately speaks up, "All women will not provide oral sex." I say, "The Hell they won't, there's no such thing as a cold woman, only clumsy men. Trust me; they will all provide oral sex." He responds, "What about my Mom"? Without thinking, I say, "Of course she will, under the right conditions." He looks at me with rage in his eyes before shouting, "You just called my Mom a cock sucker. I'm going to kick your ass." He reaches across the table to gather me up. You don't fight a guy like Shawn without a gun. Trying to match physical strength with this guy is not a good idea. Missing his initial effort to grab me, he stands up and runs around to my side of the table. Oh shit, I run down the squad bay with the enraged bull chasing me. The rest of the guys in the squad bay are laughing like Hell as they push footlockers in front of Shawn to trip him up so that he doesn't kill me. After a couple of laps around the entire squad bay, he starts laughing. Thank God.

Shawn is fighting his weightlifting buddy, Bret Wentworth, an extraordinary individual who has recently extended his military career to attend the Naval Academy in Annapolis, Maryland. The two strongest men of Charlie Company have come to blows. First, they forcibly push one another and then began trading heavy strikes to the head and body before the fight goes to the ground.

Now here's where it gets interesting, Shawn and Bret have each other wrapped in bear hugs as they roll down a steep hill. When the two combatants reach the bottom, they continue to squeeze one another with their mighty arms. Two big guys squeezing one another may not sound too significant until you realize how abnormally strong they are. The mutual chest squeezes prevent both men from expanding their lungs so that neither one can breathe. They press each other with incredible intensity. These guys have the type of power that can just shut down the entire breathing process. They are mutually disabled, but each wants badly to dominate the other; neither desires to stop fighting. They continue to squeeze each other so tight they both turn blue.

Now comes the true meaning of negotiations. One man whispers to the other, "I will let go if you will." His opponent replies, "Ok, ease off." They both slid back before standing and departing in separate directions.

The true meaning of negotiation is that no one will seriously negotiate with you unless they fear you. You must have something with which to retaliate. Your opponent must know that if he doesn't do this, then a consequence is assured. If you are powerless without options, you will never successfully negotiate. The strong men turning blue as they mutually squeeze one another provided a college-level course of the foundational components of negotiation for the observant viewer.

Liberty

Great news, we are about to go on liberty heading for Old San Juan, Puerto Rico. Oh my God, women, women, and more women. That's an excellent way of saying prostitution. We are delighted to be going, and the ladies will be equally happy to welcome us.

Based on a port and starboard liberty system, every Marine is provided two alternating days of relaxation in Old San Juan. We depart the ship in the early afternoon dressed in crisp, khaki summer uniforms. We are spotless in every respect. After saluting the flag and the officer on deck, we are on our own. We can do whatever we want until liberty expires at midnight. They call it Cinderella Liberty.

The island of Puerto Rico offers many tourist attractions, from historical forts to guided nature hikes. However, most Marines are not interested in those wholesome activities unless we can be back in town by early evening. No, we are looking to drink whiskey and spend time among the vast number of prostitutes that have come to town to meet the Marines and Sailors. I am sure this all sounds coarse in these days of politically correct speech and conduct. However, in 1964, I am a nineteen-year-old young man who could not have been happier.

We soon learn the strict rules of accepted conduct while in the company of the ladies. First, you must pay seven dollars for her services. Yes, that's correct, seven dollars. You walk out of a bar, down a sidewalk, and enter a two-story building; let's call it a motel with lots of rooms. After walking up a steep staircase and greeted by a man from behind a screen who takes the seven-dollar payment, five dollars for the lady, and two dollars for fifteen minutes of room rental, he assigns you accommodation and starts a timer. Regardless of how things go, everything must happen within the allotted time. There is not a lot of foreplay. This arrangement is quite different from an evening on the town, with wine and dining slowly working your way towards a romantic encounter. I have a pocket full of money because previously, there was little opportunity to spend my monthly compensation of 85.80, which I earn as a private first class. During recovery time between seven-dollar expenditures, I laugh and drink Cuba Libre, a drink made from rum and coke. I just couldn't be happier. Old San Juan, Puerto Rico was fantastic.

A fair question to ask would be how paying for sex with strangers affects a young man's transitions? In my opinion, to be successful in life, all of us must learn to manage two unavoidable driving forces of human evolutionary genetic inheritance. One is sex, and the other is violence. Two hundred thousand years ago, Homo sapiens began passing on traits that allowed us to survive and reproduce in a hostile environment. The more proficient a person is in first comprehending and managing those determinant influences, the better they will use their other inherited or learned talents. I am not suggesting you must learn to be violent or sexually promiscuous. I am stating that by discovering who you are and coming to accept yourself with an understanding of sex and violence's inherited impulses, the more successful, you will be in life. The bottom line, your brain will not be constantly distracted by your insecurities resulting from the stress of performance anxiety. Your mind will more efficiently utilize the possibilities of life. Now, you may be thinking, what professional authority allows me to make such statements. My source of authority stands on a prosperous life. I have been married to the same woman for over fifty years and blessed with a loving family.

Tattoos are all the rage among Marines on liberty in Old San Juan. Why don't I have one like so many other Marine grunts that proudly reads USMC, Semper Fi, or some other reference to the fact that I am a Marine? Well, I did stand in line, waiting for my turn to be branded. Yes, on the second night of my liberty, I picked out a tattoo that I thought was incredibly cool. The Marine Corps mascot, a bulldog wearing a helmet with letters USMC boldly printed under it, seemed perfect. That was my choice, and I had enough money left to purchase it. However, after standing in line for what felt like an eternity, I begin to realize that liberty will soon expire, and the tattoo artist is overwhelmed with customers. With the effect of alcohol diminishing, the idea of a bulldog's image drilled into my arm doesn't feel as vital as it was an hour ago.

How much would my chosen tattoo cost? You guessed it, seven dollars, and I had precisely seven dollars left, not one penny more, not one penny less. Time for a decision; whether to make one more trip upstairs or wait a bit longer for a bulldog to be hastily inked into my arm? Today, I do not have any tattoos because I chose option one, another trip upstairs.

That last night of liberty, another event took place that would forever change the life of a very personable and pleasant member of our platoon, Lance Corporal Venter. His amiable nature is ever-present until he drinks whiskey. Then nice guy Venter turns into an angry menace threatening everyone with aggressive behavior.

We would tell him the next day when he was sober, "You got to knock this aggressive shit off. What you become when you drink is ugly. Knock off the bullshit and clean up your act." Venter would always reply, "Sorry guys, it will never happen again, I promise. I apologize to everyone, so sorry." Unfortunately, his promise to change never takes place. When he drinks any alcohol, especially whiskey, he soon turns into a scary Cro-Magnon man. Venter is not a guy you want to go toe to toe with. He is a formable opponent, drunk or sober. On the other hand, none of us want to fight him because we all like him most of the time.

On the last night of liberty Venter is the recipient of a hands-on method of psychological change. He leaves a bar with a prostitute and proceeds up two flights of steps for his fifteen minutes of love in a rented room. Most Marines and Sailors are perfect gentlemen returning to the bar happy and relaxed. Not Venter; he somehow gets into a confrontation with the man behind the screen at the top of the stairs. Unable to settle the situation and repeated physical threats against him, the man behind the screen calls the shore patrol.

Shore patrol means that corporals or sergeants assigned to duty that night become roving policemen after being issued an official duty belt with an attached nightstick. Marines and Sailors work together because both branches of services enjoy the same time and location for liberty. However, neither of these non-commissioned officers is trained in police procedures or military legal guidelines concerning force use.

Most of the time, this all works well because their primary function is to respond to disruption and calm it down. Make the state of unrest go away, so whoever makes the complaint is satisfied, and whoever is causing the problem relocated. The troublemaker is put into a cab and sent to another location or back to the ship. No one desires to ruin your night of liberty, only to restore order, so you don't destroy anyone else's.

When the shore patrol arrives, Venter is standing at the top of a steep staircase. He is whiskey drunk, raising hell, and intimidating everyone. The two non-commissioned officers who have never met Venter walk up the steps to a small landing and then make a sharp turn before walking up to another flight of steps. At the very top, they approach Venter, who continues to be distributive. The corporal quietly says, "Hey, you need to settle down and come with us. Let's make this situation go away before you get into real trouble. So just come with us, and we will help you change locations, okay"? Venter immediately punches the corporal in the face and knocks him to the floor. Then, he attempts to kick the Marine as he lay on his back. The corporal sprang to his feet and struck Venter in the face with his nightstick. Venter drops to the floor with a fractured nose and loose teeth. The irate corporal kicks him down the first flight of steps before kicking him down the second flight and out the door to the street. Venter has hit the wrong man. The next day instead of making his usual apologies, he is in severe discomfort with a cracked nose, black eyes, and loose teeth.

Well, that was Venter's "Come to Jesus Moment." Some beautiful woman destined to become his wife will never know the Venter of yesterday. That ass-kicking cured him. Somehow his aggressive behavior, previously manifested when he was intoxicated, stopped. Yeah, he can now drink with the rest of us, and we enjoy his company. Damn, the Marine Corps could just possibly replace psychiatrists or perhaps fill their offices with incurable patients.

Short Men Are Often Big

After returning to Camp Lejeune, we enjoy our barracks' more spacious areas after living in exceedingly tight quarters on troop transport ships. However, the barracks are also overcrowded, just a large bedroom adjacent to open use showers and toilets. Living closely with forty other men will teach you much about accepting others and sharing space. Forget privacy; grunts share all activities. Never do you have the luxury of going to your private room and enjoying quiet time.

I must confess we all get frustrated with one another at times. We often return to the barracks exhausted from days in the field with little sleep and grueling long marches. Part of our training is learning how to live productively with others, work as a team, control our anger, and share space.

Becoming proficient at living in close quarters has its trials and tribulations that sometimes do result in altercations. Most quarrels are verbal, rarely coming to blows for several reasons. First, we are like family without the option of separation. Another reason for controlling our anger is that you will be punished with the loss of rank or confined to the barracks if you disobey or start a fight with Marines that outrank you.

Returning from four days and three nights in the field late one Friday afternoon, I manage to lose my temper and do get into a knockdown, "I am going to tear your head off," type of fight with the Marine that bunks below me. The space between adjacent bunks is only several feet wide and eight feet or so long. That afternoon we are attempting to remove our packs when we vigorously bang into one another. Neither of us yields space. As we exchange fighting words, we begin forcibly pushing and shoving.

I consider my opponent to be a small man because he is short in stature, maybe five feet five inches tall. I decide to attack him with a body slam. With the aid of heavy legs, I perform leg, shoulder, and hip throws well. My favorite move is to squeeze my opponent's throat and push him backward. After tilting him off balance, I leg sweep him by stepping forward with my left leg and swinging my right leg to strike just below the calves and above his ankles, forcing his feet out from under him. Without exception, everyone I have fought in training lands on their backs under my attack. They are entirely swept off their feet by the power of my heavy leg strike.

With confidence, I grab my advisory's right shirtsleeve just above the wrist and hold it off to the side as I grasp his neck. The problem I immediately encounter is my opponent doesn't have a neck, not really. His head seems to sit on his shoulders. What little bit of a neck he does offer is vast and thick. My attempt to force him to lean backward to avoid pain created by grabbing his throat is unsuccessful, as is my leg sweep. I soon discover that his center of gravity is exceptionally low, and his legs are large and muscular. All I manage to do with my tried and tested leg sweep is to infuriate him further.

He retaliates by grasping my arms with huge hands that surround my biceps. I am powerless as he lifts me as you would a child with incredible strength before thrusting my head into the angle iron of the bed frame. The rage in his eyes is more unsettling than the pain caused by my head colliding with the iron frame. Held helplessly in the grip of a man who completely overpowers me, I realize that I have written a check that my ass can't cash. Yes, this Marine is short. However, he is a big man in every other respect. When he pulls me close so he can once again thrust me into the iron frame, I bite his face. Yes, I make use of the only weapon I have available to protect my head from being repeatedly smashed into the angle iron directly behind me. I don't let go even when his blood runs into my mouth. He is instantly shocked, allowing me to break loose of his death grip and twist him off balance before we both go to the floor. I am on top of him when the platoon sergeant separates us.

My opponent is undeniably one of the strongest men in our platoon. Never again will I determine another man's power by his height. Formidable men and women come in many shapes and sizes.

I eventually realized that my mistake was to overestimate my power and abilities and underestimate my opponent completely. Learning that the enemy is more potent or has tactical advantages doesn't mean that you are without recourse. It does mean that you must accurately measure your adversary before committing those in your command whenever possible. The talent of comprehending strengths and weaknesses, be it of an individual or an enemy battalion, is foundational to success in combat. Just as I allow anger and an over-sense of confidence to motivate me to attack a man with overwhelming strength, leaders in war may make the same mistake.

In less than a year, I will lead Marines in combat. The lesson I learn from foolishly attacking the large and powerful man who just happens to be short became foundational in determining what is and is not possible.

Return of the "Space Cadet"

I have met all the requirements for promotion to Lance Corporal, E3. But, how much of that "Space Cadet" from the neighbor is still controlling my life? I am on the edge of a transition, and I don't realize it.

Sunday morning, after enjoying a great weekend visiting with my family and girlfriend, I pack my travel bag. I still have a few hours left before meeting my ride to Camp Lejeune.

I'm off to the neighborhood billiard room to shoot a game of pool and say hello to some of my old friends. When it's time for me to head home, Sonny walks in. "Hey, I got us a ride back to the base from a guy that will pick us up in town." Great news, we have a few more hours to hang out. I rack the table for another game of 8-ball. Soon, I get bored shooting pool because Sonny can magically position a cue ball. I grow weary of losing.

Sonny and I decide to go to a local bar. Yeah, have a couple of drinks before we push off for our trip back to the base. Seagram's Seven Whiskey and Seven-Up soda is our choice of beverage. I soon discover drinks of Seven and Seven can drastically alter my mind. Particularly when I drink one after another, then tell the bartender to take out the ice since it is slowing me down. We are drinking straight shots of whiskey. What got into us, what made us do that, I don't know. There is a point where we should have stopped, yet we didn't; we drank like fools.

Now it's time to leave the bar, but I am too drunk to drive. I suggest that Sonny drive my mother's car. How is that for an executive decision?

Sonny drives so fast that when the road curves, he loses control. The car sliding sideways into and then over a curb begins to roll but first hits a wire fence, preventing it from flipping. Finally, the runaway vehicle slows by sliding down a hundred feet or so of the Sinclair Oil Company's heavy-duty security fence. Eventually, we bounce back onto the road. Excited by the wild ride, we continue jamming to the music blaring from the radio, tuned to WIBG. I say, "Let's go! We have to get back to the base; I've got a promotion coming tomorrow morning."

We soon discover that the car can't be driven forward, only in circles. As we are trying to leave the scene, a tow truck arrives. Sonny immediately falls to the ground when we get out of the car; his legs will no longer support him. I throw him over my shoulder and start walking towards my home about two miles away. A car full of rescuers stops and loads Sonny and me in their back seat and drives us to my house.

I enter my parent's house to pick up my travel bag. As it would happen, my stepfather's brother and his wife are visiting when we burst in. My stepdad says, "Hey, you are late. Oh my God, you're drunk. Where is our car"? I said, "Oh, I think I wrapped it around a fucking pole on Post Road." My answer infuriates my stepfather. That type of profanity is spoken in the motor shop among men, never in our home. Characteristic of my stepfather, he says, "Get the hell out of here." I pick up my little bag and go outside just as a police car pulls up. Sonny sees the cop and hobbles down the alley to avoid him. That leaves the officer and I facing one another in the tiny front yard of my parent's home.

The police officer announces that I am under arrest, "You have left the scene of an accident." I respond, "Sir, I can't go with you because I have to get back to the base. My stepfather will take care of everything; he will go with you." He barks, "I am not asking you. I am telling you to get in this car." I tell him, "I can't do that, and I am not going to do that." He pulls out his nightstick and says, "You are resisting arrest." We both begin to circle the small front yard like two combatants. Thankfully, my stepfather comes out of the house and tells me, "Get in the car, I will go with you, and we will take care of this and get you back to the base."

All anyone has to say is they will help me get back to the base, which will satisfy my alcohol-saturated brain. Yes, back to Camp Lejeune, then everything will be ok. My stepfather and I get into the back seat of the police car. The cruiser pulls away from my home and soon makes a right-hand turn onto 9th Street. A man in a red baseball hat, a councilman, a low-ranking member of the local government, flags the police car down and announces that he has captured the other individual. When Sonny left my house, he discovers once again he can hardly walk. Trying to hide, he enters a sandwich shop. When Sonny steps out, the councilman runs across a parking lot and tackles him. Realizing he has knocked down an injured man, he calls an ambulance to transport Sonny to the hospital.

The councilman is now sitting in the police cruiser's front seat, running his mouth about how he got one of these punks and how pleased he is that the officer has captured the other. I speak up, "That guy is not a punk." He replies, "You are both punks, just two shit heads out of control." I start kicking the screen separating the front seat from the back. When you are in the back seat of a police car, you are basically in prison because a heavy wire screen separates the car's front from the back. There are no inside door handles. You are in confinement. However, by kicking the screen hard enough, you can break it loose. I did free it from its bindings allowing the screen to strike the police officer in the back of his neck with each additional kick. The officer immediately pulls off to the side of the road and opens the cruiser's back door, so my stepfather can get away from me.

Soon, four other police cars arrive and park in front and behind the one I am in. Suffering from excessive alcohol consumption, I see double images of the spinning red lights.

The local politician, the councilman wearing the red baseball hat, presses his nose against the rear passenger window of the cop car and starts screaming at me. I respond by kicking out the window. Yes, I just took my foot and smashed it through the right rear window of the police car. Boom! Now we have no window between us, making it possible for me to reach him quickly. Five police officers gather to form a half-circle next to the rear door of the car. A big burly cop opens it and screams, "Get out of the car! Get out now!" I fly out of the opened door and punch the police officer in his face. I then begin hitting all the other cops, anyone I can reach. I feel as though I am winning. I am not. They all hold night-sticks and are about to use them. Trust me, Philadelphia area cops don't hold back corporal punishment from anyone who strikes them. In the 1960s, if you punched an officer of the law, they responded with overwhelming force. When the perpetrator recovered, he would spread the word on the street. "Don't hit cops if you are anywhere near Philadelphia, Pa."

My stepfather saves me from a severe beat down. He pleads with me, "Stop, stop fighting." I can see a woodland behind the officers, knowing I will be free if I can get to it. Nobody can catch me in the woods. I have never heard my stepfather plead in my entire life. He realizes I am only seconds away from being hammered with multiple nightsticks. His pleas were like a distant voice; I stop fighting. One cop immediately positions a device over my wrist, which he then twists. The resulting pain goes into my bones. You would have to be dead not to feel it. Another cop grabs my left arm and jams it hard behind my back. A third cop starts pounding me in the chest and stomach. However, his blows are to my body, not to my head. That's because my stepfather is witnessing the entire assault. However, my stepdad's presence doesn't prevent the officers from unmerciful punching me; the cops kick my ass.

When they are tired of beating me, I am placed in handcuffs and thrown into another police car, one with its wire screen in place and all its windows intact. While en-route to the courthouse in Marcus Hook, Pa, I sit quietly, trying to recover from too much whiskey and too many well-landed blows. Subdued, not sober, but low-key, I am escorted into the courthouse and placed in an oversized wooden chair in the center hall. I quietly sit until approached by none other than the councilman wearing the red baseball hat. He leans over, gets right in my face, and begins yelling at me. I absorb his verbal assault until his eyes leave me and look towards the officers standing nearby. I can clasp my still cuffed hands together as I jump up, striking him. I miss my intended target, his neck, thank God. I might have severely hurt him. I can't assess the damage the blow creates because two police officers throw me back in the chair. I am once again out of control, screaming profanities, the nastiest words ever uttered in a courthouse.

A judge who is holding a legal proceeding down the hall is interrupted by my outrage. He is upset when he leaves the courtroom and briskly walks to my chair, where two officers hold me in place. He scolds me, "Young man, this is the house of justice. Just who do you think you are screaming profanity in our courthouse"? I shout my answer, "Fuck you, you bald-headed cock sucker." Yes, that was my answer to his question regarding respect. Oh, I am having a big day. The judge says only three words, "Lock him up." I am immediately thrown into a cell and left alone to ponder my situation. Several hours later, I awaken with a terrible headache before throwing up. I violently expel everything in my stomach. I continue to throw up even though nothing is left to throw, a condition called "Dry Heaves." I am not feeling well, but I am no longer drunk.

I begin to realize the gravity of my situation. I have reverted to "Mr. Space Cadet."

My stepfather and my stepbrother come to my cell to speak with me. They say they are going to do their best to get me back to the base. Before leaving, my stepfather declares, "Boy, you are in a world of trouble. You are at the mercy of the judicial system."

I don't remember how long I sat in silence before a young police officer takes me from my confinement to a private office. I believe it is a room where they question prisoners. He asks what happened and what is my rank is in the Marine Corps. I tell him that I am scheduled for promotion the following day to lance corporal E-3. I confess that I have just screwed everything up. I have been doing well before I came home for the weekend. He says, "You have been in the Marine Corps for less than two years, and you have made the rank of lance corporal"? I am beginning to believe this officer is a former Marine. "Yes, I was recommended by my platoon commander. Tomorrow morning, I will be promoted. Well, that is until they hear what I did this afternoon."

He gets up and leaves. I am never to see him again. Another officer escorts me back to the cell for several more hours of confinement until, to my complete surprise, my parents stand before me. It is now 11:30 in the evening. The judge has left his home and returned to the courthouse to hold an after-hours legal proceeding where he fines me three hundred dollars, a lot of money for my family in 1964. My mother, stepfather, and stepbrother now drive me to another town, Trainer, Pennsylvania, the car accident's jurisdiction. The magistrate of that town gets out of bed to hold another legal proceeding where I am fined an additional one hundred and fifty dollars. My family doesn't have an extra four hundred and fifty dollars to pay for my bullshit. They are devastated by my outrageous conduct.

Earlier Sonny's brother called Camp Lejeune, reporting that we have been in an accident. He explains to the base authorities that we will be returning beyond our authorized time of liberty. He also advises me to go to Chester Hospital's emergency room to be checked out and, most importantly, get documentation that proves I have been there. All this sounds good to me because my left arm is screaming with pain from the manhandling I received from the Trainer and Marcus Hook police. The medical staff at the hospital informs me all was well with my arm, expecting a full recovery if I rest it.

The following morning Sonny and I are on a bus heading for North Carolina. I don't know what to expect when I return. While serving on active duty in the U.S. Armed Forces, you can be punished twice for the same offense because you are under the jurisdiction of civilian and military law. I fully expect to be reduced in rank after the authorities become aware of my weekend activities.

The ride back is long, and I am extremely ashamed of myself. I have stepped on the other side of trying to transition to a better mindset. It seems I am a prisoner of my past, "A fuck up." When I enter the orderly room, the company first sergeant comes out of his office to greet me. He speaks first, "We received a message that you were in an accident. Are you ok"? I reply, "Yes, I am fine, just a bit sore." He asks, "Are you able to join the company in the field"? I cheerfully answer, "Yes." I change into my field clothes and strap on my helmet and cartridge belt. Rifle in hand, I mount a waiting jeep and soon join Charlie Company in the woodlands of North Carolina. No one mentions the accident. They know nothing of my horrific conduct.

The world had reached out to a young Marine and given him a second chance to pull his head out of his ass. Things are a bit different in 1964. Respect for service members is commonplace in a post-World War II society. There is no official recording of my numerous offenses. I am guilty of leaving the scene of an accident, destroying the police car's wire screen, and kicking out its window. As well as assaulting several police officers, a local politician, and calling the judge a "bald-headed cock sucker." Everybody is stepping up for me, yet I am screwing up by the numbers. Will I ever mature?

Our platoon's squad bay's bulletin board displays "Dear John letters" from our girlfriends. Yes, we often receive letters stating that our relationships with them are over. The basic theme of the correspondence goes about like this; "After you left town, I discovered Jody, and we have fallen madly in love. So, goodbye." To lighten the gloom, we created a contest to honor the best "Dear John Letter of the Month." A letter that genuinely stands out for being the most impactful, skillfully written, or downright gut-wrenching.

I to receive a Dear John letter. It reads in part; "Do not come home, you are not welcome, stay away." I have wrecked the family car, and my parents paid for a hundred feet of Sinclair Oil Companies' cyclone fence and the damage to the Trainer police car. They also paid fines in two different towns totaling over four hundred and fifty dollars. Not to mention how I have embarrassed them in front of our neighbors and visiting family. Due to this irresponsible behavior, my mother and stepfather have decided it will be best if I stay away. So my mom sent me a Dear John Letter. However, her Letter did win the best "Dear John Letter" of the month.

Operation Steel Pike

After my mother's written declaration stating I am no longer welcome at home, it is somewhat of a reprieve when the entire 2nd Marine Division is deployed on Operation Steel Pike[8] from October to November 1964. Charlie Company crosses the Atlantic Ocean in an APA troopship[9]. We Marines are the cargo, men dressed in olive drab utilities cramped together like sardines. The chow lines are so long they never end. Standing at the

---

[8] **Operation Steel Pike** was the largest peacetime amphibious landing exercise in history, conducted by the United States Navy and Marine Corps and taking place on the coast of Spain in October to November 1964. The operation involved 84 naval ships and 28,000 Marines of the 2nd Marine Division, and was commanded by Vice Admiral John S. McCain, Jr.. In the opening hour of the landing, two helicopters collided in mid-air, resulting in the deaths of nine Marines and causing injuries to 13 others. Another Marine was crushed to death by a tank while asleep in his sleeping bag. Operation Steel Pike | Military Wiki | Fandom (wikia.org)

[9] **Haskell-class attack transports (APA)** were amphibious assault ships of the United States Navy created in 1944. They were designed to transport 1,500 troops and their combat equipment, and land them on hostile shores with the ships' integral landing craft. Haskell-class Attack Transport amphibious assault ships (savyboat.com)

end of a breakfast line can very well mean you are in front of the same line for lunch. Sleeping quarters consist of stacked hammocks just above the floor and only a few feet from the ceiling.

What a spectacular sight it is to witness eighty-four ships crossing the Atlantic Ocean in tactical formation. First, we disembark the troop carriers by climbing down nets into landing craft. Then, after spending several hours sitting in the bottom of small boats going around in circles and watching Marines throw up from seasickness, we run across a lowered ramp onto the beach. The entire land phase of Operation Steel Pike occurs in the Andalusia region in Almeria, Spain's southeastern corner. Moving a division of Marines and their machines of war is inherently dangerous. Two helicopters collide, killing nine Marines and injuring 13 others. Another Marine is killed in his sleeping bag when a tank runs over him.

After the operation's land phase concludes, the task is to move 28,000 Marines and their equipment back onto waiting ships. The first night on the beach, we enjoy bonfires and a bit of locally purchased wine. The beach party ends when the battalion commander orders us to conduct ourselves professionally while waiting in the assembly areas. The entire 2nd Marine Division is back on the ships in less than a week, heading for different seaports. Our battalion is treated with four days of liberty in Lisbon, Portugal, and La Coruna, Spain. Neither of these ports is a typical liberty destination for Marines and Sailors. The usual diversions generally found in most seaports routinely visited by young servicemen are not available. However, we are provided with an outstanding opportunity to explore two European cities and enjoy them as ordinary tourists. Well received by the locals, we behave ourselves.

Diana and I

Shortly after the 2nd Marine Division returns from Operation Steel Pike, I depart for ten days of Christmas leave. Not forgetting that I am no longer welcome in my childhood home, I call my mother from a bus station in Washington D.C. requesting permission to visit. She grants my request after stating her unnegotiable conditions.

Following a relatively lukewarm welcome home from my parents, I go to the neighborhood auto body shop to visit friends. I soon discover Diana Ramos, a beautiful young woman with a warm and affectionate personality, is working in a department store in Chester, Pennsylvania, during her semester break from Moore College of Art & Design in Philadelphia. I immediately devise a plan to reintroduce myself by going to her workplace under the pretense that I am shopping for Christmas gifts. After discovering that she worked in the infant's department, my shopping excuse for meeting her was a bit difficult to support. However, I am delighted when she warmly responds to my unannounced presence with pleasant conversation until her supervisor suggests that she return to her duties.

That evening without notification, I drive to Diana's bus stop and wait for her to arrive. When she does, I approach and offer to drive her home; she accepts. On the way, we pulled into a drive-in restaurant and spent an hour talking and laughing.

That cold December night, as we drink cokes and enjoy our hamburgers, neither of us has the remotest realization that we will be married next summer and that Diana will deliver our first child the following February.

Diana and I first met in 9th grade and shared an easy friendship all through high school. We dated several times during my ten days of Christmas leave, including a formal diner where I wore my Dress Blues Marine uniform. Unbeknownst to me, I have fallen in love with the woman with who I will spend the rest of my life.

Dominican Republic

During the annual January to April intensive training period at Camp Lejeune, I come home as often as possible to visit Diana. We are both very much attracted to one another and patiently wait for our next opportunity to be together. I treat her like a lady and conduct myself as a gentleman. She inspires me to improve and to become a man worthy of her.

Our weekends together are interrupted in late April by a civil war in the Dominican Republic. A system of rapid response standby alerts divided into three categories, Alpha, Bravo, and Charlie, define how quickly a company assigned to each will respond. Charlie Company serving as Alpha Alert, sits packed and ready to immediately board transportation when ordered to join Operation Power Pack[10] in the Caribbean.

Charlie Company is flown to Guantanamo Bay to board missile frigates that transport us to the Dominican Republic. Not designed to transport Marines, there is no place on board the frigates for us to sleep. The sailors give us their sleeping berths. They gave us their only place to sleep because they know we are going into a fight and will need the rest. No explanation, no one asks for recognition; the sailors voluntarily give us their berths.

We will soon experience the ultimate purpose and function of the U.S. Marine Corps. Armed conflict. The Dominican Republic's small country occupies the eastern two-thirds of Hispaniola's island, while

---

[10] The second American occupation of the Dominican Republic, code named "Operation Power Pack", began when the U.S. Marine Corps entered Santo Domingo, Dominican Republic, on April 28, 1965, in the Dominican Civil War. American occupation of the Dominican Republic (1965–1966) | Military Wiki | Fandom (wikia.org)

Haiti's government occupies the remaining one-third. A civil war among the military leaders, the presiding president, and different factions of the civilian population, often led by Cuban activists, creates chaos for the U.S. citizens living on the island. After several days of the conflict, all U.S. citizens and foreign nationals desiring evacuation move to the Hotel Embajador on the western outskirts of Santo Domingo.

Charlie Company, First Battalion, Sixth Marines, and a paratrooper company from the 82 Air Borne Division dig defensive positions surrounding the hotel to protect the evacuees. Units from the Marine Corps and the Army who moved into Santo Domingo's city are soon engaged in intense firefights with the enemy. However, identifying the enemy is confusing. By the time the U.S. intervened, many civilians armed themselves with captured weapons. Adding to the confusion of who is enemy and who is not, different Dominican military branches are loyal to their generals and admirals, not their president and the central government.

As we dig fighting positions around the hotel, we are immediately plagued with small red itchy bumps caused by a combination of intense heat and dirt. Later that afternoon, I see several flak jackets covered in blood. The dead Marines who had worn them are flown back to the ships anchored offshore, but their blood-soaked flak jackets remain. A message printed onto the jackets clearly states that they will not protect the wearer from bullets, only provide moderate shrapnel protection.

When night comes, our defensive positions begin receiving small arms fire. For the first time in my life, I am under fire; I am frightened. The incoming bullets speed safely over my head; however, their intended purpose is to kill me. Our orders are to hold fire unless we have an identifiable target. The Marine Corps is all about fire discipline, one shot - one kill. Yet, the 82 Air Borne hasn't received that message. They fire with such intensity throughout the night we Marines think they must be fighting off an infantry assault. They aren't. That is just the way they roll. When those soldiers are in doubt, they shoot.

The next morning a news reporter asks several of us how we handled the previous night. When I tell him I was frightened, he seems surprised.

He must have thought he was interviewing a hard-core battle seasoned Marine who had previously fought in Iwo Jima or Guadalcanal. Looking back on my exposure to deadly force that night and comparing it to my 13 months fighting the Vietnam War, it isn't a big deal. However, if you have never been shot at, just the sound of the weapons opposing you and the fact that another human being is trying to kill you will, trust me, be a big deal. Yes, that first night guarding the hotel, I am seriously frightened. What am I so afraid of? Dying, I am fearful of dying. People are actively trying to kill me. The bloody flak jackets I recently saw were worn by healthy young men only hours before. Men seasoned in combat learn how to control their fear, but they never can eliminate it. Fear is an inescapable component of war.

Our assignment to guard the Hotel Embajador is no longer necessary after everyone who desires to leave the island is evacuated. Our next mission is to search a vast cave in a remote area suspected of holding a weapons cache.

Leaving our defensive positions surrounding the hotel, Charlie Company must somehow carry hand grenades without grenade pouches. The small canvas bags designed to hold an infantry's men's grenades should have been issued when live ammunition was distributed among the troops. But, for whatever reason, there are none. So, what else can we do except attach them to our gear or put them in our pockets? Besides, if you never had a grenade pouch, you don't miss it. That is until a horrific death occurs because of our inability to carry those instruments of destruction properly.

Walking to our destination, one of us inadvertently drops a white phosphorus grenade[11]. A young boy about ten or twelve years old who has been following us picks it up. The boy has no idea what he is holding when he manages to pull the pin. He dies a horrific death in tremendous

---

[11] The **white phosphorus (WP) grenade** is an incendiary grenade that produces intense heat by means of a chemical reaction, burning at 2,800 °C (5,070 °F). The damage potential of WP grenades comes not only from the heat it produces, but also from the chemical itself - as the body is exposed to the grenade it may absorb the poisonous phosphorus, leading to deep burns and possible organ failure. White phosphorus grenade | Metal Gear Wiki | Fandom

pain when the phosphorus burned into his chest cavity, arms, neck, and face. He screams until he dies.

After witnessing a young boy's body being destroyed by a grenade that we dropped, I begin to understand that as Marines, we are agents of death. Everything we carry is designed to kill, from the full metal jacket bullets in our firearms to the grenades in our pockets to our brains, conditioned to perform acts of violence. A company of field Marines should be avoided unless you desire to be fucked or killed. The kid had the bad luck of crossing paths with us, the men of death. To this day, I am troubled when I see children handling fireworks. More than agitated, I want to intervene immediately. I never want to see a child suffer like that again. Unfortunately, that desire is not to be. Not only will I see other children suffer, but I am destined to be the source of their suffering. War is not pretty; death and destruction of the innocent are unavoidable.

The cave is impressive but holds no arms or munitions. The mission would have been soon forgotten if it had not been for the young boy's death.

Our platoon lucks out with our next assignment to provide security for a large hotel the U.S. Government has rented for use as a command center. Our first task is to establish roadblocks and checkpoints at all the local and distant approaches. When we are not on guard duty, we enjoy many of the comforts offered by an island resort. Six of us billeted to one room slept on mattresses distributed on the floor—what a delightful change from sleeping in a fox hole. We think of the accommodations as a gift, not to mention the hotel's swimming pool complete with a diving board, which we wear out doing one and one and a half flips, backflips, or whatever else fancies us.

The Dominican Republic's civil war is responsible for the deaths of over 4,000 Dominicans, 9 U.S. Marines, and 18 U.S. Army Soldiers.

Operation Power Pack brought with it the realization that becoming a member of the U.S. Marine Corps may cost you your life just as it had for the young Marines that died there. It is uncommon in our society to comprehend at an early age that death is eventually inescapable. Although, such awareness, especially in our youth, is a powerful asset in pursuing a successful life.

Return from the Dominican Republic June 1965

Charlie Company, First Battalion, Sixth Marines returns to Camp Lejeune, North Carolina, in June 1965 following its deployment to the Dominican Republic. After meticulously cleaning our weapons and field gear, we are granted ten days of leave. Diana and I are keenly excited to see one another after several months of separation. It is a balmy evening when we drive to the Essington Boat Yard, where my stepfather docked a beautiful twenty-foot cabin cruiser he had restored with tender loving care. Walking among the array of boats docked at the pier, we enjoy a gentle breeze that bears the pleasant aroma of warm water. We boldly ignore a large sign that reads "Authorized Personnel Only" as we trespass onto my stepfather's boat. Instead, I invite Diana to the cabin below deck after gaining entry through an unlocked window. That evening we conceive the first of our two daughters and begin what will be a lifetime together.

Promotion Exam

A month after returning from ten days of leave in 1965, my platoon commander recommends that I sit for the corporal's exam. Rank advancement in the U.S. Marine Corps beyond lance corporal E-3 comes slowly. Most Marines graduate from boot camp as a private E-1, advancing to private first-class E-2 after six months. That progression is not too difficult, providing you stay out of trouble. Lance corporal, E-3, is more challenging and doesn't come easily. The rank of corporal, E-4, is a big deal. Corporals in the Marine Corps are noncommissioned officers given a great deal of responsibility and authority.

To achieve corporal E-4, you first must be recommended by your platoon sergeant and your platoon commander. You are then eligible to sit for a written exam in competition with all the other candidates. The key to the exam is the home study courses the Marine Corps makes available for every MOS. I took two, Squad Tactics and Guerrilla Warfare, which are the subject matter of many corporal exam questions. I do well on the written exam, earning the second-highest grade in the battalion. Great, I have made the first cut, and I'm now eligible for the second phase of the corporal's exam, the practical.

The week following the written exam, the practical phase is administered and graded by officers from within the Sixth Marine Regiment but not our battalion. My multifaceted practical exam begins at the weapons table. The grading officer addresses me, "Field strip the M14 rifle as you recite its specifications. Sir, the M14 Rifle is a select-fire, gas-operated, rotating bolt weapon. The effective range is 500 yards without optics; it weighs 9.2 pounds, 10.7 pounds fully loaded, fires a 7.62 full metal jacket bullet, the magazine capacity is 20 rounds, its rate of fire is 720 rounds a minute in fully automatic mode." The grading officer records my responses, not commenting on their correctness. He just makes notations on a paper with my name on it. Another officer administering the Corporal's Test sits at a table labeled "Nuclear, Biological Warfare." His first question, "What is the antidote for nerve gas, and how do you administer it"? I provide the correct answer, "Sir, use a needle to inject Atropine, a medication used to treat certain types of nerve agents, into a large muscle." Many questions about gas masks follow before being asked to demonstrate how to mount and purge a gas mask properly. Radiation fallout questions and how to protect oneself from it are then answered, followed by the next officer instructing me to respond to various map and compass skills questions. You get the picture; lots of tables, lots of subjects, and lots of questions. After completing the entire circuit, scores are compiled to determine who will proceed to the practical test's final section, the close order drill. All Marine NCOs must be proficient in close order drills.

We form a platoon for the close order drill test with other selected candidates, the final cut. If I can drill the platoon more precisely than most other candidates, my promotion to the rank of corporal, E-4, is inevitable. Hearing my name called by the grading officer, I step out of formation and command the platoon. My only opportunity is to demonstrate my ability to drill troops and show the grading officer that I can move forty-some men in all directions using various march commands while calling cadence. The challenge posed is to find a way to stand out. Every one of the candidates can drill troops. I need to take a bit of a risk and demonstrate depth in my ability to march the formation precisely. First, I turn the marching platoon with a "By your left flank, augh" command so that everyone is marching directly towards a tall chain-linked fence. Then, at the very last moment, I give the command, "To the rear, augh," that turns them just before striking the fence. That march maneuver requires exact timing and comprehension of the commands of preparation and execution. Well, you may have thought those Marines were part of a drill team when they complete the maneuver with precision.

Several days following the exam, the unsteady, trouble-prone, irresponsible "Space Cadet" will now be addressed as Corporal Mezick, USMC. I am proud.

Letter from Diana

One month after being promoted to corporal, I receive a frantic letter from Diana stating that we are pregnant. Now what? I didn't know. I go to the first sergeant's office and explain the situation. In 1965, the Marine Corps is not then a family-orientated service. He responds to my request for emergency leave by saying, "You do not have to marry this girl. We can transfer you to Japan." Duty in Japan means serving as a noncommissioned officer in a guard outfit avoiding the Vietnam War. Here is my opportunity to duck out of town with a cozy duty station sidestepping the war. The first sergeant goes on to say, "We can do this immediately. You are one hell of a Marine, and you do not have to go home to get married." I reply, "I want to be with her when she tells her parents about the pregnancy. I intend to marry her and handle this situation properly." The first sergeant reluctantly grants me ten days of emergency leave. Arriving home, I enter a sea of chaos. You can imagine how upset Diana is after realizing her college education is over and that her parents will be devastated by the news of her pregnancy and rushed marriage.

Sitting next to Diana on a park bench in Chester, Pa. I speak softly to her, "Tonight, we must tell your mother and father that you are pregnant, and we are going to marry." She says, "My mother knows; my father doesn't." I reply, "Out of respect to your family, I must go to your home tonight and tell your parents you are pregnant and inform them of my intentions to marry you. Your parents deserve respect. I intend to provide it." She agreed.

When I arrive at their home that evening, I am unsure if Mrs. Ramos has told Mr. Ramos what to expect. When I enter their living room, I immediately sense negative energy. Sitting on their couch, observing Diana's distraught mother, I realize our first family meeting is going to be exceedingly challenging.

I sit in front of their ornate coffee table, facing Diana's father standing before me. Mr. Ramos wore a tailored suit, hair, and mustache meticulously groomed.

He abruptly begins, "I understand that you have something to say to me." I look into his eyes before speaking, "Yes, Sir, I love your daughter, and I am going to marry her. I will provide for her and our child for the rest of my life." My heartfelt expression is sincere and honorable. Those words are a public declaration of my commitment to Diana and our child. The man who stands before me doesn't hear my vow; he is blind with anger and contempt. Mr. Ramos begins by speaking softly at first but soon starts screaming how disappointed he is. I only understand some of what he is shouting, words like shame, unworthiness, and lack of education. It becomes evident that Diana's father intends to do whatever necessary to protect Diana from me. He certainly isn't going to help us in our time of extreme need.

I will never totally forgive him for becoming part of the challenge Diana and I faced that evening. We are young and in need of guidance and support. Mr. Ramos has a broken heart and is devastated by my intention to marry his only daughter and become his first grandchild's father. He isn't helping at all; he is totally out of control, only speaking of his pain and disappointment. Diana's distraught father continues to scream without pause until abruptly stopping. Staring at me with a look of anguish, he reaches into the breast pocket of his suit coat. I think, "Oh my God, he is going to shoot me." I have my fingers under the coffee table to flip it into his face creating a distraction. So, where do all these thoughts of guns come from? Not from him. No, from me, because I live in a world of guns and violence. He isn't going for a weapon; he is reaching for his angina medication. The man is about to have a heart attack.

Mr. Ramos's angina attack ends the family meeting. Our situation isn't better; it is worse. During his verbal assault, he blurted out that his son, a pharmacist, can provide a corrective solution. The man never used the word that defined his suggestion—the name he can't bear to speak as a practicing Catholic, abortion. Mrs. Ramos declares that Mr. Ramos needs to rest and settle himself.

Diana and I immediately go to my father's home in Milmont Park, Pa., looking for a parent that will hopefully rescue us from our mutual despair. My Dad is an addicted gambler costing him his marriage to my mother. However, this night, when Diana and I surprise him with our visit, he is the perfect loving and guiding parent we desperately need, his shining hour. Shaken and troubled, we now have responsibilities for which we are ill-prepared.

Dad answers the door, quite surprised to see us. He had no idea we were coming. We immediately inform him and his third wife, Alma, that we have something important to tell them. Alma suggests we all sit at the dining room table and enjoy a cup of coffee and cookies. Dad is wonderful, at first visibly shocked when we tell him that Diana is pregnant, and we are planning to marry. He handles his emotions quickly and then asks us what our plans are. "Have you figured out how to marry before returning to Camp Lejeune"? I tell him, "We don't have a plan, only that we are going to marry and raise our child. I guess we have to get a marriage license"? He replies, "Of course, you have to get a license and wait three days for the results of a blood test in the state of Pennsylvania. I suggest you apply for a license in the state of Maryland. I don't think Maryland has a blood test requirement, and that will save you several days."

We spoke no more of marriage plans after his one suggestion. He gently tells us how proud he is of our decision to marry and love our child. His words of praise and respect emotionally stabilize Diana and me. This man has an undeniable problem with gambling, but he also has a lot going for him. I have rarely been the recipient of his parenting; this night, I get all of it. I stand to leave when he asks me, "Do you have enough money for the wedding and honeymoon"? I tell him I don't. He reaches into his pocket and pulls out every dollar he has. He is the owner and operator of a dry-cleaning business that deals primarily in cash. He always carries cash to make change when delivering cleaned clothes to customers. The money he carries belongs to his business. It is not profit; it is operating capital. He hands me all his cash. I respond, "Dad, you can't do this. You will need cash for tomorrow." I cut the wad of bills in half and hand it back to him. I didn't know if I got the heavy half or the light half; it didn't matter. My Dad's sincere offer to empty his pockets is a magic moment between a father and son that far exceeds the money we exchanged. To this day, I remember that night. Of all the people to stabilize our ship and reset our course, it was my Dad.

The next day I tell my mother and stepfather of my intentions to marry Diana. Joe is the first to speak, "You don't have to marry her. Boy, this happened to me. I married a woman that I didn't love and then fathered two more children before getting a divorce. Don't marry her unless you would marry her without that child. Otherwise, you will have other kids, and everything will be more difficult. That's my advice to you." I tell him, "I do love her. I am going to take care of Diana and the baby for the rest of my life." Joe and I never discussed my decision to marry Diana again. My mother also disapproves of my marriage plans. However, she does say something bizarre, "You are marrying a woman with my height, my build from our heads to our toes. Our hips and chest are so similar that I believe you are marrying the image of your mother." I say, "I am not." She smiles before softly saying, "Yeah, take a look at your future wife." She is correct, but trust me, I never consciously look at Diana and think of my mother. My Mom drove Diana and me to Elton, Maryland. Her presence is thought to be legally required because I am only twenty years old, one year too young for a male to marry without a parent's signature.

Forty-eight hours later, our marriage license is waiting for us at the courthouse in Elton, Maryland. On this day, I will be married to a young woman who I don't know well. There is no wedding reception planned for us. My mother is going to attend the ceremony, accompanied by Diana's Mother. However, that morning I receive a phone call from Diana stating that her mother isn't going to the wedding because she is upset; their family dog died. That's right; their beloved Pekingese had an untimely death the day of our marriage. We think of it as a horrible coincidence. I inform my Mom that Mrs. Ramos will not be attending our wedding and suggest that she doesn't need to drive to Elton, Maryland, and back by herself. She agrees without hesitation. Quite frankly, no one wants to attend our wedding, including Diana and me.

Never am I so aware of a life-altering transition as I am this morning. After bathing, I see my troubled face in the bathroom mirror as I prepare to shave. Overcome with sorrow. I sit back on the edge of the bathtub to reconsider what is about to happen. Part of me wants to immediately return to the base and tell the first sergeant I will accept his offer of serving in a duty station in Japan. The easy way out, I can escape a rushed marriage that no one seems to care about and avoid a combat assignment in the then raging Vietnam War. But, no, it is time to man up. Instead, I dress and drive to Diana's home. My self-pity is instantly replaced with wholesome emotion as I accept the hand of this beautiful woman in her white wedding dress. I don't remember if her mother said anything to either of us before we left her home.

From that point on, Diana and I will be on our own. No one came forward, nor did I ask how to manage the wedding or the honeymoon. After obtaining our marriage license, we decide to have the wedding in a local chapel. We aren't clear about how to choose a chapel, or an officiate for the ceremony. Our dilemma is quickly resolved when several gentlemen offer to perform our marriage. Like barkers trying to lure us into their establishments, one shouts out, "Hey, come into my chapel. I will marry you." Another man motions for us to join him from across the street, and he will perform our marriage.

Diana selects the gentleman she thinks might be a minister. He walks with us to his home, which has a façade that looks a bit like a chapel. Entering the living room, we walk past a piano to a small podium where the ceremony will take place. He is about to begin when he abruptly stops and announces, "Wait, we need a witness. Ethel, please join us." A middle-aged woman leaves the kitchen and joins our wedding party with a dish towel still in her hand. The gentleman, then having everyone assembled to marry us, begins the ceremony.

Here comes the magic, the sacred moment for me. Those words he has us repeat to one another, "For better, for worse, for richer, for poorer, in sickness and in health, to love and to cherish, till death do us part, according to God's holy law, and this is my solemn vow." The crude circumstances of our wedding no longer matter to me. During the brief ceremony, I commit myself to my wife and baby. I have no idea how I will provide for them, only a sense of confidence that I can, and I will. The intensity, I feel, is no different had we been married in the Washington Cathedral with the United States president in attendance. The room comes alive with emotion; the officiating magistrate is moved, as is his wife. Diana and I vow our dedication to one another through good times and bad. We have no idea the day we make our commitment to one another how difficult and challenging our lives will become.

Honeymoon

Diana requests that we find a quaint little motel for our honeymoon, just like the one in the movie called Psycho. Ok, fine with me. I can find one if she points it out because I haven't seen the movie. How naïve, a honeymoon without reservations or a defined destination. Our marriage begins in search of a hotel only envisioned in my bride's mind. We are two kids without a plan.

We next travel to Georgetown, a historic neighborhood in the commercial and residential district of Northwest Washington, D.C. I find a parking place on Wisconsin Avenue that is barely large enough to squeeze our borrowed car into. Trying to park, I jump the curb, startling Diana. She has a frightened expression as if to say, is this how it's going to be for the rest of my life? I feel her frustration. I, too, wonder if this is how it will be for the rest of my life? Hopefull, showing none of my internal thoughts, I flag a passing cab and request the driver take us to a fine restaurant. Moments later, Diana and I enter Blackie's House of Beef. Our dinner is delicious, and everything is perfect; it could not have been better had I made reservations.

Now it is time to go to our motel. After a cab takes us back to our parked car, I head south, searching for the motel, the one envisioned in Diana's mind. We drive for what seems like forever through a light rain on Route #95 under continuous construction for at least fifty miles. Finally, late that evening, around 10:30 or 11:00, we find a motel out in the middle of nowhere. It is precisely the type of motel Diana has envisioned. I approach what I determine to be the office. After repeatedly docking on the door, a grumpy man opens it and abruptly tells me he has a gun and is prepared to use it. He informs me that this is no longer a motel, and I should leave his property. We drive back to the Virginia, Washington, D.C. border and find a motel with bright lights. We are given the last room available after I plead with the proprietor and the middle-aged couple who are ahead of me in line. I explain that I have been married this afternoon, and this is our honeymoon. The couple smile and allow Diana and me to rent the room that should have rightfully been theirs. I wish with all my heart that I could find them today and express my lifelong gratitude. Some acts of kindness can never be repaid directly, only passed along.

Diana and I filled our finally acquired room, our bridal suite, with love. We could not have had a more romantic honeymoon night if provided with the finest accommodations. We did not choose one another from a long list of common interests, educational backgrounds, or any of the other multitude of reasons people select their life partners. However, we were always physically attracted to one another. Whatever a man and a woman physically need from the other, we provide it. Lovemaking for us is passionate.

The following day, with the aid of a taxi driver, we tour Washington, D.C. The cabbie recommends we visit the Wax Museum and then walk to the White House. The next day we visit Arlington Cemetery and the

Washington Monument before heading home. But whose home? We are now dependent on someone to help us. After considering our options, we go to my mother's and stepfather's house in Trainer, Pennsylvania. So far, my relationship with Diana's father is dangerously flawed. The reality of his only daughter marrying a corporal in the U.S. Marine Corps, especially one from Trainer, Pennsylvania, is more than he can bear. I absorbed his insults once because I owed him that respect. That was his one free bite. Far better that I stay away from him before I return to the base in just another day. My family accepted Diana and made us both feel at home. Not initially pleased with our marriage, my mother and stepfather quickly adjust and begin to help us in any way they can. Thank God Diana needs a stable place to live until I can take her to my next duty station. Maybe the Marine Corps will assign me to the base in Japan that the first sergeant initially offered. There we will live together in military housing, and I can be with Diana during her pregnancy and our child's birth.

After I leave for Camp Lejeune, Diana stays with my mother and stepfather for a couple of days before returning to her home in Eddystone, Pennsylvania. Her Dad is still unhappy but welcomes her back with open arms. I believe he hopes she will reconsider his offer to accompany him and her mother back to Puerto Rico for a previously planned vacation and terminate the pregnancy.

Orders for Vietnam

I travel to Camp Lejeune by bus arriving well after midnight. Several of my fellow Marines are playing cards with the aid of a dim light at the end of the squad bay. One of them works in the company office, where he processes orders for those about to be transferred. When he notices I am nearby, he blurts out, "Hey, Corporal Mezick, I processed the transfer to your new duty station last Friday; they're sending you to Vietnam." I respond, "Bullshit, they know I just got married and have a baby on the way." I go to bed. After breakfast, the next day, our entire company forms outside our barracks. The company's first sergeant addresses us, "The following personal are being transferred to Fleet Marine Corps Pacific.

Your orders will be preceded by thirty days of leave before departing for Camp Pendleton, California, Corporal Mezick." I am the first name on his list; he called twenty-some names; mine is the first. My assignment to Vietnam can't be authentic. The first sergeant must have called my name by mistake.

Assembled in the company orderly room for processing, the first sergeant addresses the Marines called from his list, "I have a question that must be addressed and recorded on each of your orders. Are you volunteering for duty in Vietnam? Gentlemen, it doesn't matter. You are going to be transferred to Fleet Marine Corps Pacific no matter how you answer the question. So, who among you volunteer to defend our nation in a time of war"? Nineteen hands enthusiastically thrust into the air. The first sergeant addresses me, "Corporal Mezick, you are not volunteering"? I reply, "No, I am not volunteering. I would like to speak with you before you finish processing my orders." He nods his head, "Everyone else is dismissed. Corporal Mezick, come into my office."

As I enter, he pulls up a wooden straight-back chair adjacent to his swivel chair behind his desk and motions me to sit. He begins, "Just what is your problem, Corporal Mezick"? Looking directly at him, I start my explanation, "First sergeant, I am the Marine who just returned from ten days of emergency leave to get married. My wife will deliver our baby next year in February." He must have known; emergency leave is extremely rare. He is the one who approved my leave request after I turned down his offer to be transferred to a duty station in Japan. I go on to say, "My wife is pregnant; her father is enormously upset with us. I don't have a problem going to Vietnam. That's not the issue. I only want to delay leaving until my baby is born. I am abandoning her just when I am needed the most." Again, he looks directly at me, pausing before he begins to speak, "You are a trained noncommissioned officer in the U.S. Marine Corps. If we wanted you to have a wife, we, God Damn well, would have issued you one! This conversation is over." He turns his swivel chair to face his desk and begins to work on my transfer orders. That is, the total amount of compassionate consideration I will receive before being sent to fight in Vietnam.

Transit to Vietnam

A tour of duty in Vietnam requires a Marine to spend thirteen months of service in-country. For all the other service branches, their Vietnam tours of duty had a duration of twelve months. We had to do an extra month for the Corps. Now, it's time to leave Camp Lejeune forever and all the guys I had served with for two years. There are no goodbyes, no handshakes, no going away party, just another grunt on his way to war.

Returning to Eddystone, Pennsylvania, I become a house guest in my father-in-law's home for the next thirty days. The relationship between Diana's Dad and me has improved somewhat, but not to the extent that we sit together enjoying cool drinks planning my future. None of that; let's have a beer together and get past our rocky start. Mr. Ramos is quite popular in the neighborhood, especially with the Spanish intellectual community. However, our conversation primarily consists of him telling me which of his relatives holds what college degree. Through his apparent disapproval of my academic achievements, he is lighting a fire of transition within me.

I spend most weekdays with my dad delivering and picking up clothes from his dry-cleaning customers. I had very few memories of my father before my parents' divorce when I was three years old. Our time spent together is natural and pleasant as we get to know one another through adult conversations. My dad is well educated, earning a business degree from the University of Kentucky. Through our leisurely discussions, it becomes apparent that this man has opportunities, natural talents, and skills continually marginalized by his addiction to gambling.

As an active married member of the U.S. Military, I had my benefits amended to include my wife. As a result, Diana will receive a mandatory distribution[12] each month from my military pay. If I die in combat, she will receive the insurance benefit of ten thousand dollars. My transfer orders are in my possession, as is my plane ticket to Los Angeles International

---

[12] **Marines with the rank of corporal E-4** or below with less than 4 years of service had a mandatory monthly distribution of their pay sent to their wives.

Airport. The night before I leave the Ramos home, Diana and I cuddle together to prepare for my departure the following afternoon. We both are consumed with emotion, knowing that we will not be together to share the experience of her pregnancy or the birth of our baby.

The day has come for me to leave. My mother drives Diana and me to the Philadelphia Airport. We wait tensely in the upper terminal overlooking the tarmac before called to board the jet that will transport me to California. When it arrives, and passengers began to board, I kiss my mother goodbye before taking Diana into my arms. Our goodbye kiss is an emotional expression that penetrates my soul. When we let go, she is crying, as is my mother. I am on the verge of crying, and I want to cry; I don't know how. I turn away from the two most important women in my life as I pick up my bag and begin what becomes the longest walk of my life. Striding across the tarmac to board the waiting jet, I feel like a condemned man marching towards his execution. Every step I take is in the wrong direction. I am walking away from my obligations, letting everyone down. I want to throw my seabag into the trash and rip off my uniform. Put on some jeans and a tee-shirt and start my new life. When I reach the top of the long stairway boarding the plane, I nod my head at the two hostesses who cheerfully greet me. I suspect they can see I am in grief and about to cry. Shortly after finding my assigned seat, one of the stewardesses walks up and asks if I would like a drink.

The airplane has not yet left the tarmac; other passengers are still boarding. I look up, and she repeats her offer, "Would you like a drink"? Never having flown on a civilian aircraft, I asked, "Is everyone else being offered one"? She looks rather puzzled by my reply before asking, "What type of drink would you prefer"? I request a Seven and Seven whiskey highball. She returns with a drink for a twenty-year-old on an aircraft that is not yet airborne. I had no idea she broke protocol to serve an underage passenger whiskey on the tarmac. I must have clearly shown my despair of leaving my pregnant wife the day I left for Vietnam. Once again, a United States citizen stood up to help a Marine on his way to war. During the latter months of 1965, any service's uniform is highly respected, especially those of us who wore the U.S. Marine Corps uniform. Folks reached out because they knew we might never return as so many of their fathers, uncles, and brothers had not from WW II or the Korean War.

After the plane is airborne on its way to California, I have another drink and watch a movie. I get past my emotional crisis and, for the first time, begin to seriously consider where I am going and what will be required of me before I can return. I shift gears; I am mentally back in the Marine Corps. Now, I need to focus on how I am going to stay alive. I don't know what that task will entail, but I must return, this much I know for sure.

When I arrive in California, I take a bus to Camp Pendleton and join a staging company. The Marines within the staging company do not necessarily have the same MOS. We are going to Vietnam as individual replacements after waiting a week or more to assemble the required number of men to fill the transport jet that will fly to Okinawa. As we wait for others to arrive and be processed, they have us do busywork. We are free to go to town after work hours, but very few of us are old enough to drink. However, Tijuana, Mexico, doesn't care if we are twenty-one years old before they will sell us a drink. So, where did Marines too young to drink in the USA go? They had two choices, enlisted man's club, where you may be bored to death, or Tijuana, Mexico, where you may be assaulted, arrested, or killed. The laws in Tijuana are whatever they say they are at the time of consideration. For example, you could get arrested for spitting on the street if they thought you had fifty bucks in your pocket. Your fine will be forty-nine dollars; the other buck is for cab fare to the U.S. / Mexico border.

A group of us go to Tijuana to see for ourselves just what that infamous Mexican city has to offer. Well, there is plenty of whiskey and women for sure, but not for me. I am not about to get drunk in a foreign country and a lawless city. Our Tijuana trip helps me acclimate back to being a grunt in the Marine Corps, but I am not in a party mood. I feel somewhat responsible for the younger Marines with me. The mental image of my wife crying as I left Philadelphia, Airport is ever-present. I must temporarily disregard the mindset of a married man with a child on the way and begin to accept the life of a grunt on his way to the Vietnam War. However, I have no idea how complex the mental transition will be and never consider that I will also have to transition back if I survive the war.

The only memorable event of our trip to Tijuana is that of a disappointed young Marine because he didn't buy a watch from the friendly Mexican salesman who wore many precious watches positioned up and down both arms. This young Marine is trusting to a fault. When a stranger in a foreign country offers you the deal of a lifetime, and you are not suspicious, that's a problem. Think knock-off watches. Yes, they may have the Bulova Watch Company name engraved into their underside, but Bulova's name is misspelled or blurred. A tinker-toy of a watch made to look attractive for the bargain price of just one hundred U.S. dollars. What a buy for a thousand-dollar watch. The young, gullible Marine didn't have enough money that night to purchase one. I asked another Marine in the transport company to lend me a knock-off he had mistakenly purchased for twenty dollars. Later in the week, I offer to sell it to Mr. Gullible for just fifty dollars. Everyone knows this is an object lesson except the purchaser. When he proudly displays his new watch to the other Marines, they all tell him that he might have purchased a toy. When I tell him the watch's real value is under five dollars, he takes forever to accept his mistake. After he finally realizes that he has wasted the fifty dollars and sweating him a bit, I give him his money back.

The time we spent waiting to depart El Toro Marine Corps Air Station, California, is so dull we are relieved to finally board an Air Force C-135A Stratolifter that will take us closer to war. Finally, we are on our way to an island in the Pacific with a bloody history, the gravesite of many a Marine just one generation ago, Okinawa.

During the thirteen-hour flight, I try to remember in detail everything I have learned about infantry tactics. I then face the unpleasant fact that I am a noncommissioned officer without leadership experience, promoted a mere three months ago. My platoon sergeant sent two senior corporals, both college dropouts, near the end of their four-year enlistments to a two-week leadership school for NCOs at Camp Lejeune. The company gunnery sergeant reasoned that the NCO school might convince the college dropouts to reenlist and join the Vietnam fight. Fat chance of that, the only corporal in our platoon that did go to Vietnam was the one they didn't send to the leadership school, me. Now I am about to join a grunts company with profound combat experience and function as a leader. I will have to learn the skills of combat leadership on my own. For now, I will keep reading a generic military manual about leadership that is of no assistance whatsoever. I sit for hours trying to revisit lessons taught in two years of infantry training. The one undeniable gift I possess is comprehension, and maybe that will enable me to learn essential leadership components of my corporal rank quickly.

The jet begins to jump around, one moment dropping the next shaking. Red lights flash with a warning to fasten our seat belts. The pilot reports, "we are experiencing air turbulence." On a commercial flight, an airline flight attendant would softly inform you how the rough ride is nothing to concern yourself about and will soon pass. Instead, our airline stewards are men serving in the Air Force who are not pretty or pleasant. I overhear them talking amongst themselves, "Man, this shit is heavy-duty; I hope the wings stay on." I began to think that maybe I wouldn't need that leadership school after all. I was sure they didn't teach how to survive a torn apart jet before it falls to the earth.

CHAPTER THREE

Chu Lai

Office Hours

Arriving in Chu Lai, Vietnam, on October 25, 1965, with other Marines sent as individual replacements, I am assigned to Bravo Company, First Battalion, Fourth Marines. In the company's command post, a lance corporal directs me to a squad-sized tent where I join Bravo Company's Second Platoon, First Squad.

Entering the tent and taking a seat on my assigned cot, a Marine says, "Hi," and immediately tosses me a hand grenade. He and three others run out of the tent, screaming, "Grenade, it's going to blow!" A joke at the new guy's expense. The grenade's spoon is attached, preventing it from detonating. It is harmless. When I don't fall prey to their attempt at humor, they return.

Later the same day, walking towards the mess hall, a tall thin Marine approaches me from behind. He puts his arm around my shoulders and introduces himself as PFC Spiffon, "You don't have to worry about a thing; I'm going to take care of you." I had just met the Marine that will become one of the best I will ever command in a firefight and the most difficult to control when we aren't in a firefight.

Several days later, Bravo Company deployed to Tam Hai Island off Chu Lai's coast in the South China Sea. The rains in November are relentless, often accompanied by strong winds. We have access to squad-sized tents for sleeping and relief from the never-ending rain when not sitting in wet, soggy, fighting holes performing perimeter watch or on patrols during the day or ambushes at night.

I have only been a member of one patrol before being given the assignment of leading a seventeen-man night ambush with my squad and four Bravo Company's weapons platoon members. I don't yet realize the immense responsibility of combat leadership and that I will be held accountable for every Marine's action in my command. My entire Vietnam experience thus far has seemed like a training exercise with live ammunition.

We arrive at our ambush site and set up to intercept anyone using a walking trail that leads to a small village. After several hours of waiting in our ambush, a Vietnamese man selling beer approaches us. One member from the weapons platoon dealt with the intruder and sent him off, but not before buying a quart of locally made beer. I am not aware that a bottle of smelly home-brewed beer is being passed among us until it comes to me. I decline the near-empty bottle and pass it on.

Huge mistake! I should have immediately moved the ambush team and let these Marines know that their practice of drinking beer while on an ambush is unacceptable. I said nothing except that the beer smelled terrible.

In the early morning light of a new day on our way back to Bravo Company's island outpost, my ambush team bumped headlong into a patrol led by none other than Captain Wentworth, the company commander. The two patrols heading in opposite directions on the same trail walked past one another when suddenly, Captain Wentworth barks out, "Halt, I smell beer." The Captain detected the odor of beer on the Marine, who had purchased and drunk most of it. They are both tall, and when they pass, the beer breath of one is detected by the other. The company gunnery sergeant standing next to the Captain yells instructions to my ambush team, "Everyone, of you, are on report and required to write an account stating your involvement with alcohol consumption."

Before entering the perimeter of the island outpost, I stop the patrol and bring everyone together. I begin by saying, "We are all on report, but we don't all have to burn[13]. We have two options; one, we provide details explaining who among us drank beer. Two, we tell a story that involves me, the NCO in charge, and the Marine who purchased the beer and who is also the one on whom the Captain smelled beer." Everyone agrees to

---

[13] **Burn** – Slang term for a Marine being punished by the guidelines of the Uniform Code of Military Justice.

option two because it prevents all but two of us from being punished. The Marine with the beer breath will report that he alone purchased and drank the beer. I will be penalized for providing absolutely no leadership. Leaders in the Marine Corps are always held accountable for everything that happens within their command. Therefore, I thought it better that only two of us be punished rather than all of us. That reasoning was my second huge mistake.

Two of the weapons platoon members attached to my ill-fated ambush were the first to deviate from the agreed-upon story. They wrote a debriefing report that was partially true but left out the part about their guy buying the beer. Quite frankly, I didn't know what the others had reported. I knew if I changed my story, I would make liars out of everyone who stuck to the agreed version. The truth is we are all liars, and that is mostly my fault. Trying to be a nice guy with an immature sense of fairness, I have inadvertently created a situation involving a group of men who decide to tell different stories.

Several days later, Captain Wentworth holds office hours[14] for all seventeen members of my ill-fated ambush. I am the last Marine called into the command post. Captain Wentworth addresses the two Marines standing at attention facing him. One is a corporal, E-4, that would be me. The other, a lance corporal, E-3. We are both asked to chronicle a series of events that happened during the ambush. Throughout the entire inquiry, each of our statements contradicts the other. After the other Marine is dismissed, I stand alone before the Captain. He looks at me with an expression of disgust and anger before he begins to speak, "After reviewing the entire situation, I conclude that you are a liar, that you are immature and incompetent. I will not allow you to kill my Marines with your obvious lack of leadership ability. The limits of punishment I can

---

[14] **Office Hours** - Non-Judicial Punishment (NJP) is known by different terms among the services, such as "Article 15," "Office Hours," or "Captain's Mast." The purpose of NJP is to discipline service members for minor offenses such as reporting late for duty, petty theft, destroying government property, sleeping on watch, providing false information, and disobeying standing orders. Non-Judicial Punishment Explained | Military.com

legally administer are insufficient, so I recommend you to the colonel and request that he refer you to court-martial proceedings. There under the Uniform Code of Military Justice's decree, lies the legal authority to punish you properly by reducing your rank and confining you in a brig; because that's where you belong, not here leading my Marines. You disgust me, leave, move, get out of my sight. I can't stand to look at you any longer."

After being verbally assaulted and humiliated by the Captain of Bravo Company, I walk out of the command post extremely dejected. Realizing I am in severe trouble and the penalty I will soon receive will negatively affect my wife, who expects to deliver our first child in February. I realize that I am on the path of failure, a man not deserving to be a husband, a father, or hold corporal rank in the U.S. Marine Corps. Leaving the company headquarters, I am overcome with a desire to change. I don't grow up at that moment; I am jerked up, never to be the same again. Oddly, there is another strong emotion, one of self-esteem. I am proud of my decision to stick to my lies and not incriminate the other Marines who have all agreed to the same lies.

When you step on your character, you are going down a slippery slope of internal ruin. I stood up for the untruthful description of the events we have agreed to provide as our collective statement of the incident under investigation. I am not declaring we made a correct decision by deciding to lie. However, I am defending my decision to stick with the lies. I took it on the chin. I alone am held responsible and bear all the punishment while everyone else is excused. Why? Because I was in charge. The Marine Corps is exceptionally critical of leaders who don't lead, and I am guilty of that charge.

That's it, nothing more, nothing less. You may be thinking, why would the Captain want to send me to the brig over a quart of beer shared by a group of men? The company commander knows that the lack of leadership and immaturity I displayed while in command will get Marines, his Marines, killed. That's it, nothing more, nothing, less.

In retrospect, Captain Wentworth had become and would continue to be one of the most influential men in my entire life. What he saw in me was a disaster waiting to happen, and he was correct. I could beg mercy and inform you, the reader, how I was thrown to the wolves without proper orientation and that the leaders of the Marine Corps had failed me. War does not allow for excuses. It only creates statistics of those who die and those who live. The Captain's reaction to my lack of leadership and immaturity became, for me, a beacon illuminating where I am and where I need to be.

Buoyancy Lesson

Life goes on even for a Marine who is down, lonely, and in trouble. But, before I stand in judgment before a Battalion Commander of the Fourth Marine Regiment, Lieutenant Colonel Donavan, several significant events occur.

First, I will tell you about an island called Hoa Xuan (aka "Snaggletooth"). The reason for its unusual name is its irregular shape. Depicted on a topographical map, it looks like a broken tooth. The island's distinctive shape is most likely created by the forces of erosion fueled by the South China Sea currents surrounding it.

Bravo Company, First Battalion, Fourth Marines established a company outpost on Tam Hai Island off Chu Lai's coast and a platoon outpost on its northeastern tip. A half-mile east of the platoon outpost is a small two-acre island called Dao Da (aka Stone Island), accessible at low tide by walking along the South China Sea shore and crossing a few hundred yards of wet sand. Southeast of Stone Island appears to be a river about 400 yards wide, separating it from Snaggletooth Island. However, the water between the islands is not a river; it is the South China Sea.

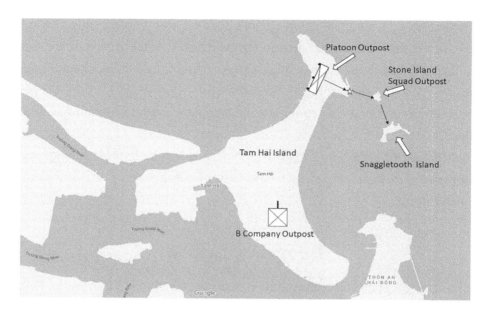

Snaggletooth Island's significance is that no Marine in 1965 has ever set foot on it without being shot at. Snaggletooth is Indian country; the bad guys own it; we only come to visit. In November of 1965, there are not enough Marines in Vietnam to permanently occupy Snaggletooth Island. So, what do we do? We hold operations on it. If we can't occupy it, we can keep its defenders busy, keep them nervous, annoy the hell out of them. They have the same intentions towards us. The expression "annoy the hell out of" means killing one another. So how do you get a company of Marines across the four hundred yards of the South China Sea that separates Stone and Snaggletooth islands? One way is to use amphibious assault vehicles called Amtraks that propel themselves through water after mostly sinking. As a passenger inside an Amtrak, you are in an iron box with small round windows submerged to water level permitting you to see bubbles created by the vehicle's tracks that propel it. The experience is claustrophobic, kind of like a nightmare of being buried alive in a watery coffin. So I am always relieved when the front ramp opens, and I got the hell out of it. However, when the door does open, everyone is clustered together, providing ideal conditions for the enemy to assault with deadly efficiency.

Approaching Snaggletooth Island by sea using Amtraks gives notice of our arrival by its loud engines' sound. The enemy hides and harasses us with small arms fire from concealed positions. They don't engage us in force, but instead, they fire at us, hoping they can lure us into one of their many minefields. Bobby traps and mines are a constant threat on Snaggletooth Island, causing multiple casualties.

Captain Wentworth is not pleased with our operations' results using Amtraks, so he tries something creative. He acquires Vietnamese fishing boats that resemble canoes but are a bit larger in length and width. The idea is to secretly position these boats on the shore of Stone Island across from Snaggletooth. Then, the boats will quietly paddle across the open water separating the islands in the dark of night.

However, there is a significant risk in putting an entire company or even a platoon in Vietnamese boats all crossing the water simultaneously. If the boats come under fire on the open water: they will be virtually defenseless. So, how do we handle such exposure? You first cross the four hundred yards of open water with a squad of Marines to put a friendly force on Snaggletooth Island. The thirteen Marines on the far side can provide cover fire for the larger group as they cross. If the enemy is waiting at our chosen landing site, they will first have to engage the advanced landing squad exposing their positions. The chosen solution poses hazardous duty for the Marines, who will be the first to reach Snaggletooth Island, but provides cover fire for the larger group as they cross the open water.

Two four-man fire teams gently position themselves into sitting positions within the advanced landing force's first boat being extremely quiet. This maneuver is not easy in the darkness of a moonless night. Everyone is heavily loaded. The combined weight of our M14 rifles, cartridge belts holding four magazines of ammunition, Ka-Bar knife, several hand grenades, two canteens of water, individual bodyweight, plus the additional heft of our flak jackets and helmets creates a buoyancy challenge. Finally, the small boat, now filled with eight Marines crammed together from bow to the stern, silently pushes off from the South China Sea shoreline.

An object will float if it weighs less than the amount of water it displaces. Rocks sink, and steel ships float due to this principle. Unfortunately, the Vietnamese boats filled with Marines' weight in full combat gear create more downward pressure on the water than the upward force created by the water displaced by the boat. As a result, our boat sank into the South China Sea.

The strong currents that flow between the two islands have eroded the seafloor creating a sudden drop-off. We are sinking in deep water just off the edge of the island. The weight of my body and that of the equipment I carry is significant. I drop fast, but I think if I vigorously kick my legs, I will return to the surface. Not so. Flipping my legs back and forth has little effect on my descent into the deep, cold, dark water. I scissor kick my legs harder and harder, but I can't stop my descent into the ocean. Surrounded by ever-increasing darkness, as the slight glimmer of surface light fades away, I begin to lose my sense of knowing the direction to the top. I can't breathe; my brain is racing as it sounds the alarm for oxygen-enriched blood, so I do the unthinkable for a Marine; I drop my rifle. I don't intentionally let go of it; some survival instinct makes that decision for me. Without the rifle, my hands and arms are free to push against my descent. Under the power of my arms and legs, I surface, taking a massive gulp of air as I loudly trash around in the water as though I am at a beach party. Thank God for preventing the catastrophe that would have occurred if the enemy were on the other side firing at us struggling Marines.

Swimming to solid ground, I immediately recall how insistent and harsh the Marine drill instructors were when they forced us to take a swimming test. Now, looking around at my fire team members and the other members of our squad, I realize no one has drowned. Yeah, everyone is safe because we were taught how to swim wearing combat gear and not panic when we couldn't breathe. My boot camp training's severity makes more sense as I experience a Marine's life in combat.

We dive deeply into the ocean with the first morning light to recover the rifles that all of us have dropped. The water is clear, permitting us to see several feet ahead as we dive towards the bottom. Not everyone can descend to the ocean's depths to retrieve their gear, so those of us who can make multiple trips. The saltwater causes our rifles and magazines to begin rusting as soon as we bring them to the surface.

The planned operation of silently assaulting Snaggletooth Island using Vietnamese fishing boats is aborted after our buoyancy lesson. We return to our base on the main island. Our squad needs to clean their rifles and magazines immediately to prevent them from further rusting. We asked our leaders where the rifle cleaning solvent, brushes, oil, and rags are to begin the task? There is no rifle cleaning equipment available, none. The ugly reality that the world's wealthiest nation has sent its young men into combat without rifle cleaning equipment is true; I wish it were not. This unacceptable condition continued to plague us for months to come[15].

What we do have to clean our rusty equipment with are mainly our personal possessions. I must use my only toothbrush to clean my rifle and magazines. The problem with scrubbing your rifle with a toothbrush is that it removes the bluing[16], a process of treating steel that, among its other effects, makes the rifle metal dull, preventing light reflection. I work for hours to remove all the rust from my rifle and magazines, only to discover the next day it returns.

Bob Hope comes to town. Yes, Bob Hope, with one of his fantastic entertainment shows, is on the mainland in Chu Lai. I refuse the offer to attend, as do most of the other men in our squad recently submerged in saltwater. Why? Our magazines are still rusty to the point of malfunction. Sorry, Bob, rust first, recreation second. Trust me, I want to neglect my gear and see the show.

---

[15] Later I shared the precious contents of a Sears & Roebuck rifle cleaning kit my wife mailed me.

[16] **Bluing** or black oxidizing is a process of treating steel to create a thin protective shell around it. It works by turning rust, into black iron oxide. The blue-black image of black iron oxide is what gives the name to this process. <u>Gun Bluing 101 – How to Blue a Gun (makerslegacy.com)</u>

Under Fire - Lieutenant Shot

There is no Bob Hope Christmas Show for those of us who stay behind removing the rust from our rifles and magazines. A wise decision because the very next day, we attack Snaggletooth Island using a new plan. This time we use the Amtraks again but with sleight of hand. We assault the island in the afternoon and spend several hours advancing through the hamlets and then board the Amtraks and leave. Our platoon hides after being left behind as the rest of the company departs. Now, if our platoon remains undetected, we will gain the element of surprise. We hide until nightfall and then begin walking to a destination known only to the platoon commander. We walk all night. I think we are lost. I have no way of knowing because we are given information on a need-to-know basis only. If we are not lost, we damn sure walk all night for some reason unbeknown to us.

During our never-ending march in the darkness, I discover that you can almost fall asleep on your feet. Almost, but not entirely. You can't fall asleep while standing unless you have external support. If you are moving, it's easy to stay awake; the challenge comes when you stop. Then you absolutely can nod off; however, as soon as you do, your brain protects you from falling by involuntarily waking you. That sequence of beginning to fall asleep on my feet and waking before I collapse happens three times; I never hit the ground. With the aid of first light the following morning, we realize that we are in the island's approximate center, surrounded by rolling dunes with light vegetation between them.

Suddenly in open terrain, we are attacked with small-arms fire from several different directions. I have been shot at before in the Dominican Republic, but I can't say for sure that the shooters were aiming at me. Now the bullets are close, and that thing about hearing bees buzzing, well, that's true. You can hear bullets buzz, and for some reason, most of them seemed to be aimed at us. Who is us? I am walking next to the officer in charge, our platoon commander, Lieutenant McMaster, the most desired target. Our officer is tall, and I must say he looks snappy. Even though he has walked all night enduring oppressive heat and humidity, the man still looks like an officer. His clothes and gear fit perfectly; he stands tall, showing no fear whatsoever. I am on the edge of panic, my brain in hyper mode. I want to run; my leg muscles are full of energy, just waiting for the release command. However, I am not allowed to run; we all must stay in formation. If we are going to run, we must run together as a unit.

Sprinting away from the main body is called "Breaking Ranks," an unforgivable sin in the U.S. Marine Corps. I control myself by drawing courage from the lieutenant's example of composure under fire. He will never know to what extent I am affected by his calmness as he stands tall quietly, giving orders. Lieutenant McMaster is commanding us in a calm voice loud enough for everyone to hear. He orders us to run together up a vast sand mound on our right flank about forty yards away. As a unit, we jog up the sandy hill taking no more than a few moments to reach the top. Once the shooting started, I am not tired anymore; I have unlimited energy. We find pre-dug fighting positions on the crest of the dune, and of course, we jump right into them and begin firing back at our attackers. I don't know or care who dug the fighting holes. I am more than pleased to get most of my body below ground level. The firefight intensifies. Man, their incoming rifle fire is incredibly accurate. How can they shoot with such precision as we present tiny targets to them in those sandy holes?

I have a bullet go by my face so close that I can feel the speeding projectile's air pressure. I think how my head would have exploded if it struck me. I throw up from fear. My mouth and nose fill with vomit; I swallow the foul bile and continue to fire my weapon. How are they shooting so accurately? Looking to the front of each pre-dug fighting position, I see a four-foot-tall bamboo pole used by the enemy as aiming markers almost invisible to us against the morning sky. The bad guys know we will advance to the high ground and take cover in the existing holes. The aiming sticks become a reference point visible to their concealed firing positions about a hundred and fifty yards away. They have only to aim to the right of the bottom one-third of their aiming sticks; that's where we are. They predicted our every move and positioned us exactly where they wanted us, a perfect example of guerrilla warfare tactics. We all low crawl out to the aiming stakes and pull them down. Our adversaries are now not so accurate.

The enemy marksman who has recently fired the round that barely missed my face continues to fire at me. I can't see him. He is well hidden, but I get a break. With the sun now high and brightly shining above us, the surrounding air becomes hotter and humid. Firing a high-power rifle causes air turbulence, a disturbance seen in high heat and humidity. It is difficult to explain the effect further, but you know what it is when you see it. I aim just below the air disturbance putting multiple rounds on that son of a bitch who has been trying to kill me all morning. I don't know if I killed him, wounded him, or just motivated him to get the hell out of his fighting position. However, I can report with complete confidence that the firing from that site stopped.

Our lieutenant observes that many of his Marines are not shooting accurately, yet PFC Spiffon seems to be on target. Our platoon commander calls out in the heat of battle, "Spiffon, what's your dope"? The firefight is raging with lots of shooting from both sides, making communication with one another problematic. The lieutenant, hearing no reply, calls out to PFC Spiffon again, "What's your dope"? The answer from PFC Spiffon, "I don't know, Sir." The lieutenant, "What do you mean you don't know? Report your dope."

Dope means the lieutenant wants PFC Spiffon to determine to what extent he has adjusted his rear rifle sites. Spiffon needs to turn his elevation control knob down and count the number of clicks until it is at the bottom and then turn the windage control knob back to its center reference point and report the number of clicks counted.

Spiffon answers; I don't know, Sir." The lieutenant; "Count them, now." Spiffon, I can't, Sir." The lieutenant; "Why not"? Spiffon, "I don't have any sights, Sir, I lost them."

PFC Spiffon is from Kentucky, and his daddy has taught him how to shoot by aiming with Kentucky windage. Using old rifles, you don't adjust the sights; you change your aiming point by guessing where to shoot next. Yeah, this much up and this much to the left or right, and that's where you aimed. So why didn't Spiffon have any sights? After being submerged in the South China Sea during our aborted attempt to reach Snaggletooth Island using Vietnamese boats the previous day, PFC Spiffon most likely had removed the sights from his rifle when he was cleaning it. I suspect he went to the Bob Hope Christmas Show, leaving his rifle sights unassembled. So now, we are in a shooting contest where the losers die. Despite our extensive marksmanship training PFC Spiffon is outshooting everyone without rifle sights. Go figure.

Shortly after querying PFC Spiffon, the lieutenant is shot in the stomach. When he gets hit, he blurts out, "The son of a bitches shot me." That is the only time any of us have ever heard the lieutenant use a word of profanity. A helicopter medevacs our lieutenant off the island; we never see him again.

His leaving is of great significance because of the pending office hours I will soon have with the battalion commander. Before you stand before an officer holding a disciplinary inquiry, your platoon commander first speaks on your behalf. His report of your performance may heavily impact your punishment. Under the Uniform Code of Military Justice, if you are not going before a court-martial, those proceedings called office hours are, for lack of a better word, a "Kangaroo Court." The officer in charge can do whatever he thinks is best for the Marine Corps within his rank's authority. The presiding officer can dismiss the entire affair or throw the book at you.

We all miss our lieutenant. He is, in every manner, an outstanding example of a Marine Officer. Our platoon sergeant, Staff Sergeant Anderson, becomes our temporary platoon commander until a commissioned officer will replace Lieutenant McMaster. An enlisted man will now testify to the quality of my performance to the battalion commander when he presides over my upcoming office hours.

The change of command within our platoon has a profound effect on my future.

Sleeping on Watch - Sergeant Jefferson

Christmas is less than a week away, and I still have not appeared before the battalion commander to address the charges against me. I fear that those proceedings will result in my referral to a court-martial to determine my punishment. So much has occurred since arriving in Vietnam. I have conducted myself so poorly as a leader that official charges have been brought against me. I have almost drowned in the South China Sea. My head was nearly destroyed by a bullet that came precariously close, and our lieutenant has been shot. Yet, the most profound change is within me as I have begun my journey into the world of leadership, violence, and fear.

No more, Mr. Nice Guy. The perimeter that protects our company's island outpost must be defended, night and day. Checking its defensive positions, I discover a Marine sleeping on watch in broad daylight. His rifle is not in his hands; it is several feet away. Sleeping while on watch is not a trivial offense; it is a significant violation of trust. Back home, if you caught a nap at work because you were exhausted, then returned to your assignment, it may not be a big deal. Well, it is a big deal here in an environment where people kill one another. Being awake and ready to fight allows others to sleep because you are protecting them.

Approaching the sleeping Marine, I begin to speak to him; he offers no response. I want to awaken him if he is only lightly dozing. No, this man is unconscious in a deep sleep. I hold my unchambered rifle by the barrel and bang him over the head with the rifle stock. Yes, he has a helmet on. I slam him with some degree of intensity. Then, of course, he awakens, and his first words are, "I am not asleep." After discussing his violation of duty, I notice that my rifle stock's wrist grip is cracked, rendering it useless.

It is now necessary to return my rifle to the armory to receive a replacement. I report my cracked stock to my squad leader, Sergeant Jefferson. He instructs me to carry the rifle to our company gunnery sergeant, who will handle the exchange process. Upon receiving my broken firearm, the armory requests a detailed explanation of how the stock got cracked.

Well, I have told enough lies for the rest of my life. After the horrible experience of lying to our company commander during my office hours, I promised myself never to lie again. So, I write a report detailing the actual events that caused the rifle stock to crack. "I broke my rifle stock over the head of a Marine who was asleep on watch to get his attention." The gunnery sergeant sends my report back without forwarding it to the armory. His instructions are, "Inform Corporal Mezick that he can't tell the battalion armory that he broke his rifle stock over another Marine's head. Tell him to come up with something else." So, I write another report declaring that I tripped and hit the stock on a rock.

Now, in my world, I am not lying. The altered report is their lie, what the world wants to hear, not what I want to report. Besides, what did I have to lose? By the way, I am not the same guy; no more casual leadership. The lesson is, "If you are working for me, you truly are working for me. I don't care who you are; I'm in charge. I got it – I got it. I'm in charge, it's my responsibility, and you will do what I say."

What I am now about to share is one of the most profound experiences of my life.

My limbo state between the company commander's office hours and the battalion commander's office hours is personally challenging. When not busy, I am down and lonely. Sergeant Jefferson, my squad leader, watches me closely. I am not describing a tender loving relationship; ours is a working rapport. Eventually, even during this challenging period, I am assigned the complete duties of a corporal.

Sergeant Jefferson never once mentions my pending disciplinary action. He never reveals any concern until the day he takes me aside for a private conversation. Sergeant Jefferson begins by asking two questions. "Do you know what you have done wrong? Do you understand why the Marine Corps is so upset with you"? I answer, "Yes, I was in a leadership position, and I did not perform as a leader. It's just that simple. I didn't take full responsibility; I was on some nice guy, boy scout kind of a tangent. That will never happen again. I totally get it." He said, "The lieutenant has been shot. That means Staff Sergeant Anderson will represent you before you stand before the colonel during your upcoming office hours. Whether the U.S. Marine Corps realizes it, whether our company commander recognizes it, or whether you know it, you are a natural leader. You have tremendous potential that will soon be wasted if you do not snap out of your shit. You need to mature now! Listen carefully and follow these instructions. Do not say a word to anyone about your upcoming office hours. Not a word."

The questions and instructions I receive from Sergeant Jefferson are incredibly significant. Career enlisted Marines have a fraternity of their own and now know in detail exactly what transpired the night of my bouched ambush. Before being called to stand in front of the battalion commander during my upcoming officer hours, my platoon sergeant will speak on my behalf. There will be no jury during these proceedings. The severity of my punishment will be in part determined by my previous record and my current performance as reported by my platoon sergeant. The career Marines in Bravo Company don't want me incarcerated; they want me to perform appropriately in a manner fitting my corporal rank.

Sergeant Jefferson has reached out to me because he sees in me a young man trying to find himself. He sees potential in me that I don't. It becomes clear to me I must come to know and accept who I am and decide for the first time in my life who I want to be.

Booby Traps

Christmas came and went, hardly noticed by most of us. The Marine Corps made a massive effort to get all its Marines in Vietnam a hot Christmas meal. Most of us appreciated the effort more than the cold, soggy dinner that reached our island outpost. Few things dampen the spirit more than spending Christmas away from your family.

January 1966, Captain Wentworth leads two of Bravo Company's platoons on a daytime patrol to investigate reported enemy activity on Stone Island positioned four hundred yards west of Snaggletooth Island. Before arriving, we are confronted with several hundred yards of open tidal land, separating Tam Hai Island from Stone Island. During periods of low tide, the tidal land provides easy access by walking through ankle-deep water. However, Bravo Company will not expose its Marines to hundreds of yards of open terrain before making sure they will not be attacked from Stone Island's southern tip directly to our front or from Snaggletooth Island to the northeast. First, a fire team will cross the open tidal land and check out the small island's southern tip. My fire team gets that assignment.

PFC Preston leads the way walking point. I am directly behind him; the other two men are behind me. We cross the open terrain without incident and begin walking the only trail on Stone Island's southern tip. After proceeding several hundred yards into the interior of the island, PFC Preston suddenly stops. The earth under the toe of his right boot has begun to give way exposing the edge of a matt. The matt looks exactly like the earth surrounding it, but Preston knows he is on the edge of a hole containing a booby trap. Depressing the matt with his body's weight will trigger explosives below it as he falls into the waist-deep cavity. PFC Preston and I stand frozen. The direction in which he next moves his right foot will determine our future; we are inches away from certain death.

A week before, during an operation on Snaggletooth Island, a member of our squad stepped on a booby trap; it blew off his right foot. Blood just poured from his shattered leg as everyone called for the platoon's corpsman to come to his aid. The wounded Marine looked up into the face of his fire team leader and blurted out, "Corporal Whitney, Corporal Whitney, I can't dance, I can't dance anymore." When his brain allowed him to sense his injuries' enormous pain, he began to scream uncontrollably.

To witness the devastation of a young man is horrific. But it is particularly horrifying when you are also in the same minefield. We evacuate the wounded Marine and then, as a unit, move forward. Every step you take might be the last one you will ever take. Now, with that in mind, just a few days later, PFC Preston stands with his foot on the edge of a booby-trapped pit.

PFC Preston is terrified. He says, "Corporal Mezick, my right foot is on the edge of a camouflaged matt." I reply, "don't move." At this moment, my four-man fire team is positioned one behind another in a staggered column. I order the two Marines behind me to back up and tell PFC Preston, "You are going to be ok as long as you don't apply downward pressure on the matt. Carefully slide your right foot back, and then I want you to turn around and walk toward me slowly." Preston is sweating, extremely stressed, but he overcomes his fear and begins moving as directed. He slides his right foot back, slowly turns around, and begins to walk toward me. He advances his left foot; he advances his right foot and left foot again, hardly any distance before stepping on the edge of another booby-trapped pit.

God didn't intend for Preston to die that afternoon. No, not on this day. Somehow, fate has allowed him to place the toe of his boot on the edge of not one but two booby-trapped pits. The camouflaged holes are skillfully positioned just where the trail takes a slight bend. This arrangement will double the enemy's chances for success regardless of which side of the trail is walked.

Realizing we are in a minefield, I take out my Ka-Bar knife and repeatedly push it into the sand as I close the distance between PFC Preston and myself. Finally, returning to my starting point several yards away, I say, "It's clear there are no booby traps between us. Now you need to walk toward me slowly. Just walk back, and you are going to be fine." He says, "I can't move." I said, "You can. Suck it up, get yourself together; I'm with you. Just start walking." Preston replies, "I'm telling my leg to move, and it won't go." The unavoidable realization that only he has the power to move his foot becomes apparent to PFC Preston, now standing on the precipice of death.

He steadies himself and carefully walks away from the second pit. God bless him, he is so frightened, and he has every right to be fearful. The Marine who recently had his foot blown off is not the only one lately injured by booby traps. We all know first-hand the savage reality of how an explosion can tear the human body into pieces.

PFC Preston, beyond all odds, has escaped death. What's next? I radio back to the company commander, informing him we have discovered two booby traps and request engineers to remove them. The Marine Corps has engineers specifically trained to disarm mines and bobby traps. The command post replies to my request by stating that no engineers are available and orders my team to detonate the bobby traps immediately.

I look at the other three Marines in my fire team and say, "We must detonate the explosives in both pits." All three look down, hoping I will not select one of them to perform the dangerous task before us. Quite frankly, none of us are qualified to carry out the order we just received. I had attended a one-day booby trap school on the mainland of Chu Lai. The instruction I received had nothing to do with how to disarm a booby trap, only how to detect the warning signs that you are in the vicinity of one. The intended victims of the booby traps are us, the Marines, not the local population. Somehow, the locals must be forewarned that a deadly device is in the vicinity. Symmetrical patterns of natural objects like sticks or stones in any structured arrangement are warning signs that booby traps are nearby. Often, stones arranged to create the shape of an arrow or just positioned one beyond the other uniformly spaced become the beacon of impending death. The point is; when you see natural objects arranged in an orderly pattern, it is in all probability a warning sign of imminent danger. The natural order of nature is disorder, one of entropy.

Well, I guess all that government education makes me the expert. I will disarm the booby traps. With that decision made, how the hell am I going to do it? I soon create a plan of action. If I make a long-webbed rope by tying two rifle slings together and attach one of its ends to the matt covering the pit, I might be able to detonate the explosives by pulling the other end. Ok, this is my plan: I will get back the length of two rifle slings, lay on the ground, and give the fashioned rope a big tug. The movement of the matt will cause the booby-trapped explosives to detonate. What can go wrong with such a fine solution to the problem of bombs in holes?

After tying two rifle slings together, I use my Ka-Bar knife to spade my way back up to the pit. I then attach one end of the slings to the matt. I am nervous as hell because I am now in danger of disturbing the trigger device that will initiate an immediate explosion. I get the sling attached and back away until all the slack is out. Then, lying on the ground, my helmet facing the pit and my nose in the dirt, I pull the rifle slings upward. Oh my God, the earth shakes. The explosion is tremendous. I don't know what the hell was in that pit, but I believe it was an unexploded bomb dropped by one of our planes. Instant headache! I feel as though the explosion has driven my brain into my skull. I am in pain; all I can hear is the ringing in my ears.

I am not going to place myself that close to another explosion voluntarily. No one can take two hammerings from my brilliant sling idea during the same morning. The four of us then discuss how I will blow the second pit. We are interrupted by a radio message from the company commander, ordering us to "Hurry up!"

I notice that off to an angle about thirty-five yards away from the second booby-trapped pit stands a lone tree. This tree is large enough to provide some protection from flying shrapnel, so I spade a safe path to it. The new approach is to detonate the explosives in the second pit with a hand grenade. After I pull the pin and release the spoon, I will drop the grenade into the pit. From the moment the spoon flies from the body of the grenade, there will be at least three seconds before it explodes. Indeed, the exploding hand grenade will move the matt with its attached tripwire far enough to detonate whatever might be in the pit. This time I will be further away from the explosion.

I spade my way to the tree to avoid running into another bobby trap between the second pit and the tree. Putting together the sequence of events that are about to occur, I go over every step of the new plan. What can go wrong? First, there is the ugly fact that some grenades have a shorter delay than the designed time of three to five seconds before they explode. Can I drop the grenade, turn, and sprint to the tree in three seconds? Probably not, but the presence of the tree makes me feel good. I get down in a sprinter's position with my left foot behind me and my right ahead. I pull the pin and let the spoon fly. I drop the grenade into the pit and start running, hoping that the dropped grenade's weight will not immediately disturb the booby trap's tripwire. It feels like a dream where you want to run fast, but your legs hardly move. My brain directs my body to pour every bit of energy available into my legs. I run as quickly as I possibly can, counting, one thousand and one, one thousand and two, one thousand three, "Oh shit, it's going to go off before I reach the tree." I dive into the sand just before all hell explodes.

Ok, no more pits, no more booby traps. What kind of feedback do we receive from our company commander? None, not a word. The Marines waiting for us to clear the booby-trapped pits then advance across the tidal land, and my fire team falls back into formation among them.

Battalion Commander's Office Hours

Finally, the day has come for me to stand before the battalion commander, Lieutenant Colonel Donavan, who will determine my punishment's extent. I clean up as well as possible to make a positive impression. My only thought is of the promise made to myself never to tell another lie for as long as I live. However, on the other hand, I can't change my story without incriminating most of the other Marines who were with me on that fateful night. For the same reason that I could not change my report during my first office hours, I can't now change my story. I dread the thought of telling another lie to anyone, especially my battalion commander. But on this day, I am prepared to lie yet again, believing that breaking a trust that you have committed to is even worse than lying—changing my story will bring down others who have made the same commitment.

When summoned, I walk into the same tent where my previous judgment occurred and stand at attention in front of the officer who will determine my immediate future. Lieutenant Colonel Donovan sits at a crudely fashioned desk. Looking directly at me, he begins to speak, "I have reviewed all the written reports of the charges against you, and I have spoken with those in your immediate chain of command. Accordingly,

I am reducing your rank from corporal to lance corporal by suspension: holding the punishment in abeyance for three months. The conditions of the suspension of your rank are to start immediately. Within the next three months, if you commit further violations of the Uniform Code of Military Justice, your rank will be reduced on the date of that judgment. Then you will be further punished per your most recent violation. In addition to the three months suspended rank reduction, your punishment will include a fine of 50 dollars held from your next distribution of government compensation. You are dismissed." I didn't say a word during the entire procedure beyond reporting to the presiding officer. I went in there prepared for the worst and only received a three-month suspended bust and a fifty-dollar fine. That means in plain language: if I get into any trouble within the next three months, I will be immediately busted back to an E-3 lance corporal and then punished for my newest offense.

However, I maintained the rank of corporal E-4; I am still a noncommissioned officer. The fifty dollars deducted from my next paycheck will not affect my wife because she will still receive her monthly mandated distribution. The fine is taken from the part of my pay that I receive. Trust me; this is not a problem because here I have no use for pocket money. Diana or no one else in my family will know of the punishment I have received. I am now on the other side of disciplinary proceedings, the other side of "Shit Bird," with a new opportunity to establish myself inwardly as well as outwardly.

Since my rocky beginning as a member of Bravo Company, I have proven myself as a leader. Sergeant Jefferson and I have gotten to know and then trust one another. We build a working relationship grounded in mutual respect and hard work. He is my immediate superior, he is my professor, and I am his motivated student. Sergeant Jefferson often asks me questions about tactics and listens intently to my responses even when he disagrees. I am changing daily, and, let there be no doubt, Sergeant Jefferson provided me an opportunity for a second chance. For that, I will never forget him, and I work every moment not to fail him.

There is no reality more sobering than the naked truth of who you are. I am not pleased with all that has been revealed, but I feel a sense of rising confidence. Not really understanding all the internal forces driving me; still, I give them full authority to enable change. Think baptism, not as a Christian, but as a fledgling leader.

Leadership Challenges of a
Non-commissioned Officer

The leadership challenges confronting non-commissioned officers in the grunts were often exceedingly difficult. You didn't get to pick and choose from a manpower pool. The Marines in your command were most likely born and raised in different geographical regions of the United States. Most were from blue-collar backgrounds, and some had less than stellar resumes. Nevertheless, young men from various races, levels of education, and faiths discovered they had much in common and got along quite well for the most part. But, trust me, we had an occasional Marine that at best was atypical and, at worst, borderline crazy.

Bravo Company, still deployed on Tam Hai Island off the Ky Ha Peninsula coast, enjoyed the privilege of squad-size tents with cots to sleep on. If not assigned to a night patrol, perimeter guard duty, or an ambush, you could sleep on those excellent cots. That's what I am doing when abruptly awakened at about 0230 or 0300 hours, 2:30 or 3:00 am, in the morning. Corporal Whitney, the first fire team leader in our squad, is standing over me and shouting, "You have to come, you have to come quickly; PFC Spiffon has gone over the top; we need you right now. I desperately try to grasp the situation as I awaken. My first response, "PFC Spiffon is not in my fire team. He is in your fire team. So why are you waking me up"? He replies, "Because he only wants to talk to you, and you have to come, this is serious."

I approach PFC Spiffon's position cautiously; he sees me and shouts, "Halt, Corporal Mezick, is that you? Who is approaching me"? I immediately respond, "Yes, it's me, Corporal Mezick; I am here to talk with you."

Spiffon replies, "I thought you were Sergeant Roberts. I'm going to shoot that son of a bitch tonight. He's going down. I'm going to put some holes right in his fucking chest." Thoroughly alarmed, I respond, "Spiffon, you got to stop talking like this. What are you saying? What I'm hearing is crazy talk." Now that he recognizes me, I approach him more closely. He doesn't have his helmet or flak jacket on; he is bare-chested, pacing back and forth, holding his M14 rifle. Coming even closer, I see his bloody face and swollen nose. I ask, "Spiffon, what happened"? He says, "Sergeant Roberts kicked me in the face. He said I was asleep. By the time I got my wits about me, he had left. Otherwise, I would have greased that mother fucker." Spiffon is furious; he is beyond my control.

Sergeant Roberts, our platoon's right guide, is quite capable of kicking anyone he discovers asleep on watch. How do I know? It's embarrassing for me to admit this, but I once fell asleep on watch. That's right. It was challenging in Vietnam to stay awake on watch because you were so tired after humping all day and then being assigned to guard the perimeter. So you had to teach yourself how to stay awake. Yes, you can teach yourself not to fall asleep even when your body and mind are exhausted.

Let me share my experience. An illumination round fired from a ship moored off the Ky Ha Peninsula bathed the fighting positions protecting our company's island outpost's perimeter with soft light. To prevent me from becoming an illuminated target, I must kneel in my fighting position. I watch the flare supported by its parachute gently fall from the sky and continue to monitor its progress. It gets dimmer and lower and dimmer and lower until just before it touches the earth, it goes out, and so do I. As if hypnotized, I am now asleep as I kneel in my fighting position. Wham, the next thing I know, I get kicked in the helmet by Sergeant Roberts and then made to do pushups while he verbally assaults me. He explains, "While you sleep on watch the Marines depending on you are also asleep. That means everyone is asleep, and we will all be killed. Your sleeping on watch can never happen again. Your conduct is unacceptable, a disgrace. I am extremely disappointed in you."

To my recollection, I never fell asleep on watch again. I was genuinely embarrassed. I forced myself to stand up in my fighting position from that night on if I became too exhausted. I would rather expose myself than fail those depending on me. That's the kind of environment we were in. Kicking a Marine in his helmet while he is sleeping on guard duty could very well have been the best thing that ever happened to him—but not kicking him in the face. What the hell happened here? Did Sergeant Roberts slip and miss his helmet? Did Spiffon happen to look up when the boot was coming? There is no dealing with Spiffon; he is not controllable.

Fearful for Sergeant Robert's life and Spiffon's future, I go to the sergeant's quarters and alert him to the situation. I explain, "I have just returned from PFC Spiffon's position on the perimeter. He has sworn to me he intends to kill you later this evening when you check lines. I don't know what happened between the two of you tonight, but he is beyond making any sense whatsoever. I must report that he is dangerous. I suggest you don't recheck his position before daylight." The sergeant replies, "Of course, I am going to check the lines. Do you think I will let one out-of-control asshole prevent me from checking the lines I am responsible for"?

The following day, the company gunnery sergeant relieves PFC Spiffon of his rifle. Ordered to sit on his cot and go no further from it than the latrine, Spiffon sits as instructed for two days; before being reinstated. That's right, they returned his M14 rifle and put him right back on duty as if nothing happened. How can you be so far on the other side of so many violations and not be punished?

Here's what happened. Sergeant Roberts is a senior sergeant, a career Marine under consideration for promotion to Staff Sergeant E-6. If accused of kicking a Marine in the face regardless of the reason, he will, at minimum, be no longer competitive for promotion and will most likely be punished. Sergeant Roberts's intentions may have been what the Marine Corps needed from an infantry NCO. However, a charge of that nature, should it be entered into his official record, will prevent him from being promoted, possibly for the rest of his career. I suspect the gunny realized that PFC Spiffon could not be charged without charging Sergeant Roberts as well. PFC Spiffon is reinstated to his regular duties and carries on as though he is innocent of all charges.

Shortly thereafter, Spiffon's fire team leader approaches me with a twenty-dollar bill and an offer, "You take PFC Spiffon, and I will accept any man you want to swap from your fire team. Plus, I will give you twenty dollars." I said, "I'm not taking Spiffon for twenty bucks." He says, "Fifty, I got fifty for you." I refuse, "I'm not taking him for fifty dollars either. I don't want to be responsible for him. You do realize, Spiffon is nuts"? He agreed and left disappointed that he could not unload PFC Spiffon. I should have accepted his last offer because Sergeant Jefferson eventually assigned him to my fire team, swapping one of my good men for him. When I speak of good men, Spiffon is the best Marine ever if you happen to be in a firefight. Hell, he is worth two men. No doubt about it, he is the man you want with you in a fight. The problem is if you aren't in a firefight, you can't control him. The Marine that Sergeant Jefferson swapped out of my fire team is rock solid all the time.

PFC Spiffon, now a member of my fire team, went about his business somehow, not realizing he sidestepped a court-martial. Preoccupied with unrelenting rain, most of our platoon never learned of the incident between Spiffon and Roberts.

The rainy, cloudy weather we endure during January creates an ominous threat, body fungus. All types of bacteria thrive in areas of our bodies not exposed to open air or light. Taking a bar of soap to a mud puddle, we washed our feet, genitals, and butts with fresh rainwater. My responsibility is to make sure everyone in my fire team complies.

PFC Spiffon is the only member of my team that has not stripped down and washed as ordered. I approach him in a low-key fashion, "Spiffon, let's get this muddy bath over with so I can report that everyone has washed." I leave him, hoping that nothing more will have to be said. Yes, I give him a little extra time. Why? Because he is PFC Spiffon. However, he doesn't comply. At this point, I have no choice but to break hard. He doesn't have the right to pick and choose which orders he will follow. He is also prone to the same debilitating funguses that the rest of us are.

The conversation goes like this, "Spiffon, strip down now. Here's your soap, take it, get into the water, and wash, now." He stands there. I look him in the eyes and say, "Do it and do it now." He picks up his M14 rifle and points it at my chest as he forcibly states, "I'm not washing in a mud puddle, and don't you ever tell me to do that again." I reply, "Spiffon, now that you have explained how you feel about washing, I get it. I understand. Thanks for breaking it down for me." I walk away from the Marine, pointing a rifle at my chest, and go directly to our acting platoon commander, Staff Sergeant Anderson.

I report that PFC Spiffon is unmanageable, out of control, and a danger to others. Staff Sergeant Anderson doesn't hesitate or even ask me what happened; he doesn't care. Spiffon has been warned that if he threatened anyone again, he would be out of Bravo Company. I didn't tell the acting platoon commander that Spiffon had pointed his M14 rifle at me. I figured if I could get him out of Bravo Company, they would find a suitable assignment for him. I didn't want to put a nail in his coffin. I hadn't forgotten how much we all appreciate him in a firefight.

Several days later, PFC Spiffon is reassigned to work in the Chu Lai Combat Base's mess hall. His new job; wash dishes in the mess hall. Now, how could he possibly screw that up? He did! Here's the situation as described to us: A company of Marines returning from an extended operation stands outside the mess hall's locked screen door that prevents them from sitting down to a hot meal. The Marines are wet, tired, and hungry. The evening meal has a start time and an end time; it was then several minutes after the posted end time. PFC Spiffon met the Marines at the screen door and refused to open it. Instead, he shouted to them that the evening meal has been secured three minutes ago and informs them that they are welcome to come back for breakfast. One verbal exchange leads to another before the grunts pull the screen door off its hinges and grab Spiffon. His dishwasher buddies come out, the cooks come out, and there is an explosion of physical and verbal assaults.

I believe that it doesn't matter if PFC Spiffon is in the Marine Corps or becomes the chief executive of a finance company or a truck driver; he will always be the same PFC Spiffon. God bless him. I hope he goes on to a long and prosperous life.

Outpost Attacked

The headache I received from detonating the two booby-trapped pits went away in a day or so. However, the ringing in my ears continued loudly for over a week and has never totally stopped. I continuously hear a low-frequency buzz in both ears. You somewhat get used to the condition called tinnitus as your brain attempts to compensate by ignoring that annoying sound.

Sad booby trap reports: the last we heard of the Marine who had his foot blown off on Snaggletooth Island is that he is in worse condition than we first thought. He is suffering from shrapnel wounds throughout his body, and the explosion has blinded him. Several weeks after PFC, Preston fatefully avoided detonating two booby trap pits; another Marine patrolling Stone Island stepped directly onto a camouflaged mat before falling into the hole below it. The air turbulence from the explosion was so powerful it tore his body to bits, literally to bits. The fragments of human flesh deposited on nearby vegetation rotted in the heat and humidity. The resulting stench was horrific.

Bravo Company regularly holds operations on Snaggletooth Island to prevent it from being used as a launch site to attack the Chu Lai Combat Base on the Ky Ha Peninsula with heavy weapons. Unfortunately, the airfield is vulnerable to such weapons, mainly 128 mm rockets or 120 mm mortars. In addition, booby traps and minefields continue to plague us on Snaggletooth and Stone Islands.

Battalion needs to establish a company size outpost on Snaggletooth Island to prevent Stone Island's several acres from being continuously booby-trapped. In this way, Chu Lai Combat Base with its airfield and aircraft will be protected, and Stone Island will also be secure. Great idea; however, there are not enough Marines in Vietnam during the first months of 1966 to establish a permanent outpost on the large Snaggletooth Island. Such a deployment requires our battalion to have a fourth line company assigned to it; that request is denied. The next best solution to securing Snaggletooth Island with a company of Marines is to have Bravo Company spread itself even thinner by establishing a small outpost on Stone Island. Every two days, the assignment to defend the new outpost on Stone Island rotates amongst the three squads of the platoon assigned to the outpost on Tam Hai Island's northeastern tip.

The squad of Marines reinforced with an M60 machine gun and a rocket team defending the tiny island outpost wields a considerable amount of firepower. However, there are severe vulnerabilities to its defenses. The fighting positions dug to protect the island are nothing more than holes in the ground without any concertina wire or early warning devices forward of them. The entire island is flat with a large wetland to its west. Wherever we establish our defensive positions, their locations are exposed by the Vietnamese who live on the island.

Defending the remote outpost on Stone Island is dangerous and challenging. From a private to a general, Marines then and now receive and carry out orders. They don't discuss the why of their orders. They accept them and begin working on how to accomplish the task before them.

The saga of that tiny island with its new outpost continues with many unfortunate events.

I am approached early one morning by a machine gunner from our weapons platoon. He comes to me to confess what he considers to be a crime of morality. He declares, "Corporal Mezick, I am going to die." I say, "What are you talking about"? He repeats himself, "I am going to die. I am totally fucked." This man is serious and upset. He is on the verge of a mental crisis. I ask again, "What are you talking about"? He yells out his reply, "We had Stone Island outpost last night, and a boat came right at us. We ordered the boat to stop, but it kept coming. The boat wouldn't stop. I'm not sure that the people in the boat could understand us. The boat kept coming. I was ordered to fire my M60 machine gun at the boat, and I did. I burned it up. I killed every damn one of them." I say, "Were there any bad guys in the boat"? He cries out, "I don't know how the hell would I know. I couldn't hear anything while I was firing, and when I stopped, I could only hear people moaning before they drowned in their sinking boat. No one survived. That's wrong, and God knows it's wrong, and God is going to punish me. He knows it's wrong, and I know it's wrong, now I'm done. There is no way I can survive because what I did, is not right. I'm going to the captain right now and tell him that it isn't right." I said, "Hey, settle down. There is a name for all this killing; it's called war. We must understand; sometimes, it's them or us. What if the boat had been full of bad guys hell-bent on attacking the outpost, and you didn't fire on them? Would you rather be dealing with that decision this morning? Your sergeant had little choice but to order you to fire on the approaching boat. How fair is it that your sergeant had to order you to fire"?

He looks up with tears running down his cheek and says, "All I could hear were women and kids moaning and crying after I shot them. I am going to tell the captain what I did, how I killed all those people." I tried one last time to console him, "Listen, everyone who is supposed to stop this shit, all the politicians, they blew it. Now we are here, in a place without compassion. People you don't know will blow your ass away on sight, and you have no choice but to blow their ass away. Don't ever stop being aggressive because as soon as you do, that's when you are going down." As he predicted, he died during a night attack on Stone Island outpost only weeks later.

Since my battalion commander's office hours, I continue to improve; I am on the other side of my rocky start. The squad leader of the third squad has completed his thirteen-month tour and rotated back to the states. I am selected to replace him. The promotion comes fast, considering I joined the company in November, and it is now early January. The squad has requested that I become their new leader. Being recommended to lead by your peers is a high honor, especially so in a war. Leaving the first squad to take command of the third squad, Sergeant Jefferson walks up and shakes my hand. After a moment of silence, he tells me how proud he is of me. I will never forget that handshake.

Shortly after being promoted to squad leader of the third squad, my platoon rotates to the outpost on Tam Hai Island's northeastern tip. During that week, late one afternoon Sergeant Jefferson's squad is getting ready to depart for the remote outpost on Stone Island. Before he and his men leave, we are all treated to a hot beer, courtesy of the U.S. Government. I don't know how this came to be, and it only happened in Chu Lai. Yeah, we got a hot beer ration once a week. I can't possibly tell you how awesome it was to get that can of hot beer. It was like gold, like Glenfiddich Single Malt Scotch or something equivalent. We all eagerly opened our beer, and no sooner than we could take a couple of sips, Sergeant Jefferson's squad is ordered to "Saddle Up." One of the Marines who I had recently served with as a member of Sergeant's Jefferson's squad looks at me and says, "Here, have mine." The gift of his hot beer is a genuine gesture of friendship. Hang on to that thought.

That night I am asleep in a pup tent when roused by our platoon's right guide[17], Sergeant Roberts. He orders me to assemble my squad and lead them on patrol around the entire outer perimeter of the platoon's outpost. I am told that Sergeant Jefferson's squad has been fighting on Stone Island, and we have lost radio contact with them. The Marine Corps' radio used to communicate with its reinforced squad defending our most distant outpost is called a Prick 6. First used in World War II and then in Korea, they are nothing more than little walkie-talkies. The Prick 6 radios we use malfunction so often you can't tell if your lack of communication is another malfunctioning radio or if the radio operator is dead. Our guys have been in a fight at the remote outpost. Did they need help? What is their status?

At first light, our command post is still unable to contact the outpost on the small island; my squad is ordered to find out why. Walking north adjacent to the South China Sea, we see a man without a weapon approaching us. The lone man is our platoon's corpsmen. Before he can speak, I notice that his skin color is gray, and he wears an expression

---

[17] **Right Guide** – A sergeant acting as an assistant platoon sergeant. His chain of command is above the three squad leaders in an infantry platoon and below the platoon sergeant.

of extreme anxiety. This man is in shock; something is seriously wrong. Finally, he begins to speak, "Don't go down there, don't go there. We need to go back and get everyone. We got attacked last night; everybody's dead. Fucking dead." Hearing the situation report, the battalion commander sends us Amtraks to transport the other two squads of our platoon to the remote outpost.

Upon arrival, we discover a horrific scene, one of carnage. The outpost has been attacked by sappers[18] that threw knapsacks filled with TNT explosives into each fighting position. The defensive positions were overrun; the squad is mostly dead. Between the hours of two and three in the morning, every defensive position was approached by sappers silently moving a few inches at a time. When the sappers reached their final attack positions, they coordinated with their leader by blowing into a specially cut leaf to create an insect's sound typical to the island. All the defensive positions, each containing two Marines, one on watch and one asleep, were assaulted simultaneously with TNT explosives. The enemy knew the exact location of every position. Ninety-eight percent of the Marine casualties occur the moment the attack begins. The sapper attack is followed by an infantry assault completely overrunning the outpost. The squad of island defenders is defeated before knowing they are in a fight. The sapper attack is a cruel example of why we must be 100 percent on our game, constantly ready to fight. Most of the Marines who were not dead were suffering from concussions. Some of them are walking around totally incoherent.

One Marine, Corporal Hernandez[19], managed to escape injury during the initial attack. Surrounded by death and destruction, he alone mounts

---

[18] **Sapper** - A Viet Cong or NVA commando, usually armed with explosives. The purpose of NVA/VC sappers was to penetrate an American defensive perimeter in ADVANCE of a ground attack by another NVA/VC unit. The sappers would initiate battle from WITHIN the American defensive perimeter at the SAME time another unit would attack the American perimeter from WITHOUT. Military Thoughts: Sappers.

[19] **Corporal Hernandez** - Was awarded a Bronze Star for his actions during the sapper attack. He was credited with saving the lives of the wounded by driving the enemy out of the overrun outpost. If ever a Marine deserved to be recognized for bravery, it surely was this man.

a counterattack. After being awakened to sheer chaos, he hides in the darkness behind a tree armed with his M14 rifle and one magazine of ammunition. Everyone around him is speaking Vietnamese. Hernandez goes on the offensive killing the guy he figures is the leader because when this man barks commands, everyone else listens. Corporal Hernandez put him down with one shot and immediately moved before the tree he hid behind was saturated with return fire. Aided by the darkness of a moonless night, the only Marine capable of fighting moves and fires and moves and fires from different locations. He appears to the enemy to be a more significant force than one.

The fact that he killed their leader is substantial because their rank and file were very dependent on their commander. They became confused and didn't continue to pursue their ghostly adversary, who has only several rounds of ammunition left. The leaderless attackers picked up anything they could eat or shoot. They also captured the squad's Prick 6 radio; good they could keep it. They didn't linger for two reasons; first, they were under fire from a Marine they couldn't kill. The second reason; their machine gun that had been continuously firing from Snaggletooth Island during the attack to protect the Tam Hai Island platoon's approach route had stopped.

Now, it is time to collect the remains of our dead Marines. Among them, to my extreme grief, lay Sergeant Jefferson, my mentor. The Marine, I thought, was unkillable. The career Marine, the black belt in Judo, the man that reached out to me when I was in need. Sergeant Jefferson is the epitome of a Marine, and now he is dead. Not only is he dead, but his body lay broken, twisted in an unnatural position. A human body can't be in such an arrangement without having a broken back and broken legs. He looks like a rag doll. Staring down at Sergeant Jefferson's body, I am overwhelmed with a humiliating response to his death. "Better him than me." That's what I am thinking. Oh my God, where did that come from? I later learned not to be ashamed of such a response. It's a normal survival instinct. It surfaced every time I was in the presence of violent death. We are all descendants of those who survived the violent history of human evolution. Our brains are naturally wired to preserve us from extinction to perpetuate our species.

Had it not been for my promotion to squad leader of the third squad less than one week prior, I would have been here, most likely laying among the dead. Tears fill my eyes and roll down my cheeks. That would be the first and last time I will cry during the thirteen months I spent fighting the Vietnam War. I admired and respected the man that then lay dead before me. I am stunned because I think a Marine of his caliber can never be killed.

Then came a profound transition. I promised the dead to make their death my battle cry, my Alamo. I will have no problem killing the sons of bitches who did this. Not that I have a problem so far. I have been swapping bullets with the enemy with no difficulty. But from this day on, the war becomes personal. I commit to using every ounce of my physical and mental energy to kill. What kind of transition is this? I leave it to you to put a label on it. I will only declare from this day on; I continuously put myself and those in my command into situations where we kill with the greatest efficiency.

After loading the fallen Marines into Amtraks, everyone else leaves Stone Island except for my squad and the platoon's right guide, Sergeant Roberts. We are ordered to stay and defend the island from the same fighting holes attacked the previous night. Holy shit, we are sitting in the same holes where our mates got blown up the night before. Why? Because it is an order. We will die in rank; we will die fighting for each other; we will do as ordered. Our training is to do, not to question. Quite frankly, I am looking for a fight anyway. I am not too worried about myself; I want some payback. I feel an intense desire to see those responsible for the death of my fellow Marines in my rifle sights as I squeeze the trigger.

Realizing how exposed the rest of us are, I quietly sit in a fighting position and begin to consider how we can better defend ourselves. Directly to my front, I see something peculiar on the ground. I pick it up and rub it between my index finger and my thumb. It feels hard and rough on one side, with a somewhat slippery texture on the other side. I recognize what I am holding is a piece of a human skull. Looking closely, I observe hair. Then I realize it belongs to my friend. The Marine who gave me his beer before he left the platoon outpost to come here. The last time I saw him, he handed me his beer; the next time I am in his presence, I hold a piece of his skull. Now it is my turn to spend the night in the same God damn hole where he was blown to pieces the night before.

Sergeant Roberts interrupts my moment of personal reflection, "Select several members of your squad for a dangerous assignment." I think shit, can it be any more dangerous than our present assignment?

The Amtraks left us with two cases of hand grenades still packed in their shipping canisters. Think of a cardboard container with a circumference that will not allow the grenade's spoon to move even in the unlikely event the grenade's pin separates from it. The cardboard canaster, because of its design, can be used to booby trap the grenade. We secure the canaster holding a grenade with a pulled pin between two stakes and support it above ground with a C -Ration case box. A string is attached to the grenade, pulled halfway from its canaster, and strung to another stake approximately twenty yards away. Anyone approaching, especially in darkness, will push or pull the taut string causing the grenade to slide out of its cardboard canister. Within the next three to five seconds, the grenade will explode.

The booby-trapped grenades work both as an early warning of approaching enemy and as a lethal weapon. They are also a vivid example of how dangerous the squad size outpost on Stone Island has become. Working in two-man teams, we deploy several booby-trapped grenades before our hazardous task is interrupted by an order from battalion headquarters instructing us to return to the Tam Hai Island platoon outpost. We carefully pick up our booby-trapped grenades and reinsert the pins. Somehow that task has come to seem normal.

Several days later, our company commander, Captain Wentworth, arranged for a Chaplin to visit our platoon. The captain's intentions of helping us deal with the death of our fellow Marines are well-intended. However, he steps on any religious sentiment by preceding the Chaplin with a presentation of his own. He refers to the dead Marines as having "Bought the farm." Whatever he meant by this expression, it hurt most of us. Considering the loss of my fellow Marines on Stone Island, the captain's words are cold and insensitive. I see and hear a man internally struggling with the order he gave to establish a semi-permanent remote outpost on flat ground, protected with static fighting positions without any wire, early detection devices, or defensive armaments.

Many of us Marines preferred to put our terrible defeat out of mind and carry on as if nothing happened. Not me; I transitioned into a mindset of critical analysis. I went over every detail of how we defended our remote island outpost and pondered each element of how the enemy successfully attacked it. I learned how challenging it is to look at a situation without bias. To not sugarcoat facts and forgive mistakes made by men you respect. My pursuit of analysis is not to determine blame for decisions made in the past. Instead, I desperately want to learn how not to repeat them in the future.

Brenda Born February 21, 1966

Late in January 1966, during Operation Double Eagle the First Battalion Fourth Marines and two rifle companies from the 7th Marines are given the mission to secure the entire northern half of the Chu Lai area of responsibility, AOR[20]. Bravo Company is pleased to be done with Snaggletooth Island. However, five infantry companies covering such a large area are spread thin. Our leaders attempt to minimize this challenge with aggressive patrolling and ambushing. When defending static fighting positions, early enemy detection is a form of offense. You can't sit in the same hole night after night and prevent an attack. We are all painfully aware of how Sergeant Jefferson's squad was destroyed by sappers throwing satchels full of TNT into every defensive position.

Small squad size operations are the backbone of Marine Corps tactics in Vietnam. There were thousands and thousands of small unit engagements without names remembered only by those involved for every huge battle

---

[20] **Area of Responsibility** - The geographical area associated with a combatant command within which a combatant commander has authority to plan and conduct operations. Also called AOR. area of responsibility (US DoD Definition) (militaryfactory.com)

with its name recorded by history. Sergeants and corporals leading lance corporals and privates experience Vietnam up close. After three months of familiarity, I am beginning to learn about Vietnam as a combatant. My thoughts are no longer dominated by my recent marriage and our expected child. February 22, 1966, my squad is about to return from an ambush when we hear movement. The sounds seem to be of a small unit walking towards what I consider a perfect ambush site, a small pocket of trees and underbrush overlooking a footpath between two small hills. I whisper into a radio handset and request to extend the ambush for several more hours. After that, whoever is approaching must have turned onto another path. A lucky night for them, a long night for us. Yes, I have mentally transitioned into a Marine in combat and further away from my life before Vietnam.

After returning from the ambush, I am directed to report to the battalion headquarters communications tent. I am informed that my wife Diana has delivered our baby at the Naval Hospital in Philadelphia, Pa. The officer on duty asks, "Would you like to speak with your wife"? Astonished, I reply, "Yes, if that's possible." Today's technology that enables immediate worldwide audio and video communication was one step beyond a miracle in 1966. Somehow, contact is established from Chu Lai, Vietnam, to Philadelphia, Pa. Diana is surprised to receive a transpacific phone call from her husband on the other side of the world. To this day, neither of us remembers the words exchanged beyond the news that we have a baby girl, and everyone is healthy and doing fine. Our call seems surreal; two people who have spent so little time together as husband and wife are now forever connected by the birth of their daughter. Ending the call with Diana, I want to be home to begin providing for my new family. No man should ever have to miss the magical moments when his wife delivers their child. That night, I have no idea of the magnitude of what I had been denied until the birth of our second daughter eleven years later.

After the call, I feel a new burden of accountability and responsibility. Ready or not, I am the father of a child who is dependent on me. Here, in Vietnam, I am not sure I can lead a squad of Marines in combat. When or if I ever return to Eddystone, Pennsylvania, I fear I will not feel the compassion of a loving father and husband. Before returning home to my family, I must survive in Vietnam. Only then can I begin to experience the tenderness of a devoted father and husband. To get back home, I must get good at being here. To survive the challenges of a grunt fighting in Vietnam, I must first become proficient in the talents of human destruction.

Our entire battalion is relieved on March 6 and assigned to III Marine Amphibious Force Reserve. Our new role as a battalion in reserve means that we will be sent to the next significant battle anywhere in the entire I Corps Area of the northern section of South Vietnam. After relocating to Chu Lai Airfield, we have only to wait four days before heading north to a major battle.

CHAPTER FOUR

Phu Bai

The Street Without Joy – Chin An Hamlet

March 13, 1966 Alpha and Bravo Company of the First Battalion Fourth Marines leave Chu Lai and go to Phu Bai. We board C-130 four-engine heavy-lift transport planes. Flying in any aircraft is not a bad thing. Any time a grunt isn't walking, that's a good thing. We are not particular about the mode of transportation, gladly accepting a ride in an airplane, helicopter, Amtrak, truck, whatever. It is a relief not to be walking. Most of the time, we don't ride in anything. We walk everywhere!

Flying to Phu Bai is pleasant and comfortable, although we are a bit concerned. What's going on? How come they must get us to Phu Bai so fast? It's only eighty-five or ninety miles from Chu Lai to Phu Bai. We don't know because the officers don't tell us anything; they think we don't need to know. We later learned that an Army Special Forces camp in the A Shau Valley was overrun on March 10th. The camp had approximately four hundred defenders, mostly South Vietnamese serving in the Army of the Republic of Vietnam supported by Montagnards and other nomadic tribes that populated North and South Vietnam's highlands. The Army of North Vietnam, officially called the People's Army of Vietnam, PAVN, overran the camp.

Marine and Air Force aircraft did what they could to support the Army Special Forces camp's defenders despite punishing ground fire and the terrible weather conditions during the monsoon season. Marine Medium Helicopter Squadron 163, known as HMM-163, did a heroic job of evacuating many of the camp's defenders before the North Vietnamese gained control of the A Shau Valley. We are sent to Phu Bai to become part of a Marine offensive to retake the Army Special Forces camp. That counteroffensive was canceled after our battalion commander, Lieutenant Colonel Donavan, flew over the A Shau Valley and evaluated

127

the situation. He determined that two understaffed companies of Marines were insufficient in number to retake the fallen camp. His official report noted that nothing less than a regiment containing 1,500 to 2,000 Marines would be required.

After the A Shau Valley counteroffensive operation was canceled, Alpha and Bravo Companies became a reactionary force. There were reports of a significant enemy buildup within striking distance of the Marine Combat Base in Phu Bai. The Marine Corps has a highly effective defensive aggression philosophy that prevents an attack by making the would-be attackers defend themselves from an attack. Well, that attack first tactic is us. We are about to go to Operation Oregon.

For me, Operation Oregon started on March 18th when I was ordered to report to our platoon's command center by the following command, "Squad leaders up." We still don't have a replacement for Lieutenant McMaster since he was shot on Snaggletooth Island. Our platoon sergeant, Staff Sergeant Anderson, continues to perform as our platoon commander, Sergeant Roberts, the platoon's right guide, is second in command.

I notice when Sergeant Anderson briefs the platoon's squad leaders; he is intense. Using a stick to draw four straight lines, one above the other, he labels them A, B, C, and D before he begins to explain the platoon's battle plan. "The choppers are going to put us in below line A where we will form an online[21] frontal assault formation and sweep forward. We are one hundred percent certain of making enemy contact somewhere between lines A and D. The enemy is estimated to be of platoon strength, forty to fifty men at most. Corporal Mezick's third squad will be our left flank and form online with the company's second platoon. The second squad led by Corporal Dickens will be on our right flank and form online with the company's third platoon. The first squad led by Sergeant Costa will form online behind second and third squads

---

[21] **On-line** - Everyone facing the same direction adjacent to the person next to you on either side with several meters of distance between persons.

in reserve. When we make contact, Sergeant Costa's squad will attack aided by Corporal Mezick's and Corporal Dickens's squads, who will lay down suppressing fire[22]."

Think about that plan for a moment. Consider going to work today, and your boss orders you and your coworkers to walk forward until someone gets shot and then further orders everyone to attack by running at the people shooting at you. Yeah, welcome to the Marine Corps. That's precisely the way it went down.

On March 19th, we went out to the tarmac of the Phu Bai Combat Base. The weather changed to rain, with low thick cloud cover preventing jet pilots from providing air support. They just couldn't see, so Operation Oregon is delayed another day.

Alpha and Bravo Companies are now available to attend a USO Show[23] that happens to be performing later this afternoon. The show features Ann Margret. She is in the prime of her career, but somehow, she has come to Vietnam to entertain us. That last statement may not sound all that relevant. At first, you may think, what's the big deal? Listen, it isn't just that she is sexy and beautiful, and it isn't only that she cared enough to come to Vietnam and perform. The power of her presence creates a connection to all of what we had left back home. The Marines referred to back home in the United States as the world. Yeah, back in the world because they considered Vietnam to be some other planet. To us, this place, Vietnam, can't be part of the real world. Not the world of our mothers, fathers, sisters, brothers, girlfriends, and for some of us, our wives. Ann Margret is the last European woman that nineteen Marines of Alpha and Bravo Company will ever see again because nineteen of us are about to

---

[22] **Suppressive Fire** - (commonly called covering **fire**) Basically, pin the enemy down with overwhelming fire power to prevent them from firing as you advance towards them.

[23] **USO** - United Service Organizations Inc. (USO) is a nonprofit-charitable corporation that provides live entertainment, such as comedians, actors and musicians, social facilities, and other programs to members of the United States Armed Forces and their families. https://en.wikipedia.org/wiki/United_Service_OrganizationsUnited

die the next day[24]. Ann Margret, just the name, makes me smile. I doubt very seriously she will ever read or listen to this man's remembrance of the day she performed in Phu Bai. But, just in case she does. "Thank you from the bottom of my heart. Thank you."

On March 20th, it is still rainy, foggy, and overcast in the morning. We form helicopter boarding formations again on the tarmac and wait to enter CH-46 helicopters that will take us into battle. There is no change in the weather, so we just sit on our equipment and continue to wait.

Later in the afternoon, we get the green light. We are going. Once we enter the helicopters' interior, the noise produced by its engine and rotor blades is overwhelming. It becomes impossible to speak with anyone without shouting. It's not like you are sitting on a comfortable seat in a commercial airplane. No, you are sitting on a net. You sit with your rifle between your legs, muzzle pointing up, your helmet secured with a chin strap, your standard-issued combat equipment, your two canteens of water attached to your cartridge belt, and your thoughts. Unspoken thoughts of fear and death create intense facial expressions from the other Marines that reflect your intensity. Body temperature rises due to an increased heart rate producing noticeable beads of brow sweat. You know you are going into a fight, and that fight has only two rules, kill or be killed. Some of us are going to die today, and we know it. That's what it means to be a Marine. Don't let anyone bullshit you. "Marines fight their way into Hell. Marines Kill-Marines Die." Grunts have a name for that exact situation. We call it "Going into the shit."

When you land in a helicopter, the last thing you want to hear is gunfire because that means you are entering a hot landing zone. Yeah, a hot LZ. Not good!

---

[24] **Most accurate history of tactics and casualties during Operation Oregon** https://1stbn4thmarines.com/?page_id=1104= directs the reader to an article written by Ralph E. Sullivan, Ph.D., Licensed Consulting Psychologist, the battalion commander of the First Battalion Fourth Marines during Operation Oregon. See his report for the concerning tactics and casualties.

As we approach the landing zone, we hear rifle fire before the helicopters touch down. It isn't like crazy amounts of rifle fire, but it is rifle fire for sure. Helicopters have a big problem, bullets go right through them, and if they crash, the fuel ignites, and you burn to death. When you come off the helicopters, even those with the large exit ramps, everyone is close to each other creating irresistible targets for the enemy. We need to get out of the choppers and spread out.

There is no hesitation after landing. We spring into action. We take our fear and convert it into fuel to perform as trained. My orders are to move my squad off the helicopter and run towards the shooting, connect with the platoon on my left and form an online frontal assault formation. That's exactly what I do. I make the connection to the platoon on my left. The third squad that is to form to our right flank is still coming off the helicopters. Advancing with the platoon on our left flank, we hear a massive explosion to our left front, somewhere in a rice paddy. Yeah, we are in the middle of a vast, unharvested rice paddy. The stalks of rice are about two feet high, so you can somewhat conceal yourself if you get down low. The rice paddy's water is shallow, only a few inches deep, but full of leeches. To our front is a hamlet surrounded by trees and low, thick bush. You can look through the vegetation and see the thatched huts of the Vietnamese peasants. (What I call a thatched hut is what the Vietnamese peasants call home.)

In the rice paddies to our left front, mines are exploding. I don't know if they are being detonated remotely or from tripwires, but to be sure, mines are exploding. A heavy gun that sounds like the U.S. 50 caliber machine gun opens up to my front. I know it is a heavy gun because it doesn't fire fast, making a regular machine gun sound, "brrree." No, it has a slow thumping sound, boom, boom as it shoots a huge round. Trust me, the sound of a 50 caliber-like machine gun firing at you is the nightmare of every grunt. We are also attacked with light machine guns, small arms fire, 60mm mortars, and 82mm mortars. You can tell the difference between the mortars' size by the sound they make, leaving the tubes used to launch them. This place is rocking, and we are on the bullseye. We are precisely in their preplanned fields of fire, and we are getting hammered. Bravo Company is taking a lot of casualties. You can hear the screams of men in pain. That's right, in combat, you experience what they don't show in the movies because they wouldn't sell too many tickets. These are the actual sounds of men screaming after their bodies are torn apart by the weapons of war. Some of these wounded Marines are going into shock. You never forget the sounds of screaming and dying men. It imprints into your brain.

This place is rocking and rolling; we are shooting back, but it is difficult to see who's shooting at us. We soon discover that the enemy is firing from "Pillboxes," a World War II reference to concrete enclosures. Yeah, they have thatched huts placed over brick-fortified bunkers that make them look like ordinary Vietnamese homes. Their bunkers protect them from artillery and airstrikes, let alone small arms fire. We find ourselves in a preplanned kill zone with interlocking fire. The enemy is relentless as they continue to punish us with mortars, machine guns, mines, and small arms fire.

South Vietnamese troops, ARVAN, join us on the battlefield. They retreat immediately, refusing to fight or help evacuate our dead or wounded. The South Vietnamese Army ran away from the fight, leaving us to die for their country. I briefly consider shooting them.

To my right front, I see an NVA Officer go from a crouching position to almost standing. He is visible because his khaki uniform is in contrast with a somewhat white building behind him. I can see the officer inspecting the entire battlefield with binoculars. He is a leader, an infantry officer for sure. I rise to a kneeling position executing proper marksmanship alignment to perfection. I have my right elbow pushed up by my right ear with my left elbow directly under my M14 to support and steady it. I let out half a breath and then stop breathing to prevent the rifle's muzzle from moving. I put all my rifle training into this shot as I squeeze the trigger. Wham! My fired round hits the officer's chest. He goes down. Wham! I immediately get shot through my left sleeve.

While I was aiming at the North Vietnamese officer, someone was aiming at me. We both fired at almost the same instant. His aim, "Thank God," is a little bit off. The bullet, I suspect it was a 30 caliber AK47 bullet, went through my left sleeve. The turbulence that the striking bullet creates is tremendous as it tore through my shirt. Had he aimed a little to his left, I would have been struck in my left arm, most likely shattering the bone. A bit further to his left, I would have lost my life after being shot in the heart. Convinced I am hit, I lower myself in the unharvested rice paddy. But no, I don't have a scratch on me. That bullet never touched my skin. Looking up, I see a standing Marine looking down at me. He is exposing himself to hostile fire, repeatedly asking, "Corporal Mezick, are you hit? Are you hit?" He looks concerned. I said, "No, I'm not hit. Get down for Christ's sake, get down!"

The entire rice paddy is raging with death and destruction. That's the way it is. In the middle of all this shit, I have a Marine standing over me asking if I need help. That's the bond between Marines in combat. I don't know how to explain the connection, the driving force that motivates one Marine to come to the aid of another in the heat of battle. **I don't think that bond is explainable, only experienced**. I can report with complete confidence that a Marine receiving or providing aid in the face of death will never be the same again. Some events in life, once experienced, will never be forgotten. Your life, from that moment on, will forever change. Yes, another transition in the life of a young Marine.

Oh my God, in the middle of all this, Sergeant Costa is executing the original plan. Recall, the first squad of our platoon is in reserve. The plan is for them to attack any small force of resistance. Yeah, attack that small force as the other two squads put down a base of fire. So there they go running right through the second and third squads attacking the enemy. The understaffed squad of only ten Marines doesn't know that they are attacking approximately three hundred enemy combatants of the 802nd VC Battalion led by North Vietnamese Army officers.

The VC Battalion has heavy machine guns and just about every other weapon you can think of. Costa's squad charges them like they are a lone sniper. "Oh, Shit!" I order my squad to lay down, suppressing fire to pin down the enemy. Both second and third squads are now pouring hundreds of rounds into the fortified positions producing as much suppressing fire support as two squads possibly can. We roll on them. We just fire them up. The Marine that had come to my aid is only a few feet to my left. As he fires, the ejected rounds from his M14 rifle go down the front of my flak jacket and burn my chest and stomach. The muzzle blast of his rifle thunders into my ears. The noise is tremendous and debilitating. But ears ringing and a headache are the very least of my problems on this day.

Sergeant Costa's squad continues to charge, closing the distance to the enemy. One individual in his squad charges the VC Battalion faster than everyone else. Shot through the heart about thirty yards from the enemy, he screams and dies instantly. The rest of his squad fights its way back to our position with the cover fire we provide and the firepower they provide for themselves. Somehow, they get the Hell out of there. The fact that they only lost one man is a miracle. I like to think that we hammered them down, making it possible for Costa's squad to get back. They were all within thirty yards of certain death. Yeah, they had knocked on the front door of the 802nd VC Battalion's fortified positions.

The other two platoons of Bravo Company are also fighting for their lives as the battle continues. The sound of helicopters evacuating the wounded adds to the noise created from gunfire, exploding land mines, and incoming mortar rounds. A Marine provisional artillery battery from the 4th Battalion 12th Marine Regiment comes to our assistance, striking the enemy with 105 and 155mm howitzers. Naval gunfire from the destroyer USS Richard B. Anderson DD 786 bombards the communist positions. All supporting fire exploded less than one hundred yards to our front. This battle is raging, and we are not in control of how long it will last. Neither side is in control. Everyone on both sides is fighting for his life.

Then I see a little Piper Cub, a small single-engine airplane just like the one at your neighborhood airport, suddenly above the enemy. His approach comes out of the sun, invisible to anyone looking in his direction. The VC battalion doesn't hear or see him as he slowly flies, put-put-put, right over the top of them, and drops smoke grenades, marking their positions. Following the tiny slow-flying Piper Cub comes a jet that drops Napalm on the smoke. Two others, all dropping Napalm, followed the first jet. Thank God! The 150-pound barrels of Napalm tumble end over end before smashing to the earth and bursting into a roaring inferno. All available oxygen in the immediate area is consumed by the firestorm leaving the enemy breathless. The fighting stops immediately. The delivered Napalm has the effect of throwing cold water on two fighting dogs.

We are within 100 yards of the Napalm inferno. Marine Air Support calls that type of close air support "Danger Close." What does that term mean to the commander requesting the Napalm bombs; "Are you sure you want a jet flying at hundreds of miles an hour to drop a sticky fireball of death less than one hundred yards from your Marines"? Upon confirmation from Lieutenant Colonel Donavan, the Napalm is dropped exactly on target. Bravo Company withdraws to a tree line about fifty yards back from our previous position. The Marine Air Support we receive is a blessing. If I ever meet the pilots who flew the jets or the Piper Cub, I will somehow try to find the words to thank them. Something like, "One free beer on me. Let me shake your hand and try to express the respect and the gratitude I have for your talent and bravery; you saved the lives of many Marines. You saved my life."

The hamlet where the primary battle of Operation Oregon takes place is officially called Ap Chin An, located in a province called Thua Thien (Twa T end) on Quang Tri province's southern edge. The area is well known to French military history as "The Street Without Joy."

For the moment, the battle is less intense. Bravo Company continues to exchange small arms fire with the enemy, but neither side fires with the intensity that existed before the jets came to our aid.

I had not seen anyone in my chain of command since we got off the helicopters until our platoon sergeant orders, "Squad leaders up." Staff Sergeant Anderson says we must go out and retrieve the man that is down. He repeats himself. "We have to go out and retrieve the man that is down. We don't leave anyone behind. He's down, and we are going out there and get him." I reply, "that's impossible. He's 30 yards in front of the enemy. Does anyone realize how many gooks are in front of us? We are going to lose more men trying to bring him back. I believe he is dead." Sergeant Costa speaks up, "Yes, he's dead. I'm positive he's dead." I declare, "We are not going to leave him, but do you want to retrieve his body, now? There's no way in Hell we are going to get within thirty yards of their bunkers without losing more men as we try to drag him back."

Sergeant Anderson takes a deep breath and says, "That's our orders, and that is what we are going to do. Go back and get your squad ready to move out." I reply, "I understand. I will get them ready, but we need a plan. I recommend that both squads go out together, firing and maneuvering our fire teams until we get within crawling distance. Then, both squads will lay down suppressing fire. Sergeant Costa, he's your guy, so you can send someone out to drag him back. But I'm telling you again; we are going to lose Marines if we try to bring him back now." Regardless of my apprehension, the retrieval of the dead Marine is still a standing order.

I go back to my squad and tell them what our orders are. Their reply, "You got to be shitting me." One of the three fire team leaders went on to say, "There's no way in Hell we can get anybody back that close to the gooks. He fell right in front of their rifles. Even if he is wounded, we can't get him back. But he's dead. Trying to bring him back now doesn't make any sense. We got one guy out there now they're going to have us all out there if we try to bring him back before we get the gooks out of those bunkers." I step forward and say, "Listen, I did my best to make that point; I was overridden. We're going. Saddle Up!" **They said, "Ok, we'll do it."**

They know it is dumb. I know it is a wrong decision, and for those of you who have never served in the U.S. Marine Corps, this will be difficult to understand. We don't choose and pick the orders we prefer to follow; we follow all orders. We are on our way, and not one man said he wouldn't do it. Every Marine in my squad has just come out of the "Shit" and knows his life might end in just a matter of minutes.

I form the third squad's three fire teams online and prepare to reenter the rice paddy from Hell. A runner suddenly appears and says, "Stand down the order has been canceled." You can't imagine how relieved we are.

There is sporadic shooting between the warring sides now about 150 yards away from one another. The accuracy on both sides is poor; no one can see their targets very well. However, we notice one point within their defenses where we frequently see enemy movement.

Soldiers are going in and out of what appears to be an underground ammunition bunker. Our company commander sends a battalion sniper and his spotter to our position in the tree line. The sniper sets up, and I watch him kill four men in about two minutes. He clogged the steps of the bunker with dead bodies. The spotter sees it all through his binoculars. He repeatedly calls out. "Headshot! Headshot!" The snipers are just incredible marksmen, deadly accurate, particularly so with the aid of a rifle scope. Every Marine can shoot well. The Marine Corps goes out of its way to teach all of us to be marksmen. However, the snipers have a natural God-given gift for rifle shooting.

To my amazement, I see Alpha Company preparing to charge Chin An Hamlet from the south side of Route #597. They form online and charge its fortified bunkers screaming as they run through the rice paddies. Bravo Company is ordered to ceasefire, and we do. Our battalion commander or our company commander is responsible for the order that directs us to stop shooting, so Alpha Company Marines won't be killed by Bravo Company Marines providing suppressing fire. We, Bravo Company, are directly in front of the fortified hamlet. Perpendicular to us, Alpha Company Marines are charging the hamlet's southern flank. We are their only opportunity for suppressing fire, and we are ordered to stop shooting. We need to do just the opposite by hammering those bastards with intense suppressing fire.

It can't get any worse for the guys attacking; they are already in deadly fields of rifle and mortar fire. Bravo Company should not stop shooting at this point in the attack because Alpha Company receives more intense fire when we stop. Now we must stand down and watch. Some of the attacking Marines from Alpha Company get through and over the barbed wire and the thorny vegetation that protects enemy fighting positions. We can hear the different sounds made by Marine's M14 rifles and the enemy's AK 47 rifles. Unfortunately, we don't hear enough M14s. From the battalion commander to the company and platoon commanders, nobody in a command position seems to know just how many gooks they are attacking. They still don't understand the scope of the battle we are fighting.

Some of the Marines from Alpha Company shoot their way into the hamlet and shoot their way back out. Others die fighting in the hamlet. "Alpha"

Company is unable to overrun the defenses of Chin An Hamlet. Why? The study of military tactics provides historical ratios defining how many men you need to attack a fortified position with charging infantry compared to how many defend it. The lowest ratio that I am aware of is 3 to 1. You need at least three times the number of attackers as defenders. In both Alpha and Bravo Companies, we have just over 200 Marines due to a lack of replacements. Alpha Company's 100-man infantry assault across rice paddies using 200 fewer attackers than defenders has little chance of success.

When some of the Alpha Company's Marines penetrate the Chin An Hamlet's defenses, I know they are fighting for their next breath. I feel no fear. I want to get back into the fight, and so do my men. Yes, we are ready to fight to the death. Why? It doesn't have a damn thing to do with politics. Our guys are fighting for their lives, and my God, it is time for us to get back in the fight.

Had I been leading the battle, I would have ordered Bravo Company to attack, forcing the enemy to defend itself from two directions. The battalion commander now knows better. He now more accurately understands the opposition's fortifications, firepower, and manpower. Our commander must accept that the number of men defending the hamlet far exceeds the number of men attacking the hamlet. Those facts may sound relatively easy to gather, but not in a raging battle. War is noise, confusion, screaming, and fear. Attempting to make correct assessments and decisions in that environment is and always will be extremely difficult. The definition of a battle plan is an agreed-upon starting point because combat is so dynamic, changing minute by minute. It would have been foolish to have the outnumbered Marines in Bravo Company join the second attack on the hamlet. Even if we succeed in overrunning its defenses, a counterattack will destroy us. Then where will we be without additional Marines in reserve to counter that attack? That's why battalion commanders are lieutenant colonels, and squad leaders are sergeants and corporals. Emotion alone cannot carry the day.

That evening, all shooting stops, creating an ominous silence broken only by insects' mating calls and the sounds of lightly falling rain. One hundred and fifty yards now separate the warring sides, a standoff. We all know in the morning, we will once again attack Chin An Hamlet.

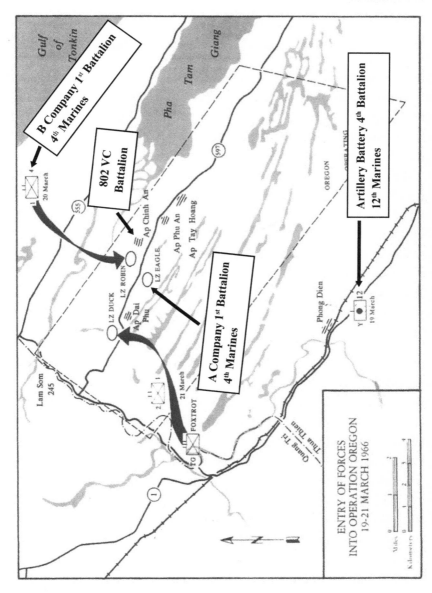

Gulf of Tonkin

Pha Tam Giang

B Company 1ˢᵗ Battalion 4ᵗʰ Marines

802 VC Battalion

Artillery Battery 4ᵗʰ Battalion 12ᵗʰ Marines

OREGON

OPERATING

20 March

555

597

Ap Chinh An

Ap Phu An

Ap Tay Hoang

LZ EAGLE

LZ ROBIN

LZ DUCK

Ap Dai Phu

A Company 1ˢᵗ Battalion 4ᵗʰ Marines

Phong Dien

12

19 March

Lam Som 245

21 March

FOXTROT

TG

Quang Tri

Thua Thien

1

ENTRY OF FORCES INTO OPERATION OREGON
19-21 MARCH 1966

Miles

Kilometres

Phu Bai

Queries of Death – Point of Insanity

It's dark now; Bravo Company is still in the tree line hunkered down. We are ordered to eat our evening meal but not expose our exact positions by smoking or using heat tabs to warm our food. I pull a C-Ration meal from my backpack, hoping to get one designated, D -1, containing a can of fruit. So, what do I get? I get the other side of the best selection. I get what they call "Ham and Lima Beans." The grunts call them "Ham and Mother Fuckers." They are just about inedible if you can't heat them to dissolve the dense grease. Any Marine that can eat a cold can of "Ham and Lima Beans" earns the title of "Hard Core." It is a term reserved for one Marine to another; it means Marine's Marine, a Marine right to his core. If you can eat an entire can of cold "Ham and Lima's," you must be "Hard Core." Well, my dinner is cold "Ham and Lima Beans." I eat about half of them before realizing that one more spoonful of cold grease and I will throw up.

In total silence, I stare into the night, enduring a misty rain with a light wind, perfect conditions for someone to sneak up on me. For some illogical reason, I am not worried about a night attack. I feel it isn't a good idea for either side to attack in the dark. Sleeping, well, there is not a lot of that going on. The weight of death hangs in the air creating an environment equivalent to a condemned man on death row the night before his scheduled execution. Everyone knows that in just a few hours, we are going to attack Chin An hamlet again. The cruel reality of advancing across open rice paddies into interlocking enemy fields of fire is no longer something imagined. We believe more of us are going to die in the morning. I should be exhausted, but I'm not because I am still on adrenaline-high, wide-awake thinking about tomorrow's attack. I know that in the morning, we will be back in the shit.

Earlier that evening, I heard battle accounts from some of the other members of my platoon. One story was particularly unforgettable. A wounded Marine was being carried off the battlefield by four other Marines, each holding an arm or leg. Blood seeped from his mouth as his lungs lost their ability to sustain him. He tried to speak but was barely audible. One of the men carrying him bent over and put his ear close to his mouth to listen. "Sorry, I got hit." The wounded Marine was apologizing for leaving the battlefield. He was apologizing for dying.

I learned more about the Army of the Republic of Vietnam troops, the ARVAN, assigned to join us in the Chin An hamlet attack. I believe their participation was an influencing factor in our commander's ratio assessment of attackers to defenders. What my squad witnessed of their battlefield performance was also reported by others. They were useless, totally useless. They ran away. They left the battlefield, refusing even to help carry out our dead and wounded. They just ran; we never saw them again.

Sitting alone, surrounded by the darkness of a misty night, I am deep in private thought. Tomorrow I will again be ordered to attack the fortified positions of Chin An hamlet. The three fire teams of my squad will look to me for leadership and inspiration. We will survive only by our ability to work as a team delivering pure coordinated violence. I must not fail them!

The rest of the night, I think about what it is like to die?" Is there a God? What happens to you after you die? Is their judgment? What happens to your soul? Who will be hurt by my death? This consideration of death, the words so frequently used to describe life hereafter now have a profound impact, they are no longer just words used to describe a far distant event.

There must be a "Creator." Yes, some energy that is responsible for everything. But God doesn't seem to care about what we do to each other. If he did, he would stop this killing right now. That's just the way it is. God doesn't interfere.

What about judgment after death? Is there someone at the entrance to heaven with a judgment sheet? You know, a list that reports all the good stuff and all the bad stuff you did in life. Here's your score. Is that how you get into heaven? I don't know the answer to judgment after death, but I know about judgment before death. I must not die a coward tomorrow.

So, I pray. "Please, God save me, but if that is not your will, let me die fighting and proud." What will happen to my soul? Before I can answer what will happen to my soul after death, I need to understand what a soul is. Do I possess a soul, is there a part of me that isn't physical, can't be weighed, touched, or dissolved? I accept my soul to be life beyond my physical existence. But I don't know why.

Who's going to miss me when I die? My death is going to be devastating to everyone, right?

First and foremost, I thought about my daughter, born exactly one month ago, and my wife. I have spent less than forty days with Diana as a married couple before leaving her standing pregnant and crying in the Philadelphia Airport as I began my Vietnam journey. Next, I consider how my death will affect my mother, father, brother, sisters, and all the people in my life that I am close to. Then I realize that the only person about to die is me. Yeah, that's right when your heart stops, I'm doing fine. When my heart stops, I die, not you. We are all in this universe by ourselves. Relationships are required and desired, but you are one on one with the reality of your existence.

This night, considering all that happened this day and what is about to happen tomorrow morning, I am never again the person I was before Operation Oregon. The raw experience of violence, death, and fear have profoundly changed me. In March 1966, I was twenty years old, not old enough to vote or to buy a glass of whiskey back home. The transitions of a young man accelerate under the influence of my struggle to comprehend life before I learn first-hand the meaning of death.

The next morning good news. Sergeant Costa and his squad, in the darkness of the night, crawled within thirty yards of the enemy's position and dragged back our dead Marine. Oh, my God. Great news! The other great news, we all receive freshwater and replacement ammunition. In combat, you may not get hungry, but I guarantee you will get thirsty. The order is passed down to eat breakfast. I can't eat. I sit waiting for the order to attack the "Hamlet from Hell," my pulse rate is noticeably increasing, knowing what is coming next. Daylight is breaking, and the low-hanging fog is lifting, allowing us to see Chin An hamlet.

To my amazement, one of the grunts gets out of his position in the tree line and walks out into the rice paddy. He is now thirty yards in front of our lines where we can see him, and the enemy can see him as well. This Marine is angry, screaming at the VC across the rice paddy in the hamlet. He tells them that he has been wronged and what has happened to him isn't right, not fair. "I'm pissed, and I'm going to kill every son of a bitch on the other side of this fucking rice paddy. I'm taking you down. I don't need the rest of these assholes; I'm going to kill all of you myself. What you did is unacceptable." Then he holds up a can of peaches for everyone to see. The peach can is mangled, filled with bullet holes. That's right, yesterday during our attack, a burst of fire from an AK47 had raked his backpack, destroying his can of peaches. He has spent the entire night thinking, before I die, I'm going to have a can of peaches in the morning. When he goes to open his beloved peaches for breakfast, he discovers that all he has is a shot-up can. His peaches are beyond recovery, and those men on the other side of the rice paddies are responsible. That's why he completely exposes himself, shaking his fist, giving the entire 802nd VC Battalion the finger, and telling them how he is going to kick their ass. Our entire Company witnesses this, and everyone starts laughing, uncontrollable laughter, a spontaneous release of tension and fear.

Can you imagine the effect? We took our fear and turned it into laughter. The sounds of our laughter take the enemy's fear and turn it into additional fear. Quite frankly, if confronted with troops about to perform a frontal infantry assault against my fortified position and they are laughing about it, I don't want to meet them. I never forgot the positive effect the laughter created in everyone who watched the crazed and pissed-off Marine bitch about his shot-up peaches. Months later, I used laughter as a psychological weapon to prevent a counterattack during an ambush. The Vietnam War is a never-ending study of tactics, survival, fear, aggression, and courage.

Our attack begins early in the morning with artillery support from the 4th Battalion 12th Marines Provisional Battery. The 105 and 155mm Howitzers do a great job of putting rounds on target. No air support because it's still too cloudy, but the artillery does a fine job. They just bang the hell out of

Chin An hamlet. I feel good about the artillery bombardment. However, there is a consistency problem with artillery in 1966. Field artillery is not a precision science. Some of it comes a little closer than comfortable even when other rounds fired within the same fire mission are on target. We called this effect "Short Rounds." An artillery round has no friends when it blows; shrapnel flies everywhere, not selecting good guys and bad guys. Our artillery support pounds the hamlet, for that we are grateful. God bless the men behind those guns.

When the artillery support stops, Company B advances online by firing and maneuvering its three platoons, the three squads of each platoon, and each squad's three fire teams. My position as the squad leader is direct to the rear and center behind my three fire teams. I order one fire team to move forward while the other two teams provide suppressing fire. We all advance towards the hamlet with the sound of rifle fire and the commands, "Third-team move, First-team move, Second-team move." The order of commands to advance the fire teams is mixed as not to create a predictable pattern for the enemy. The entire Company moves with precision advancing and shooting towards the fortified positions of Chin An hamlet. All of us, Marines, are full of fear but somehow use its energy to perform perfectly. What an unforgettable sight – a company of Marines firing and maneuvering into a point of no return.

We fire our rifles in an orderly manner, not wasting ammunition but providing enough suppressing fire to allow us to advance. What ammunition we have is all we are going to get for this fight. We have a machine gun shooting at us but with less intensity than during yesterday's attack. Our assault feels doable, but I fear the machine gun directly in front of my squad will destroy us as we advance. About forty yards from the objective, when I order "Second Team Move," the machine gun opens up, shooting high. Then I order, "Third Team Move." Again, the machine gun fires before being silenced by the "Second Team," providing cover fire.

Take a moment and wrap your mind around what's happening here. The enemy is shooting at you from fortified positions, and you are charging them. You are firing and maneuvering to the point of no return. That's what they call the "Demarcation Line," where everyone gets up and charges the enemy. There is no more cover or suppressing fire, just men from opposing sides coming face to face trying to kill one another. Reaching the all-out attack point, we rush directly into the wire and thorny brush, determined to kill, or be killed. That's what we did on this day.

Listen to these words closely; "I have canceled fear." All my life, I have been conditioned to be afraid. As a child, I didn't talk to strangers as I walked to school, didn't walk in front of a moving car or truck, didn't try to swim the ocean, didn't walk off the roof. However, such conditioning does not allow me to charge men who are shooting at me. To cancel a lifetime of conditioned fear, I must abandon all fear, and I am here to tell you with absolute confidence that mindset is a point of insanity. Yes, insane because I have canceled my natural reaction to fear and said yes to death; kill me, or I am going to kill you. I am coming now; I'm ready to die. **I reached a state of euphoria when I canceled all fear.** Yes, a point of blissful insanity after utterly abandoning a lifetime of conditioned fear response and entering an unnatural mental condition for a human being. One committed to killing and accepting death without fear.

We force ourselves into Chin An Hamlet past the wire and thorny bush. The first Marines push it down; the rest of us jump over it. Now we are inside their positions, thank God. When you overrun the enemy, it is not a time for celebration, not a time to give high fives and slap one another on the back, milling around like you just won a football game. Why? Because you are then very exposed to a counterattack. When the defenders can't hold their fighting positions under the military discipline of your advancing formations and firepower, they often will fall back and wait. They let you think you have won. Then they counterattack and sweep across the flank of your unstructured celebration. A moment ago, you were an unbeatable military machine, but now you are just a bunch of guys milling around giving each other congratulations. Preventing a counterattack wasn't taught during my infantry training. In combat, it's not over until the enemy says it's over. You are not in charge of anything. You need to kill him or destroy his will to continue fighting. I don't consider the immediate danger of a counterattack, but the staff NCOs and officers do. They order us to stay organized and maintain military discipline.

After breaching their fortified defenses, we sweep across Chin An hamlet. Most of the dead and wounded had been removed by the VC the previous night. The repulsive odor of burnt bodies from yesterday's Napalm attack is obnoxious, as are pieces of human flesh decaying in the surrounding vegetation.

The machine gun's position, the one that was direct to my squad's front, during the attack is observed by Marines advancing online on the right flank as we sweep across Chin An hamlet. Thank heaven it was shooting high, and my squad was able to kill the gunner before he adjusted his aim. This weapon could have very well destroyed my entire squad. A young man's body was reported to be lying close to the machine gun. Most likely, the defenders forced this young man, probably not a soldier, to fire at us. They only wanted him to slow our attack and provide more time for their primary group to escape. They didn't care if he could fire the weapon accurately. It was not his idea to oppose our advance. The VC would have killed him if he stopped shooting at us, and we killed him because he didn't stop shooting at us. The poor bastard behind the trigger had no idea how to aim it properly.

Operation Oregon is not over. We return to the original plan that directs us to sweep through and clear two additional hamlets, Ap Phu An and Ap Tay Hoang. We advance through both, encountering no resistance. We see no evidence of military positions; they have not fortified these hamlets. We continue sweeping through the area, trying to find what is left of the 802nd VC Battalion. The locals report the retreating enemy carried away many dead and wounded.

Before sundown, we stop and dig fighting positions to defend against a night attack. My squad is deployed to my front with two men to a hole. I am in the squad leader's position directly behind them when visited by Sergeant Costa. I think he has come to compliment us about the cover fire we provided for his squad yesterday. Nope, he has no words of praise for us. He doesn't seem to notice when I profusely compliment him and his men for retrieving the dead Marine this morning. Instead, he is demanding his socks back. That's right, his socks. Sergeant Costa claims that he lent me a high-quality, dam near new pair of socks. To an infantryman in Vietnam, his two pairs of socks are critical.

While he is chattering about his socks, a grenade goes off about thirty-five yards to our front. Then, we receive small arms fire just above our heads, and then another grenade explodes. Costa says, "That's nothing. They're just making sure we stay in our holes. They're coming out of their hiding places, and they don't want us chasing them. Now back to those socks". I realize he hasn't lent me any socks; he just came here to socialize; he came to chat. This is Costa's idea of a thank you, his way of showing a little respect and gratitude for the fire support he received from my squad. So, I flip it around and tell him. "I don't have your socks. You have my socks, and I think it's high time for you to return them." We are sitting in a hole, and the VC are throwing grenades and shooting small arms at us. How do we react? We joke about socks.

During the first two days of Operation Oregon, the change within me has been exponential. Facing extreme fear and surviving intense combat has two significant effects. One, it creates a sense of confidence. Successfully enduring and performing in such an ordeal instills a sense of pride and self-confidence, "You have faced the bear." Number two, it creates a sense of guilt. Why me? Why has fate selected me to live?

Flanker – No Relief

Operation Oregon lasts several more days, ending officially on March 23rd with 19 dead and 45 wounded Marines, mainly from the March 20th assault on Chin An hamlet.

During the last few days of Operation Oregon, I order a Marine to flank our movement as Bravo Company walks on Route #597. Marines walking the flanks' objective is to detect an enemy attempting to attack the main body from either side of the road. There is little challenge to walk on the road, but the flanks are often overgrown with heavy vegetation obscuring uneven terrain beneath them. In addition, the day is sweltering and humid; soon, the Marine I ordered to walk our flank needs rest. Unfortunately, I am oblivious to his exhaustion and forget to relieve him.

The flanker eventually staggers out onto Route # 597 and finds he has fallen behind our platoon to the one following us. A lieutenant brings him forward and asks if I am the NCO responsible for not relieving the Marine walking the flank? After replying that I am indeed accountable, he orders me to walk the flank. I know his order is an object lesson; he has no intention of relieving me because he returned to his platoon. I am full of enthusiasm, and as a matter of fact, I am embarrassed. However, it isn't long, even aided by my state of mind from being disciplined, before becoming extremely tired, and I can no longer keep up with my platoon. I eventually must walk out onto the road away from the flank. I discover that the Marines I am now joining are not from my platoon. They are not even from my company. It must be Alpha Company. I fall in next to a lieutenant who immediately inquires who am I and what is my assignment? I told him that I was ordered to walk the flank of the road by an officer after he discovered that I ordered a Marine to walk the flank and had not relieved him.

We were then walking the road together, and after a period of reflection, the officer offered a casual, father-like presentation about the privilege of leadership. He began to speak slowly without judgment. "Leaders can never stop thinking about what is happening, what can happen, or what did happen. You must feel the burden of the physical and mental challenges of your orders. You stopped thinking about the Marine you ordered to walk the flank, forgetting that he was obeying your orders. Now, if you entirely understand your leadership mistake and that miscalculation only cost you the price of one flanker being physically exhausted and nobody was killed. In that case, you are having a good day. One to remember. Some of us are not so fortunate, not so blessed to pay such a small price for such a huge lesson in leadership." I looked at him and nodded, realizing the officer beside me had paid a much higher price for the same lesson.

I left and rejoined my unit. Never was another word spoken of this except for me telling the Marine I had assigned to walk flank I would never send him to walk flank again without relief. The success of yesterday's leadership, all the good stuff. All the rock-solid leadership I provided during the assault on Chin An hamlet is now history. The next day is another challenge for leaders in combat.

Recon Hill

Following Operation Oregon, Bravo Company, First Battalion, 4th Marines deployed as a rapid reactionary force supporting Marine Force Reconnaissance units operating in the Co Bi - Thanh Tan Valley named for two nearby hamlets running east to west in Thua Thien Hue Province.

After a week or so of patrolling the valley, our platoon provides security for a reconnaissance radio relay station[25] located on the top of an enormously high hill. Where I come from, they call that kind of hill a mountain. Walking to the top, or I should say humping to the top in Marine jargon, is "Totally a Bitch". We had to zigzag and hold on to small shrubs so we wouldn't fall backward as we hauled ourselves and our unit load[26] toward the top. The temperature and humidity of the day added to the challenge of the climb. Our chests are pounding, and our leg muscles are screaming in pain from accumulated lactic acid. Just as each man crests the top of that never-ending hill, he encounters Staff Sergeant Anderson,

---

[25] **Reconnaissance Relay Hill** - A high hill or mountain used to receive line of sight radio signals from Marine Reconnaissance teams and retransmit the messages to distant locations.

[26] **The unit load** - was the standard equipment that Marines carried. Just to name a few items: rifle, ammo, grenades, helmet, flak jacket, two quarts of water, and a backpack containing poncho, C-rations, extra socks, and an entrenching tool.

who provides no help whatsoever to anyone. After each of us fight our way up and over the crest of the hill, he shakes our hands as his eyes lock onto ours with a penetrating stare that goes right into your soul. Words are unnecessary for Staff Sergeant Anderson to convey his message. He is accepting each of his men, now unquestionably combat tested and physically strong enough to hump that hill into his Marine Corps. His personal Marine Corps. We called it "Hard Core."

Recon Radio Relay Hill

Well-fortified defensive positions constructed by Combat Engineers or Seabees protect the radio relay station located on the hill's summit. Grunts using entrenching tools could not have built these bunkers whose size and structural integrity can easily withstand the pounding of artillery, rockets, or mortar rounds. The designated fields of fire are unobstructed by any vegetation providing perfect visibility to crush anyone trying to attack from below. Sitting in the bunkers, you look down the "mountain" at fifty-gallon barrels of Napalm that can be detonated from your position. Complementing the Napalm bombs is an interlocking array of Claymore anti-personnel-mines[27] whose kill range is six and a half feet high and fifty yards wide at fifty-five yards. Each bunker contains multiple firing devices called "Clackers" connected by a long wire to a blasting cap inserted into the Claymore mine. I feel a sense of confidence and security, knowing that if attacked, I will be shooting downhill from the comfort of a fortified, professionally constructed bunker supported with individually controlled barrels of Napalm and Claymore mines. I have not felt this safe since I left home.

Our platoon is getting a well-needed rest after being assigned in pairs to the array of bunkers. All we must do is sit and watch. Many of us have sores between our toes called "Jungle Rot," a condition caused by prolonged wet and dirty feet in constant darkness within our boots. Our new assignment's static position on top of the hill provides an opportunity to heal the sores. After removing our boots and socks, we spread our toes apart with small pieces of paper as we sit with legs extended to expose our bare feet to the healing effects of sunlight.

The fortified hilltop's view provides a breathtakingly beautiful panorama of the Co Bi- Thanh Tan valley. A branch of the Ho Chi Minh Trail leads into the valley, becoming a major North Vietnam infiltration route to South Vietnam. The valley provides a direct approach route for Hue or

[27] **Claymore anti-personnel mines** - were extremely effective when used in defensive positions or as an offensive weapon in ambushes. They weighed about three- and one-half pounds and were formed in the shape of a bowing rectangle about eight and a half inches wide and five inches tall. The side of the Claymore intended to strike an approaching enemy was marked with a warning molded into the plastic cover that read, "**Front – This Side Towards Enemy**". Inside the Claymore plastic housing was C4 high explosive and 700 one eight-inch steel balls. Upon detonation the effect was equivalent to shooting seventy-eight twelve-gauge shotguns each firing nine 00 buckshot at once.

the Marine Combat Base in Phu Bai. Recon Marines patrolling the valley gather real-time information to forewarn an enemy approach.

Our relaxation period is soon interrupted with assignments to conduct squad-size patrols in the valleys below the surrounding hills. Nature abhors a vacuum; well, the U.S. Marine Corps abhors a sitting and resting Marine, especially a Marine grunt. The area's hills are mostly barren on the top and sides, only supporting small scrub brush. The valleys between the hills are thick with tall grass that often grows to over seven feet. We call it elephant grass. The high temperature and muggy humidity within the grass require anyone attempting to patrol within it to be in excellent physical condition and hydrated.

The daytime patrols' purpose is to forewarn and disrupt enemy buildup below the recon relay station. I soon realize that I am damn near incompetent in using a topographical map and a compass to determine my position or the location of what I observe at a distance. No satellite navigation using GPS technology was available to us in 1966. Calling in land, sea, or air support requires you to determine your exact position using a topographic map and military-issued compass. A wounded Marine's life depends on the leader's ability to call in a medevac to his location. Co Bi - Thanh Tan Valley is valuable as a classroom for navigation because you can always look up to the recon relay hill to relocate yourself.

Sergeant Robinson is assigned to accompany my squad when it is my turn to lead a patrol. I suspect he is present to evaluate my ability to navigate. I ask him a lot of questions and thus totally expose my limited navigational skillset. Better to expose my ignorance today than not know tomorrow.

Sergeant Costa led a three-day reconnaissance patrol through the hills and valleys, displaying enviable competence in his abilities to navigate and tactically maneuver his team. The members of the patrol return to recon hill in total admiration of their leader. I silently promise myself that I, too, will reach his level of expertise. There is much more to combat leadership than knowing how to fight. I often feel challenged and secretly insecure.

Powerful Leadership Lesson

The radio relay station positioned on top of the highest hill in the Co Bi- Thanh Tan valley allowed its operators to receive status reports from the Recon Marines patrolling the valley. Radio signals transmitted from low in the valley would often bounce off the hills and become garbled or too weak to be received by Phu Bai leadership. The relay station significantly increased the ability of the patrolling Marines to report their status. In Phu Bai, Recon Marines tracked each deployed team's progress and location by recording their reported positions on a map as the teams progressed through a three to five-day mission.

It is great fun, exciting, and entertaining to go to what we call the "Radio Shack" and sit and quietly listen to the recon teams call in their status reports. Early one evening, something incredible occurs as I visit with the radio operator.

A Marine recon team is in deep shit; they are calling for help. They are calling for immediate extraction; they have wounded and are in an intense firefight. The team further reports that they are moving east from their last reported position. The radio operator relays the urgent message to Phu Bai and receives confirmation that his transmission is understood. We wait to hear what will happen next. How will the recon officer in Phu Bai respond? What order will he give to assist his team? No response. The radio relay operator sits anxiously waiting to receive a message to transmit to the distressed team. Nothing, no reaction from Phu Bai. A few moments later, the recon team calls again, this time barely audible over the rifle fire. They aggressively request immediate extraction. "Heavy contact - we have wounded - we are moving east, we are moving east." The "Radio Shack" operator relayed the repeated request to Phu Bai and received confirmation that his message is copied. Silence, no response from headquarters. Nothing! A third call from the recon team repeating their request for immediate extraction is received and relayed to Phu Bai. After receiving confirmation from Phu Bai of the received message, there is no response, no orders. Just silence.

The radio operator and I look at one another in disbelief. No one is ordering any type of assistance to the recon team. Now the relay radio operator on the hill breaks protocol and asks the radio operator in Phu Bai if an officer has received the team's request for extraction? The answer comes back from the officer in charge, **"Let them fight."** That was all he said, not another word from the commanding officer. In a state of confusion and disbelief, I turn to the radio operator for an explanation. What does he mean, "Let them fight"? What the hell kind of support is that? Why is he not sending in the calvary to save his Marines? In my opinion, a reaction team should now be boarding helicopters to come to the distressed Marines' assistance. I would order them to go out there and get those guys out of that mess.

It takes me a while, and then I figure it out. The recon team's situation is so dynamic that the officer can only wait and react to what will happen next. In the next few minutes, he will know how to respond. The officer in charge has a reaction team, and he has aircraft, but he doesn't have unlimited resources. Right now, the situation is changing so quickly he can't extract them. Before he can issue an order that will help, he must wait for this situation to do whatever it will do. The immediate future of his team is out of his control.

Take a moment to consider the recon officer's dilemma. For his ordered response to be effective, he must think beyond the present and into the future. The situation is too dynamic for him to respond immediately. Combat leadership is not always about issuing instant orders or plans of action. It often requires the leader to stay calm during an ongoing battle and coolly develop the next course of action.

He is correct in his decision to wait. Finally, the enemy breaks contact; the team moves west and is extracted by helicopter without deploying his only reaction team. I continue to this day to hear his words, "Let them fight."

The patrolling experience below the radio relay hill provided me with the best map and compass navigation course I would ever attend. I became aware of my incompetence to navigate over land and addressed it.

The Force Reconnaissance officer provided an example of leadership under pressure. I began to understand that to provide quality leadership, I will have to develop a heightened level of emotional control. I must stop letting raw emotions dictate my thought process. Emotion like fear is an unavoidable human motivator that must first be understood before used as an instrument of leadership.

Stupidest Thing I Have Ever Done

The cozy assignment of defending the recon radio relay hill lasts less than two weeks. My platoon rejoined Bravo Company and soon conducted another operation with a forgotten name. Some of these "Sweep and Destroy Operations" are given names you will never forget because they are so impactful. However, there were lots of operations with names lost from memory. For most of us, they are just another day in the field.

Our battalion is frequently moved by helicopter to conduct operations in the extreme northern section of South Vietnam just below the Demilitarized Zone[28], referred to as the DMZ. The country of Laos defines our western border. By the way, the DMZ and the border that separates Laos and Vietnam are not identified with signs that read, "You are now leaving South Vietnam." The provided topographical maps barely delineate the immediate area. Only the officers have large-scale maps. If we are conducting operations within the DMZ or in Laos, we can't determine that. Quite frankly, we genuinely don't care. The North Vietnamese don't like us being in their backyard, so their snipers shoot at us during the day, and we are routinely mortared after dark. However, they avoid engaging us in large-scale head-on battles.

---

[28] The **Vietnamese Demilitarized Zone**, was a demilitarized zone established as a dividing line between North and South Vietnam as a result of the First Indochina War. During the Vietnam War, it became important as the battleground demarcation separating North from South Vietnamese territories. https://en.wikipedia.org/wiki/Vietnamese_Demilitarized_Zone

Returning to Bravo Company after a leave of absence to attend his father's funeral, Corporal Whitney replaces me as the third squad leader because he is senior to me even though we are both corporals. I am not fond of the leadership change, and neither are the men in the squad; we have shared much during Corporal Whitney's absence. Being replaced as the leader of the squad is a mixed blessing. On the one hand, it feels like a vacation to be relieved from the burdens of leadership. Although, on the other hand, I am not ready to accept someone else as my squad's leader.

Under the command of our new leader, Corporal Whitney, our squad is assigned to perform an all-night ambush. We can't predetermine the route to the ambush site during daylight hours without losing the element of surprise. Even with a small topographical map we use to navigate that evening, we cannot locate our assigned destination. So, we decide to set the ambush at a crossroads of two trails best described by drawing an X starting with a line from top right to bottom left. The following line ran from top left to bottom right, but instead of crossing the first line in the middle, it struck about one-third of the way down. The space at the top of the X is smaller than the space at the bottom.

We set the ambush in a defensive and offensive formation, simultaneously creating a half-ass defensive deployment and a half-ass offensive deployment of our men and weapons. Grunts frequently conduct night ambushes, but they are not good at them. Crude in most respects when contrasted to Marines who specialize in the "Art of the Ambush."

The squad's firepower is deployed as follows: We position an M60 machine gun and the second four-man fire team facing the trail in a staggered formation above the trails' crossing point on the left side of figure X they form. Their intended zones of fire are direct to their front and their right side. The squad's third four-man fire team positioned on the backside of the crossing trails facing away from everyone else defends the main force's rear approach. My fire team, including the squad leader and the radio operator, set up to face the two trails' intersection twenty yards back. After determining that too many of us are too close together, I move out to their front, just a few yards from where the two trails cross.

There is no concealment at my new position, so I sit in the dark without any cover whatsoever.

Yeah, I guess it is dark enough to hide my presence from an approaching enemy. I don't care because I am so discouraged and resentful after being replaced as the squad leader I foolishly position myself directly in the kill zone of the M60 machine gun, two fire teams, the squad leader, and the radioman. The stupidest thing I have ever done in my entire life! One step away from committing suicide.

About 0230, 2:30 in the morning, three VC appear out of nowhere. They have not used either of the trails. Instead, they approach from an open field and then turn onto the trail just below where I am sitting, walking towards me. I look up and see not one, not two, but three AK 47 rifles pointing directly at me less than two yards away. They don't see me – they don't know that I am so close - sitting right next to them. Time for a life or death decision. Can I shoot three men in the side at point-blank range before one of them lets go with a burst from his automatic rifle[29]? No, impossible! Another challenge, the safety of my M14 rifle is on[30]. When the safety is released, it makes a click sound. When it does, I must be firing, or they will be the first to shoot. My trigger finger says yes, and my brain says no. Maybe if I let them walk past me, I can start by killing the last man in line, and then the rest of our squad will kill the VC in the front and work backward. Yes, that will work. We can put all three of them down before they can return fire.

Here is the problem: I am sitting directly across and in front of my fire team, the squad leader, and the radioman blocking their line of fire. I am also positioned in the M60 machine gun's and the second fire team's direct line of fire. If I initiate the ambush, I will be immediately killed by one of the three VC, my fire team, the squad leader, the radio operator,

---

[29] **Several months later a Marine serving in a Combined Action Platoon found himself in this exact situation.** Both he and the VC directly across from him fired their weapons. Both died.

[30] **It is impossible** to release the safety on an M14 rifle without making a clicking sound even if you try to ease it off with two fingers the way you can with some firearms.

the M60 machine gun, and its supporting fire team. Why would everyone fire on me? Because I am in the same physical space as the VC. I have stupidly put myself directly in front of everyone else's line of fire and straight to the side of three VC that are about six feet from the tip of my nose.

Another consideration. Is this trio of VC the point for a larger group of approaching enemies? If it is, then we all need to let these three continue walking and engage the larger body, or they will be forewarned and flank us. All these variables take only fractions of a second to consider. My heart is pounding so hard I feel sure that the three VC just a few feet away can hear it thumping as blood hammers through my arteries.

Now, I must make a critical decision. Do I begin firing? The VC walking at the front of their column is exceptionally tall, well over six feet, almost unheard of for Vietnamese men. Here, in this country, he is a giant. The other two VC are average in size, but the middle one looks directly at me. He is looking at me as I am looking at him; our eyes are locked. I realize that he sees me because I see the fear in his eyes. We both must determine if we can kill the other without being killed by the other?

So why don't the machine gunner and the second fire team with no idea of my exposed position begin firing? One possible explanation; the squad still considers me their leader even though Corporal Whitney is. They most likely think there must be a reason the three VC have not been attacked and hold their fire. The VC walk through the entire ambush site unharmed.

Writing this account today, I hope the VC that looked me straight in the eyes is writing his version of that night. I wish him well, and I further hope he has reached his senior years as I have. If I were to meet him today and identify myself, I feel confident that he will also remember that fateful night of decision. Yes, I will be pleased to buy him a beer and wish him and his family good fortune.

I realize that the night of the ambush, the squad functioned poorly because of the transition of squad leaders, and that was mostly my fault. I was upset about being bumped from the squad leader position and allowed negative emotions to override our mission to the extent that I chose to foolishly reposition myself. Fate, God, destiny, or whatever gave me a second chance. An opportunity to comprehend and hopefully learn from my outrageous mistake. An opportunity denied many.

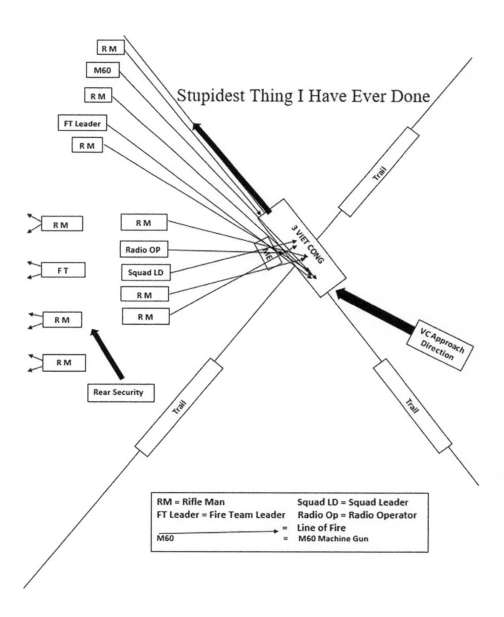

The Morality of a Marine

Another operation, I think they called it Operation Cherokee, or maybe it was Operation Wayne. The truth is, we pay little attention to the names of the operations. We are mainly concerned with the immediate 1,000 yards around us, the land of sniper and mortar fire. After a few weeks and then months, it is all about the surrounding one thousand yards. Yes, one-click out. Choppers frequently relocate us, and it is often rumored that they are coming to pick us up and take us to a rear area for a rest. They never do; they take us to another operation with another forgotten name.

During a "Search and Destroy" [31] operation, our platoon comes under fire from a sniper on our flank. He is not shooting directly at most of us when he fires on our forward squad. The sniper has two other Marine squads adjacent to him; this guy has made a colossal sniper mistake by firing from his hiding place at the bottom of a drainage ditch covered in tall grass.

Two fire teams from Corporal Whitney's squad cross the ditch and prevent the sniper from retreating to his rear. My fire team flanks him from our side of the ditch. We hear Sergeant Roberts, the platoon's right guide, screaming at the sniper to drop his rifle. A captured sniper is far more valuable than a dead sniper. Sergeant Roberts is repeatedly ordering him to drop his weapon. I am reasonably sure this guy doesn't speak English, but it is pretty much universally understood that you would put your rifle down in this situation.

On this side of the ditch, my fire team can see a path of matted down tall grass he created by trying to escape up the ditch bank. The sniper encountered the other two fire teams of Corporal Whitney's squad and

---

[31] Search and Destroy, Seek and Destroy, or even simply S&D, refers to a military strategy that became a large component of the Vietnam War. The idea was to insert ground forces into hostile territory, search out the enemy, destroy them, and withdraw immediately afterward.

Sergeant Roberts at the top of the ditch. The four of us in my fire team can see him standing in front of Sergeant Roberts, ordering the sniper to put down his weapon. He is screaming, "Drop your rifle – drop your rifle!" The sniper is now in a very precarious position. From my fire team's side of the ditch, the sniper has three semiautomatic M14 rifles and one fully automatic M14 rifle aimed directly at him. To his immediate front, Sergeant Roberts's 45 caliber pistol is pointing at his head. Roberts repeatedly screams at the sniper, who continues to hold his rifle with both hands in a firing position. This man will not drop his weapon and appears to be deciding if he wants to kill the sergeant before he dies. Sergeant Roberts becomes highly anxious, realizing he is about to lose his life. Staff Sergeant Anderson walks up behind my fire team, assesses the situation, and barks the command, "KILL HIM!" One 45 caliber pistol and four M14 rifles immediately fire, killing the sniper. He is dead before he hits the ground.

Five of us killed the sniper. Just how does a young man's mindset change from compassionate consideration for others to a man who will kill on command? Trust me; Marines will kill on command; they will kill instantly. Starting in boot camp and continuing after that, they are trained, or if you will, brainwashed to follow orders. They do not form committees to discuss alternative options. They didn't formulate differential equations to model the merit of their orders mathematically. They execute orders immediately.

Leaders issuing orders to kill beginning with noncommissioned officers and most certainly commissioned officers are literally in charge of combat morality. That may sound a bit strange, ethics in a war. I mean, after all, war is all about killing people. What the hell is moral about that? Every group within a society has its morality within that group. From the Baptist Church to the Hells Angels motorcycle gangs, all society units have a sense of moral values. Albeit a different definition of morals, but morals, nevertheless. So do combatants. That's right; Marines in combat have a moral obligation just like everyone else. It sounds weird. After all, you are in the military whose entire mission in a war is to destroy and kill, and I'm talking about morality.

Yes, I am most definitely talking about morality. A combat unit's morality from a squad to a division stands on the foundation of military discipline and quality leadership. However, combat leaders are not provided with a manual that defines a combatant's morality—no, only made aware of conduct punishable under the Uniform Code of Military Justice dictates. So, just what the hell is moral and immoral for a Marine in combat. For me, killing the enemy is not a problem; killing civilians surrounded by those shooting at me is not a problem; killing non-combatants because I am angry, afraid, or desire revenge is always immoral.

When you function within the accepted morality of a combatant, you will feel proud of your service. Conversely, if you perform outside the accepted morality of a combatant, that type of conduct has the potential to destroy you from within.

Squad Leader Reinstated

During the Spring of 1966, the 1st Battalion 4th Marines, or 1/4, continued to conduct operations in the northern section of South Vietnam. Of all United States forces in South Vietnam, the 1/4 Marines are the farthest troops north. The battalion is on the move, and our company is assigned to walk the point position. There are about five hundred men in a battalion. Our company of about 150 men walks the point position for the battalion, and our platoon consisting of approximately 43 men, walks the company's point position. Our squad of 13 men walks the point position for the platoon. My fire team consisting of four men walks the point position for the squad.

That's right; we are the tip of a human spear moving in the extreme northern section of South Vietnam. We don't know where we are, only that we are somewhere close to the DMZ to the north and Laos to the west. That's it. That's all we ever know of our precise location, just never-ending rolling hills to ascend and descend in the scorching heat. Think hot, hot, hot.

After hours of humping up and down hills, the entire battalion takes a break. Corporal Whitney, our squad leader, asked if I have a cigarette.

I answer, "Yeah, I do, and you are welcome to one if you walk over here to get it because frankly, I am too tired to walk to you. You are the one asking, so if you want a smoke come over here and get it." I offered him a cigarette with an outstretched hand. As Corporal Whitney walks towards me, he steps on an antipersonnel mine. That's the bad news - the good news - the mine mostly malfunctions. The explosive force from the mine is much less than its design. Corporal Whitney could have died or lost a foot or leg from the explosion had it functioned as its maker intended. I'm not saying the mine didn't work at all; he has a severely damaged knee and lower leg. However, if the mine functioned properly, it most likely would have killed or wounded Whitney and those of us close by.

The last memory I have of Corporal Whitney is of him sitting on top of a tank about thirty yards away, staring at me as I stare back at him. The tank gradually pulls away as he slowly raises his arm with a closed fist, and I do the same—our way of saying goodbye, our way of saluting. To be sure, when Corporal Whitney returned from his father's funeral, I resented him as the third squad leader. But I never said he wasn't capable. He can lead any squad in the Marine infantry. For Whitney, his tour in Vietnam is over. I just got a reset; I am once again the squad leader of the third squad.

Leech Ambush

Bravo Company continues to perform search and destroy missions during the day and ambushes at night in the northern provinces of South Vietnam. My squad is assigned a night ambush that is challenging due to extreme rain and total darkness. Yeah, it is raining in May; it is raining buckets. We must conduct a night ambush regardless of the prevailing conditions, making navigation damn near impossible. It is so dark we have to hold onto the Marine's shoulder in front of us to know where he is.

So, how do you find your way under the conditions of intense rainfall and total darkness? Earlier that afternoon, after receiving the ambush assignment, I got together with some of the other NCOs, and we plotted the route to my ambush site. We used a method of navigation that enables the use of a compass in total darkness.

The dial cover of the standard-issue military compass has a short fixed luminous line on its underside. The entire cover is attached to a movable bezel ring. The first step of preparing the compass for night navigation is to rotate the bezel ring until the cover's luminous line is over the compass's fixed black index line. Next, the starting azimuth of your route is divided by three because each click of the bezel ring represents three degrees of azimuth. The result is the number of clicks that you must rotate the bezel ring. If the desired azimuth is smaller than 180 degrees, the number of calculated clicks of the bezel ring movement must be in the counterclockwise direction. After moving the bezel ring, hold the compass level to your front as you turn your body until the luminous north pointing arrow of the compass needle aligns with the luminous stripe on the bottom of the movable cover. Counting your steps as you move in the direction you are now facing will determine the travel distance on the selected azimuth. This compass procedure works if you pay close attention and plan your route. We did plan well, and it did work even under the conditions of driving rain and complete darkness. We successfully navigate to our assigned site.

The rain continues as we set the ambush on the edge of a ditch, covering a trail to our front. No one is wearing a poncho because when the rain strikes its rubber coating, it makes a pitter-patter sound that may expose our position. Better wet and soggy than dead.

As we sit in the flooded ditch, blood-sucking leeches surround our lower legs. Normally our trousers are bloused by an elastic band holding the trousers tight around our boots. The blousing bands create a barrier to any plant, insect, or other animal trying to reach the bearskin of our legs. It is a sound system until you wear the same trousers so long that they tear, or you lose or break your blousing bands. Under these conditions, it is not difficult for the leeches to find soft skin to bite, and they do.

Sitting in our ambush site, we can't make any noise or quick movements by going after the leeches crawling up our legs. Yes, the rain, then varying in intensity, provides some sound cover, but additional noises or rapid arm or leg movement will expose our ambush position. Soon, everyone discovers that if you quietly and slowly reach down your leg, you can gently pick the leeches off and give them a little chuck. Well, that is until the leeches attach themselves to you. You see, a leech has a round mouth filled with teeth. When he bites, he also secretes an enzyme that causes you to bleed profusely. Once he has attached himself to your body, you cannot forcefully pull him off without creating a round hole left by his circular mouth being ripped away from your body because his teeth are still embedded. The resulting wound bleeds freely and is difficult to stop because the circular hole's edges will not come together to block the flowing blood. The bottom line, you never want to pull a leech in such a manner. So, you must sit all night and quietly take off the bloodsuckers that have not yet bitten into you and gently pet the ones that have.

We all anxiously wait for the morning light to become bright enough to light cigarettes without giving away our ambush site. Then we can begin removing embedded leeches by touching the red-hot end of a cigarette to their bodies. Burning the embedded leeches in such a manner will eventually motivate them to release their teeth and drop off. As darkness yields to the first light, we can see the leeches sucking blood from our legs, but it is still too dark to conceal a lit cigarette. Seeing the leeches and not being able to remove them yet requires a considerable amount of restraint. Only personal discipline prevents you from immediately grabbing the leeches and violently pulling them off.

One of us has a phobia about leeches, so severe that just the leech's mental image will create deep anxiety within him. He manages to handle his fear the entire night, but when he can see them in the early morning, that is too much. He pulls off an embedded leech, creating a hole in his leg just above his boot. We cover the bleeding hole with a large bandage and tie it in place. Then we go about the business of removing the leeches off ourselves. Looking back at him, we are amazed to see the entire bandage we have just applied to his wound is full of blood and leaking into his boot. He can walk back and rejoin our platoon, but we can't stop his leg from bleeding. Several corpsmen work tirelessly to prevent blood loss without success. The bleeding Marine is medevacked to a rear area medical facility.

Controlling fear in Vietnam was not just how well you faced the enemy. Many different situations would test your composure. For some, a firefight or mortar attack is less of a challenge than having to endure an entire night of leeches attached to your body sucking blood.

"To Let Them Know, That We Know, That They Knew, That We Were There"

Great news our platoon receives six replacements! We have lost men from small arms fire, mortar attacks, booby traps, sickness, and troops' regular rotation completing their 13-month tours. The field conditions are harsh for a grunt in Vietnam. Weight loss is significant due to a diet of C-Rations only and the vast amount of physical exertion performed day and night. The six replacements are not enough to fill all the vacancies, but much appreciated. Oh, my God, we truly need them.

One of the Marines who joined our platoon is a second lieutenant fresh out of officer candidate school. He is the replacement for our platoon commander, who was shot several months ago in Chu Lai. Lieutenant Garner is his name. He is being thrown to the wolves to be tested under fire as he takes command of a platoon of combat seasoned Marines as his first assignment.

Lieutenant Garner is not with us more than two days before he notifies me that he will be accompanying my squad on a night ambush. He further says that I am to lead the ambush as though he isn't present. "I'm coming along to monitor and get a feel of what happens on these ambushes." I reply, "Sir, that's fine with me, but you might consider carrying a rifle." Marine officers typically carry a 45-caliber pistol for personal protection. Their job is to lead, but if the new lieutenant wants to join us tonight in any other capacity, I can use another Marine with a rifle. He replies, "Tonight, I will only carry my pistol." Ok. It isn't my job to tell him, and maybe he already knows that two different ambush teams were attacked on their way back to the platoon in the previous two nights.

One of the recently attacked Marines has qualified for a Purple Heart medal after being wounded by a grenade that deposited shrapnel in his upper leg. Our platoon's corpsman tending to the injured Marine explains that he is not hurt badly, but he does need medical attention. The corpsman went on to declare, "I can feel the piece of shrapnel, and I can take it out right here and now, but it's going to hurt like hell. I don't have any way of numbing the flesh surrounding it. So, you qualify for a Purple Heart, and you have earned a ride on the next supply chopper to a rear area medical facility where they can remove the shrapnel professionally." The wounded Marine told the corpsman, "Do not put me in for a Purple Heart. Guys hit hard deserve the recognition. Besides, I consider a Purple Heart a marksmanship badge for the enemy. These guys barely hit me at all. Hell, this little bit of metal in my leg, this ain't shit. I do not want a Purple Heart for this little bit of nothing. This whole leaving thing, no way. Doc, here's the way this is going to work. I'm going to turn my head and look away, and you are going to take those plyer things, squeegee things, or whatever the hell you got in your bag and reach in and grab that shit and pull it out. So, let's get started."

The transitions of change come in different ways. When a grunt is in the field, all he thinks about is getting the hell out of the field. But if he leaves his outfit before everyone else does, he feels like a moral obligation has been broken. He feels like a "Non-hacker." In the mindset of a Marine, those words "Non-hacker" are toxic and insulting. Kind of hard to explain, but trust me, those emotions are real and robust. The wounded Marine's verbal suggestion concerning his medical treatment and not awarding him a Purple Heart medal are honored by the corpsman.

That night, my squad, including the lieutenant, proceed to our ambush site and soon discover that the preselected terrain provides a perfect environment for an ambush. The area borders a wetland full of green vegetation. The marsh is wide and long, but it tapers down to a width of 30 to 40 yards. Anyone walking towards us along the marsh's edge on either side will be naturally channeled to the narrow portion of the wetland. Perfect, now I know the enemy's probable location and distance from us. I set the ambush in a linear-shaped formation with security posted on both flanks and center rear. The kill zone is to our front on either side of the marsh at its narrowest point. What can go wrong?

After sitting in complete silence for several hours, I hear what sounds like low-volume voices. For some, the sight of leeches sucking blood from their bodies gives them creeps. For me, hearing enemy voices thirty to forty yards away causes my heart to race and my mind to go into hyperdrive. Well, I have no visual targets even though they sound close. Why not? I should be able to see them.

My squad anxiously waits, hoping the invisible enemy will funnel into our kill zone. After twenty minutes, nothing changes, although I can sometimes hear noises. They are not moving. Have they chosen an ambush site on the other side of the marsh? Why not? If this side of the swamp funnels anyone walking next to it, so does the other side. Oh, for God's sake, we have most likely been followed, and our prey is set in an ambush to attack us when we leave.

We are now in big trouble facing a counter-ambush of undetermined size and exact location. Ambushes are all about surprising your enemy with violent aggression delivered from a position to their flank. However, once you select an ambush formation, your firepower is statically committed; you can't maneuver well from a fixed position. It's challenging to get your team up and react to an attack from another direction. A detected ambush is a dangerous predicament; it's no longer an ambush. I need to get my squad out and away from the enemy's preplanned fields of fire.

I order the two Marines to my right and the two Marines to my left to throw hand grenades. Yeah, throw them one at a time, one after another, as far as they can to the other side of the marsh. The grenades explode, kaboom, kaboom, kaboom, kaboom, providing a surprise distraction allowing us to move. I order our squad to stand up and move back and around the funnel point created by the narrowing swamp.

Safely out and away from the ambush site, I call in a status report to our company command post informing them that we have left the ambush site after throwing four hand grenades. They reply with military jargon, "Say again your last."

In the military, they don't routinely use the word repeat in radio messages. The word repeat is reserved to repeat a requested fire mission from aircraft, mortars, or an artillery battery. You don't want someone else to use the word repeat and have it mixed into your radio transmission while your people are moving into the most recent impact zone of fire. You never use the phrase repeat unless you want a fire mission repeated. You use the words "Say again your last" when you need a verbal message to be retransmitted.

Well, in this case, say again your last means – what the hell are you doing? What do you mean you threw four grenades and left the ambush site because it was compromised? That's what they are asking. I reply, "We threw the four grenades **to let them know, that we know, that they knew, that we were there.**"

That status report became famous. All I heard for the next few days was, "To let them know that we know, that they knew, that we were there." However funny it may sound, it worked!

I began to comprehend the probability of success and failure as men attempt to kill one another in close contact warfare using modern weapons. Disciplined aggression is the foundation of success in combat, but it must be understood. Attacking from a mindset of aggression only, without a battle plan and an expectation of probable success is leadership failure.

Corporal Hernandez

In late May 1966, the First Battalion Fourth Marines walk the rolling hills that define the terrain somewhere close to the border that separates North Vietnam from South Vietnam. That's about all we know of our present location because we have no large area maps showing bordering countries.

Our battalion has stopped marching late in the afternoon and digs in for the night. "Dig in" means you use your entrenching tool to dig a hole deep enough to allow your entire body to get below the surface of the earth. So maybe you don't get wasted by a mortar attack that will surely come before daylight. That's right; our battalion gets mortared every night. Sometimes the mortars strike down the line and don't concern you too much. Mortar attacks are not a big deal unless they are close to you, but they will be close to someone, and you never know if that someone is going to be you. The only way to protect yourself is to dig a hole deep enough to get below the air turbulence of the explosions and the flying shrapnel. Not such an easy task because the ground is dry and hard. I have dug in directly behind my squad's three fire teams, where I can see everyone's position.

To my surprise, I get an unexpected visit after dark from Corporal Hernandez, who is upset. We don't usually have a social hour after dark because when darkness falls, everyone gets quiet. Light or noise will provide the enemy mortar crews a fixed position to aim at. So we sit still and rotate watch with our fellow Marine sharing the same hole.

Hernandez begins to speak, "Corporal Mezick, I need to talk with you. I'm feeling bad. I'm in a bad way." I say, "Sure, I'm honored with your presence, and please excuse my lack of accommodations and refreshments. I wasn't expecting company." Corporal Hernandez isn't impressed at my attempt at humor. He looks at me straight on and says, "I am ashamed of my Bronze Star," and the disgrace of my cowardice for not doing more the night Sergeant Jefferson's squad got attached on Stone Island. Hernandez's voice breaks and trembles with emotion as his feelings surface. I suspect this is the first time he has revealed the mental hell he is silently enduring. I am honored that he chose me to help, but I am hesitant and downright frightened that anything I have to say may create more damage than good. I speak with him the only way I know how, with brutal honesty.

Hernandez performed that dreadful night when others could not. Anyone who survived the attack on that two-acre island outpost off Chu Lai's coast owes their life to Corporal Hernandez. Hearing and feeling his pain, I can only ask, "What the hell are you talking about"? He replied, "I could see them when they left, and I could have killed more of them, but I was too scared to fire." My reply, "If it's ok, I'm going to reach over and push my finger against your knee." I did without getting his permission. I told him, "I want to make sure that I am not dreaming. Look, I think about that night a lot. I left Sergeant Jefferson's squad one week before all this all went down. I got promoted to be the squad leader of the third squad on Sergeant Jefferson's recommendation. Every time I think about that night, I think of your courage." Hernandez replied, "You don't understand. I could have done more."

"Ok, Hernandez, let's break it down, no bull shit, just the facts. The outpost was a static defensive position with no wire, no early detection devices, no claymores, fucking nothing. All you were was a reinforced squad with fixed positions known by everybody, especially the gooks that wanted to kill you. Oh, let's not forget that tiny island outpost just happened to be a few hundred yards away from Snaggletooth Island. As I recall, no Marine had ever visited that island without getting into a firefight. Under the darkness of a moonless night, sappers crawled up to every position, and at a prearranged time, they threw satchel charges, a pack full of explosives, into every fixed position. Ninety-five percent of all the Marine casualties happen at the same time. The squad was beaten before they could fire the first shot. Those not dead or wounded were suffering from a concussion caused by the explosions. Of the few surviving Marines, most could not stand, or if they could stand, they were walking around in circles, unable to realize that they had been overrun.

Now you had gooks in the wire, except you didn't have any wire. You woke up to death and destruction, and somehow you managed to grab your rifle and move. No cartridge belt, no more magazines of ammo, no grenades. You got eighteen rounds in your M14 rifle surrounded by gooks that had overrun your position. Somehow you managed to control your fear and start killing those fuckers. You are the only one shooting. Every time you shot, your muzzle blast gave away your position, so you had to move and fire from a new location. You kill the guy giving orders. Yeah, the guy running his mouth – the guy controlling the whole thing. You realize that he is the leader, and you put him down. Without their leader, the rest of the VC lost composure and became unorganized, leaving prematurely. They pick up weapons, food, and by the way, the only radio, the squad's walkie-talkie, a piece of shit PRC-6.

"Now, after you killed the leader and prompted the other gooks to leave prematurely. You feel bad because you didn't fire on them with the few rounds of ammo you had left? Look above and beyond committing suicide; you could have motivated them to turn around. They could have killed or captured disabled Marines. You deserve your Bronze Star, and quite frankly, I'm proud to know you! More importantly, Sergeant Jefferson, the Marine who mentored both of us, would be your best advocate and sponsor."

Hernandez looked up and caught my eyes with his. A full minute goes by in silence. Finally, he nods his head, stands up, and leaves without another word. To this day, I don't know if I was of any help. Corporal Hernandez rotated back to the states a few days later. So, what's this all about? Guilt. Why? Because he was selected to live while others were chosen to die. Please don't ask me to tell you who makes those selections. That answer is far above my intellectual capacity. Yes, Hernandez was selected to survive, but a piece of him died that night, and the rest of his living parts are now barely hanging on. He knows he is going home and feels that he is abandoning the dead. Hernandez stands on a fence, one side depression and guilt, the other side pride and confidence. I do not know what happened to him, but I will side with pride and confidence. Why? Because men like Corporal Hernandez survive life's challenges by putting their left foot in front of their right. I suspect he handled the challenge of returning home and adjusting to a non-combat environment just like the night of the attack. Head high and proud.

Education - Personal Discipline

Many of the skills a combatant will learn and the transitions he will make during his time in combat will affect him for the rest of his life. Yeah, think, education. The Vietnam War created the most intense learning environment I have ever experienced. Everything is so acute. So tremendously in your face, you need to learn immediately! Not learning the very minute you are exposed to new information may cost you your life. The environment of violence and fear creates a heightened awareness of everything you see, hear, smell, or touch.

Odd as it may sound, there are many lifelong benefits from attending the college of applied death and destruction. The most apparent change, confidence; you begin to believe in yourself. Yes, I would suggest that my self-confidence is unnaturally high. Not for everyone; some people buckled under the stress of war and were forever affected by post-traumatic stress. By the way, succumbing to trauma can happen to anyone. When the strongest people in the world are in a weightlifting contest, someone will eventually win. However, the competition never runs out of weights for the winner to continue lifting. We humans have a limit on the amount of stress we can endure before suffering mental damage.

Most Marines don't succumb to stress. They return to civilian life with an unnaturally heightened sense of confidence. Why? Because they faced their fear and survived. Trust me, successfully facing extreme personal challenges will enable you to understand and, most importantly, accept yourself. In combat, you find out exactly who you are. Generally, you discover you are not the strongest, wisest, or toughest individual walking through the valley of death. However, knowing and accepting who you are is a tremendous personal advantage. You are at peace with the only person you can never escape from, yourself. Now, you are free to function for the rest of your life without being in a state of personal insecurity. The way I see it, well-rounded people all have at least two things in common. First, they stand on a foundation of self-confidence and are at peace with three unavoidable human issues – fear, sex, and violence. Their heightened sense of confidence allows them to succeed and achieve where others suffering from insecurity will fail. The opportunity for education is everywhere if you care to receive it.

There is another highly advantageous personal attribute attained from combat, "Personal Discipline." The ability to say no, to delay gratification. Excessive anything can negate everything else you have accomplished. Too much food, alcohol, sex, drugs, tobacco, or gambling is devastating. Uncontrolled yielding to compulsive behavior can destroy the quality of life for you and your family. Destroy you professionally for sure.

Some people are born with a natural sense of personal discipline, allowing them to say no to excess. However, most of us must learn to control our desires by experience.

I obtained personal discipline by learning to control the strongest of all human desires, thirst. Forget about hunger, sex, anger, or love. Severe dehydration will make you crazy before it kills you. Humping through the rolling hills of the northern section of South Vietnam under a blistering sun enduring high humidity in temperatures exceeding one hundred degrees Fahrenheit brought me face to face with my body's total dependence on water. We are water; we are all about water; life is wet. When you walk over those sparsely vegetated hills and then descend into the valleys, you become surrounded by tall, thick grass. No air circulation as you fight your way through vegetation that often exceeds the height of seven feet. The extremely high humidity causes you to expel water by sweating profusely—only replaced with the two canteens of chemically treated water carried on your hips. The chemicals in the water kill the bacteria, but it makes the water taste and smell horrible. If the air temperature is over a hundred degrees, Fahrenheit so is the water in your canteens.

The little bit of water you carry is hot, smelly, and tastes awful. It is also your most precious possession. All you can think about is reaching back and grabbing one of the canteens and bringing it to your mouth to suck it dry. Yeah, bring it up and drink it dry because you need it. You are dying of thirst. Why wouldn't you do that? What the hell? It's your water, and God knows you deserve it. You are extremely thirsty, and you should be able to hydrate yourself, right? What's the problem? The problem is that there is no more water until the next ration is provided, and when is that going to happen? Nobody knows. Where will you get additional water if you come under fire and resupply becomes impossible? Are you going to ask your fellow Marine to give you some of his water because you drank yours, and now you want to drink his as well? Good luck with that. He will share his water if you are wounded or dying of heat exhaustion, but you can't ask because you are thirsty.

Quite frankly, I have no idea how anybody else mentally handled the extreme desire to drink their canteens dry. I can only tell you what I did. I created a game designed to distract me from overwhelming thirst and prolong the time before taking another drink from my depleting water supply. It was a game of visualization.

I mentally create an exact image of my childhood home. I imagine myself standing in front of our old Crosby refrigerator in the kitchen, a big round box. It has a large door handle that pulls to the left, allowing the door to open to the right. When it does, a light comes on, revealing all its dietary treasures. I visualize all this as I mentally look inside, and there, sitting on the top shelf, is a watermelon. Oh, it is beautiful, looking so cold and promising copious amounts of sweet watermelon juice.

A sequence of movements within the imagined kitchen begins to unfold. I mentally move around the table and chairs to retrieve a large plate from an overhead cabinet to support the melon before cutting it with a butcher knife. Every move is slow and deliberate as my mind reveals the finest detail of all the objects. Everything imagined happens slowly. I desperately try to consume as much time as I can between water drinks from my depleting supply. I must overcome the incredible temptation to drink the remaining water too quickly. My right hand holding a knife cuts the watermelon in half, and then I cut in half the piece still held by my left hand. I bring that wet treasure to my face and bite into it. The juice from the melon is cool and sweet, deliciously moist. Some of the imagined watermelon juice runs down my chin, and it is terrific!

If I make it this far and only if I can visualize every detail of every sequence from the beginning. I reward myself by slowly reaching back and unsnapping the cover of my canteen. Gently I pull it out and bring it to the front, ever so slowly unscrewing the cap. Then, and only then, after completing the game of visualization. I get the canteen to my mouth and take a little swallow. Just a tiny taste of water is plenty for this drink. I slowly put the cap back on, reach around and return the canteen to its cover, snapping it closed.

If at any time the visualization sequence falls apart, no reward. I will have to start over again from the beginning. All the slow imagery takes considerable amounts of time and mental focus. The entire purpose is to keep me from grabbing my water and drinking it all to quench my incredible thirst. The visualization game provides me with delayed gratification – It provides the foundation for learning in-depth the true meaning of "Personal Discipline." Such a valuable life-enhancing lesson etched into my psyche.

Most have witnessed the pain of those who have lost their marriage, their children, their home, and eventually their self-respect because they could not say that's enough. Too much gambling, smoking, drinking, drugs, eating, you name it, and you can do too much of it. What controls your natural desires for more? Personal discipline. That's what prevents you from buying everything you think you need today and saying no to instant gratification. Life is much less expensive when you are not paying copious amounts of interest to someone who does have self-control and makes money selling money to those who don't.

Personal discipline permits you to postpone instant gratification and endure discomfort. Through water deprivation, I learned how to say no to temptation and indulgence. After completing my tour in Vietnam, I began life without unnecessary loans with crippling interest rates. Self-confidence and personal discipline have enabled me to succeed in endeavors that I did not have the education or the experience to accomplish. Through the ability to mentally focus away from the desire to quit and concentrate on what I needed to achieve, I became the man I sought to be. The self-confidence of knowing who I am as a man allows me to absorb others' ridicule as they witness how hard I try when they quit. Many highly educated professionals know little about personal discipline and often struggle with insecurity.

Combat, weird as it sounds, is a tremendous learning opportunity that you can benefit from for the rest of your life. Education is where you find it – your life is your university.

Mortar Attack / Talking to God

Occasionally, the First Battalion Fourth Marines get a short helicopter ride to a new location within the I Corps Tactical Zone, but mostly, we keep humping—no breaks since March. Late in early June of 1966, we are lean, physically and mentally. We walk during the day and dig in at night.

Mortar fire continues to harass our battalion at several locations along our lines every night. The rolling hills that dominate the terrain make direct return fire at the mortar crews impossible because they attack us from behind the hills to our front. The mortar shells go up, and they come down. You can't shoot directly at your opponents with a rifle because they are out of sight, behind a hill. We can only reach them with our mortars or artillery that can drop shells on the far side of the hill. For most of us, mortar attacks are not the end of the world. Our battalion stretched a long way when spread out with Marines positioned in fighting holes about twenty yards apart. However, several different locations along the line are sure to be mortared every night. Would they strike my position? Who knows, besides, what's the problem if they do? If I dig a hole that enables me to be below the earth's surface, they must drop the mortar round pretty much into my hole to harm me. When that happens, forget it, lights out, I am history. The mortar attacks killed Marines, not every night, but they were not without effect.

Late one afternoon, after we had stopped walking and dug fighting holes to protect ourselves, the brass, for some reason, decided to shift the entire battalion of dug-in Marines two hundred yards to the left. Now that's no big deal unless you are in the unlucky unit positioned on the left flank. Everyone else shifted into previously dug holes by the Marines that shifted left. We are on the extreme left flank, so there are no previously dug holes for us when we shift out of our holes. We have to dig new fighting positions.

Digging a hole deep enough for two men to get below the earth's surface is not a trivial task. It is dry this time of the year, and the ground is hard, rocky, and arid. You adjust your E-tool (entrenching tool) to fold down the spade part of the small shovel to be at a right angle to the handle. Now you can use it as a pick. Swing it hard, strike the ground, and it bounces back, causing a tiny chip of earth to loosen. That's it, a small chip that is your reward for hitting the ground so hard your entire arm vibrates as the ground seems to swing back at you. Well, if you move enough chips, you eventually make a hole. We get it done, not easy considering it is our second hole the same afternoon.

An hour later, another command, "Shift left two hundred yards." One of the squad's fire team leaders grumbled, "You got to be shitting me. We got to dig a third position before nightfall with totally worn-out arms and hands." Everybody is bitching; I come down hard on my squad to motivate them to dig yet another fighting hole before dark. The palms of our hands are blistered and painful to the touch. It is a massive challenge for our fingers to wrap around the wooden handle of the E-tool. We keep changing hands to decrease the pain from swinging twice with the same arm. Trust me when I tell you our E-tools are just bouncing off the hard, dry, rocky surface. So, I must push my squad relentlessly to dig a third hole before nightfall. They do it.

What about me? How deep is my position? Not very deep at all. I had spent too much time pushing everybody else, and maybe I needed someone to drive me. My fighting position is just a tiny scrape in the ground that wouldn't protect a miniature dog. I hastened to improve my fighting hole, but before I make any progress in that endeavor, I receive the command, "Squad leaders up." That means I must stop digging and report to the platoon command post.

Darkness soon falls, no more digging, no smoking, no lights of any kind. We don't want to expose ourselves to enemy spotters who will record our exact positions and relay that information to their mortar crews. Under cover of darkness, the spotters will sneak to the top of the hills so they can watch the mortars strike and then send back aiming instructions to adjust their point of impact. Yeah, send back information that will change the elevation and azimuth of the mortar tubes used to launch the projectiles trying to kill us.

I don't have a fighting hole. I have a half-ass scrape that is not large enough to protect me, and it is too late to improve it. I am exposed. Well, how bad is this? The entire battalion is strung out online; what's the odds they will strike my exact position? I mean, there are lots of other places they can hit. The odds of them striking my exact location are slim.

That assumption is wrong, wrong, and more wrong. At 0200 hours, 2:00 a.m., the mortar attack begins; the first rounds explode one hundred yards directly in front of my position. Then they begin to walk the rounds in. Walk the rounds in means that a spotter provides aiming instructions to the mortar crews who adjust their weapons to strike their targets more accurately. Those intended targets are us! The next volley of incoming mortar shells hits fifty yards directly in front of my position, followed by a third volley, twenty yards straight to my front. I can feel the air turbulence caused by the shrapnel flying directly over my head. The roar of explosions is horrifying, as is the sound of flying metal, whoosh, whoosh, just above my exposed body. I push down into the earth as hard as I can. I am unprotected; my entire body is above the ground. "Oh my God, I am going to die." I realize that the next volley, the next set of rounds, may come down directly into my position, and when they do, I'm done. Why am I so exposed? Because I am lazy. I didn't do what I ordered everyone else to do, dig in!

Maybe, I can jump in and share someone else's hole? No, impossible for a whole host of reasons. I pray to everyone and everything; to God, to Jesus, to the stars, to the universe, and to anyone or anything I think can impact my destiny. "Oh God, please let me live. I promise never to be lazy again." The next volley of rounds falls thirty yards behind me. The enormous noise and turbulence from the explosions create immense fear within me. I am afraid of the flying shrapnel, and my eardrums ache from being hammered by air turbulence. I also fear an infantry assault; ground forces move under cover of exploding mortars, knowing you are hunkered down. The next volley of incoming motor rounds strikes our ammo dump, causing artillery and mortar rounds to explode. The detonations create a fire that causes more explosions, then more fire, then more explosions. The night is full of enormous noise, flying metal, and death. I keep watching for an infantry assault. I just know it is coming, and everything is about to get worse. I keep repeating my prayerful deal with God. "Oh, please let me live. I will never be lazy again. Starting now – starting right now, I will never be lazy again."

Daybreak, I began digging with great enthusiasm. I don't make a hole; I make a motel. My squad begins to gather around, staring down at their leader, digging a massive fighting position. No one says a word until finally, one of them speaks up, "Corporal Mezick, why are you digging? You know damn well we are going to be moving out any minute now"? I break a long period of silence before looking up and say, "Shut up, I made a deal."

Leaders are not immune to the hazards of war just because they oversee others. Those in command positions must learn how to motivate themselves without external influence.

When you face your death, you will consider, without shame, the true meaning of God. How others answer God's existence and significance will be of little use to you as you are about to enter the realm of the unknown.

Frame of Mind

Home is a long distance away; everyone knows that. Hell, it's basically on the other side of the world. But now, mentally, it is even further away. Back in the real world, I have a family, a wife, and a baby girl. During the last ten weeks, I have written very few letters. Beyond the apparent difficulty of writing a letter while constantly moving around the northern provinces of South Vietnam, there is another reason. I have transitioned into a Marine in a war. You want to stay alive; understand, and accept what's happening here and now. As much as possible, try not to think of the folks back home. The two different frames of mind are mutually exclusive as one weakens the other. The only way to get out of Vietnam is to get through Vietnam. I must first embrace my environment and then master it by continuously studying everything I can see, hear, or touch.

Pig's Buffet

Fate can select you to have a bad day. Our platoon has entered a village where everything is normal except no people. Not one person; that generally means VC control the village.

Before I share the "Bad Day" incident, I must disclose that I have been suffering from abdominal distress for several days. Battalion headquarters thought it would be terrific to set up a field kitchen to provide hot meals for the troops. Sounds great, but it didn't work. The food preparation tent got mortared, the food was worse than C-rations, and many of us got the runs.

Now, back to the VC-supported village. We check out the huts and the bomb shelters adjacent to them, trying to discover hidden weapons or munitions. What I call huts the Vietnamese call home. They are just grass structures, and the bomb shelters are nothing more than holes in the ground with an earthen cover that provides some protection from whatever hostile fire finds its way into the village. The peasants living in the hamlets and villages of Vietnam are caught in the middle of a colossal mess, only trying to survive. They don't care much for the French, the Americans, or the North Vietnamese. The South Vietnamese government in Saigon is also beyond their interest or control. The driving force of their lives is to plant and harvest rice to feed their families. They have no electricity, running water, or sewage system beyond a shared trench used by men, women, and children. Most of them are not educated beyond the level of primary grammar school. Modern medicine and its power to cure disease and set broken bones are not available to these peasants. The concept of illness caused by bacteria, viruses, fungi, and protozoa is unheard of or just another foreign idea. The villagers live as did their ancestors and are largely resistant to change.

After carefully examining the huts and bomb shelters, the platoon loosely assembles in the hamlet's center, waiting for an order to move out. It is at this time that I feel the sensation of an oncoming bowel movement. When anyone suffering from dysentery first becomes aware that they may need to relieve themselves, it's only a matter of seconds before they explode from their bottom end. You don't have time to select a private location that will be much more appropriate for such an activity. You drop your trousers immediately before you crap in the only ones you presently own. Field grunts have no laundry service, don't wear underwear, or have access to a shower. None of these amenities are available to me.

I can't drop my trousers until I unsnap my cartridge belt. When I finally get it released, it hangs down and behind my body, supported by shoulder straps. The hefty weight of four fully loaded M14 magazines, two canteens of water, several grenades, a pouch full of first aid equipment, a Ka-Bar knife, and a bunch of other stuff tries to pull me backward. I immediately open my belt buckle, allowing my trousers to drop around my ankles as I squat, trying not to fall back under the weight of the hanging cartridge belt and the pack on my back. My bottom end violently releases the contents of my very unhealthy digestive system. At the mercy of an uncontrollable condition, I continue to blast away with a never-ending flow of smelly fluid in clear view of thirty or so of my fellow Marines.

Can things get any worse? The answer is yes – they can get a lot worse. A pig, a massive pig, runs across the courtyard, sticks his huge ugly nose under my butt, and begins consuming everything I am discharging. My testicles are now resting on the pig's nose as he is pushing me backward. If I tumble, his mouth will be between my legs as I sit in a pile of liquid excrement. Within reach is a big stick; think baseball bat size. I grab it and begin to hit the pig as I hop backward with a stream of never-ending fluid pouring from my intestines. The pig keeps coming. I continue bouncing back with little bounds, all the while whacking the hungry pig as thirty or so of my friends laugh and laugh some more. Hell, I can still hear them laughing. Now that's a bad day!

Bad Order / Atypical Marine

A few days later, our platoon is assigned to check out an area about three miles north of our company's position. Staff Sergeant Anderson calls up his three squad leaders and reports that neither he nor Sergeant Roberts will be making the patrol. Anderson and Roberts, the two senior noncommissioned officers of our platoon, are suffering from the same abdominal distress that has affected so many of us. Anderson says, "Be careful out there, and above all, don't let Lieutenant Garner down by following a misguided order. Do you understand?"

Whoa, he has just asked us to use our judgment concerning a legal order coming from a commissioned officer. Back in the world, this is a punishable offense that may result in a court-martial. Over here, all three of us squad leaders understand his request. Experience-based guidance is what Staff Sergeant Anderson typically provides as the platoon sergeant, especially with a new lieutenant. He can't go on the mission, so he wants us to step up in a manner that respects the lieutenant but keeps us from getting killed by following an order that the lieutenant would not give after he passes through the new guy period.

On patrol, a couple of miles from the company position, the platoon comes under light sniper fire from a tree line about two hundred yards away on our left flank. The sniper fire is not yet effective, but someone will eventually be hit if the shooting continues. So, we need to stop him. Sound logical to you? Well, Lieutenant Garner thought so. He orders my squad to advance across two hundred yards of open ground to engage the sniper in the tree line. That order is a perfect example of what Staff Sergeant Anderson meant by following a misguided order.

I turn towards the lieutenant and raise my left hand as though I have something important to say. I slowly walk to his position and whisper, "Sir, this is a trap - we have seen it before. When we get within twenty yards of the tree line, that lone sniper will be joined by others. Now we will have dead and wounded on the open ground directly in front of them. Sending the first and second squads to aid the third squad is just what they expect. They are playing us. They are betting on our reputation of aggressiveness and using it as a tactic against us."

After my explanation, our destiny is in the hands of the lieutenant's comprehension and fundamental acceptance of the information given. Will he be insulted that a corporal questioned his order, or will he be forever grateful? It is now the lieutenant's call; school is over. As the third squad leader, I will carry out his next order. I wait for his decision.

He smiles, nods his head slightly as I turn to walk back to my squad and begin the attack. Then the lieutenant withdraws his previous order. He loudly shouts, "Corporal Mezick, turn your squad on the oblique and move out."

The lieutenant or I never speak of our private conversation. I realize that I have just witnessed a transition of change in our new platoon commander. From that moment on, I believe that the lieutenant will mature into a fine line officer, and he did. Our brief conversation is another example of young men going through transitions that can build or destroy them. The rocks, the hills, and the heat don't care.

Our destination is nothing more than a small area of grass and trees several acres large. Just before entering this island of vegetation, the platoon receives small arms fire from its interior. We close with the shooters but find nothing; they have disappeared. Our mission is to discover how and where they vanished and then destroy them. Lance Corporal Downs is the only member of our platoon that can see the camouflage mats that cleverly conceal the shooters.

Lance Corporal Downs requires a few words of explanation because he is atypical. When a movie producer or a promotions agent for the United States Marine Corps selects individuals to represent a Marine's image, they will never choose Lance Corporal Downs. He weighs about one hundred and twenty pounds, and he is maybe five feet six inches tall. Everyone thinks of him as a little guy because of his diminutive stature. Worse for the Marine image, he speaks very slowly, a country boy.

However, it is Lance Corporal Downs' keen eyes that discover a sniper pit. Think hole in the ground with a mat designed to blend in with the surrounding area flawlessly.

The sniper shoots from the hole and then gets down into it and pulls a camouflaged carpet over himself. Perfect concealment, you can look directly at the mat like carpet or even step on it and not notice that it conceals a sniper.

To everyone except Lance Corporal Downs, the sniper pit is invisible. Downs begins talking to the ground, "Get out - get out – hands up." Nothing happens. Downs fires multiple rounds from his M14 rifle, killing the sniper in his hiding position. He advances to another location, repeating the order to get out, and then kills that sniper. The Marine that speaks so slowly and by all accounts is not what you would call a fine physical example of a man and most certainly is not the movie image of a Marine in combat takes out two enemy sniper positions by himself.

There are movie images of Marines, and in contrast, there is the real world. Lance Corporal Downs had a lifetime of challenges. Small boys get pushed around by big boys unless they learn to fight, knowing that they will most likely lose every time they do. When they ask a pretty girl to go to the prom, she most likely replies, "No, I am going with someone else." Young boys who learn to handle fear discover they are as powerful as everyone else with a weapon in their hands, regardless of their physical size.

But wait, these individuals are way ahead in combat because they better comprehend the art of "Fear Management." Combine that talent with an inherited human trait rarely spoken of. The "Capacity for Violence" and, in Lance Corporal Downs's case, a massive capacity for violence, and you have a hardcore Marine regardless of his slight physical presence.

Blocking Force / Dead Baby

Some transitions of change are a matter of accepting responsibility for our actions. We find ourselves in a universe that is not fair, not warm, kind-hearted, or compassionate. No one is watching over us to prevent horrible things from happening.

Bravo Company is the blocking force for another Marine unit driving North Vietnamese troops into our positions. The tactic is called "Hammer and Anvil," which very rarely worked on a large scale. However, it often produces results on a limited scale. We never seem to catch the motherload of fish, but we generally find some. It is that some that provide me with the challenge of learning to accept responsibility for unintended results.

The pushing force, the hammer, begins to receive small arms fire when approaching a small settlement below my platoon's position on a hill. Shooters in the hamlet below our platoon are firing at the advancing Marines.

My squad is assigned to move into the hamlet to engage the shooters. We maneuver down the hill and discover that the shooting that previously came from the east flank of the small settlement is now coming from its west flank. Not knowing if we have two active enemy firing positions, I leave the first and second fire teams at our present location and lead the third fire team to engage the shooter or shooters on the west flank. Just as we form an assault formation, the firing that has been coming from the west flank stops, and another shooter begins firing from a grass hut to our right front. Now, do we still have shooters firing from three different locations? I can't be sure, so I prepare to engage in all three directions. I leave the third fire team to attack the shooters on the west flank, and I assault the shooter firing from the grass hut.

Removing a grenade from its pouch, it immediately falls into two parts. The grenade's body falls to the ground as I hold the spoon and the detonator in my right hand. The grenade has somehow become unscrewed. I pick up the body and screw it back unto the spoon and detonator, pull the pin, and throw the grenade directly into the front door of the hut. Perfect pitch, a strike right down the middle.

Screaming like a mad man, I charge the shooter in the hut, firing my M14 Rifle as I burst through the open entrance. The interior is full of smoke and floating debris from my exploded grenade. I can barely see. I don't know if I have a dead, wounded, or perfectly healthy shooter or shooters within several feet of me. I spray the entire interior of the hut with multiple rounds of semiautomatic rifle fire, guessing where to shoot because the smoke and floating grass prevent me from seeing anything in detail. The rifle assault produces more dust and debris, causing the air to be unbreathable. I step outside to catch my breath and clear my burning eyes. After collecting myself, I reenter the hut to discover there is no one inside. I have just shot up a grass hut.

Soon joined by the rest of my squad and some of the driving force Marines, we all begin to look for the shooters and discover a bomb shelter about ten yards away. Maybe the shooters are in it? With the aid of an interpreter, we demand that anyone in the bomb shelter come out. Immediately a woman does, holding a dead or essentially dead baby suffering from shrapnel wounds from my grenade.

The baby dies in its mother's arms, who is in terrible emotional distress, weeping uncontrollably. Staff Sergeant Anderson, our platoon sergeant, approaches and asks, "Who killed the baby"? I look straight at him and say, "I did – I think." He replies, "What happened?" I tell him exactly what took place with obvious distress in my voice. He puts his hand on my shoulder and explains, "There's a thin line, a fragile line between super outcome and shit outcome. Here is what I know. We had Marines coming across those paddies with numerous shooters trying to kill them. I ordered your squad to engage, and you shut them down. No Marines were killed or wounded. That's your only concern. You and your squad accomplished your mission; you silenced the shooters. We are done here. Do you understand? We are done here."

All that logic made sense, and it still does to this day. Well, most of the time. You see, killing a baby is not a natural event, not even in a war. I must come to terms with the fact that the baby was alive until I killed it.

Given the challenge of taking down an active shooter today, I would conduct myself in the same manner, only changing the part where my grenade needs to be reassembled. I believe the mother is the shooter who fired from a position outside of the hut with her baby close. After the grenade exploded, she took her wounded child to the bomb shelter as I attacked the grass hut.

What about the transitions of change within a young man? From where to where? Are you ever the same after you charge into a building trying to kill before you are killed and discover the only thing you accomplish is the death of a baby? To answer that question, I will leave it to the reader.

Some transitions are not a change in one's approach to life but rather the recognition of reality.

I had changed to understand only this. If you don't want babies to die, do not shoot at Marines with a baby next to you. Better yet, get rid of all wars and all the killings. Until that utopian condition comes to fruition, be thankful that some of us will fight to our deaths to keep others with those marvelous dreams alive. Many of the men and women who have accepted the ultimate commitment are United States Marines.

Rotate / Third Time Asleep

The 1st Battalion Fourth Marines has been on continuous operations in the northern provinces of South Vietnam since leaving Phu Bai Combat Base for Operation Oregon last March. We are now a bunch of skinny hard-core Marines. Our clothes are torn and worn after more than ninety days in the bush; our field gear is ragged and broken, held together with C–ration wire. So yeah, we grunts are repairing our field gear with wire initially used to hold cases of C-rations together.

Most of us have only one toothbrush, which we use to remove rust that daily forms on our rifles and magazines. You must keep your rifle working perfectly because your life depends on it. Focus on your rifle, to hell with your teeth. Rusty M14 rifles can't be relied on to perform the required mechanical cycles of chambering and extracting multiple rounds of ammunition. Rusty magazines may not feed the next round.

No one gets a shower because there is no shower. We haven't worn underwear since we arrived in Vietnam; it gets too nasty. Once during the three months we operated in the northern provinces of South Vietnam, we discover a large pool of water and use it bath after stripping down and walking into the stagnant water to make our way to the other side. For most of us, the water level is about chest-deep. We thrash around washing our private areas in the front and the back to get some of that nasty ass bacteria off our bodies. Coming out of the water, our mates knock the leeches off the backsides of our bodies. Our job is to get the leeches off the front of our bodies before their circular mouths full of tiny teeth bite into us. The large pool filled with stagnant water is the extent of our hygiene in the field.

After six months in the country, in combat, from Chu Lai to the northern limits of South Vietnam, I have matured. No longer are my youthful experiences the dominant determinants of who I am. I haven't missed a day in the field for any reason since I arrived in Vietnam. I have suffered from diarrhea, basically dysentery, but I never asked to be declared sick. I just gutted it out. Sleep deprivation is devastating, especially during the last ninety days. I lost body weight, trading it for maturity and focus. I am a seasoned Marine Corporal, a squad leader accepted and respected by my superiors and the men in my command. Spared a wound of any type, although attacked by bullets, mortars, bobby traps, and exotic bacteria. We work in an environment where killing is expected and accepted.

Chronic stress is debilitating, resulting in a condition that never allows your body to recover fully. No time off because you experience a horrible event, no time to recover from a traumatic experience like civilians do back home, no such consideration for Marines in Vietnam. None of that, "Don't drive the car for a while because you had an accident. Take a couple of days off and rest up, get yourself back together." Bullshit, not here, no scheduled downtime for us. It's just, "Man Up, Hack It, Saddle Up, Lock and Load," that is our life.

I am the sum of all my experiences in the last six months. Take all those individual days, put them together, and that's who I am. For sure, I gained personal confidence beyond any other point in my life. Hell, I just may have found something that I was good at. Well, at least everyone else seems to think so. Secretly, I pray for courage and guidance. A combat leader gives orders; his men follow those orders, then you must live with the results. Combat leaders need all the divine guidance they can get.

Trucks meet us on the road; I suspect it was Route #1 or Route #9. We climb aboard, and they drive us south through the cities of Quang Tri and Hue to the Marine Combat Base in Phu Bai. Our battalion has been relieved, and we are about to be given a much-needed rest and receive

Marine replacements to fill our depleted ranks. Manpower in every unit within the battalion is understaffed; we desperately need replacement personnel.

Just how do you rest, Marine grunts? Picture an airbase with runways long enough to enable jets to take off and land. The aircraft and airstrips are protected with a high cyclone fence buffered on both sides with concertina wire. Between the fence and the runway are fighting positions manned by Marines who serve in the base's interior. Rest for us grunts is to man the fighting positions on the far side of the cyclone fence and concertina wire. We are the first line of base defense.

We gladly accept this duty and think it's excellent! Oh my God, we are so pleased, so fortunate, so happy, to be out of the field. The best part; after several days of manning those fighting positions, we get to rotate inside the defensive positions of the base to squad-size tents constructed on platforms raised above the ground with cots to sleep on. Trust me; a cot is a big deal after months of sleeping in the dirt and mud. We now use field showers to wash with clean water and soap that lathers up. All this is just awesome! The base provides us the use of a mess hall complete with tables and chairs. For the first time in months, I get to eat a hot meal on a plate with real utensils. Ooh-Rah – this is heaven. They even have a little house where you can sit down and relieve yourself. It doesn't get any better than this for a Marine grunt.

After several days of luxury living within the base, we rotate back to the fighting positions on the other side of the fence. Not a big deal for most of us, but it is for the new replacements. The new guys come in looking strong and fresh, perfect specimens of raw manpower. We need them to get up to speed by adjusting to their new home and responsibilities. The replacements have no combat experience, and they consider those fighting positions on the other side of the fence surrounding the airstrips as a tough combat assignment. Well, it is, after all. Many bad guys on the far side of the fence would love to destroy the airfield and blow up the aircraft, especially the jets. The enemy is not without success attacking the planes and the runway. Yeah, they can strike in the day or the night, so the airfield is protected around the clock 24/7.

There is nothing in front of you except more Vietnam as you sit in the fighting positions on the far side of the fence. For those of us who have spent the last three months in the northern provinces of South Vietnam, and before that in Chu Lai on an island next to the infamous VC-controlled Snaggletooth Island, this base protection assignment is not at all scary. For the new guys, this is their first combat assignment. They all handle their excitement and fear in their own way.

One of my responsibilities as a squad leader is to go out and check the lines several times during the night to make sure someone is awake in each fighting position. The squad's three fire team leaders also check on their teams throughout the night. By repeatedly checking each post, we make sure someone is alert and ready to fight. In each defensive position, the two men decide the rotation periods of sleep and watch, generally about two hours.

Sleeping on watch is not a minor infraction of someone else's rules; it is an unacceptable offense. Everyone depends on you to be awake while they sleep. No one on watch can sleep, nap, doze, snooze, or however else you want to describe not being alert. I certainly learned the enormity of this responsibility as a new guy in Chu Lai when the platoon's right guide kicked me in the helmet to wake me up and then verbally abused me. The violation of sleeping on watch can never be trivialized or tolerated.

How does a squad leader manage a situation when he discovers a sleeping Marine on watch? Every leader has his method. The official procedure is to report all such incidents to the platoon commander. Most, if not all, of the squad leaders, handle these situations internally, only sending an offender up the chain of command if necessary. Here's why, if you send the violator to the officers in charge, you may never see your much-needed replacement again. The task is to train this person, mold him into the man you need. Unless the new guy is unfixable, none of us squad leaders want to lose a precious manpower resource by sending him up the chain of command for punishment.

Speaking only for myself, I would approach and stand close to the violator and make a soft sound, like a light cough or clearing of my throat. The

Marine who is asleep, the guy that is supposed to be on watch, generally will wake up and realize that I know he has been sleeping. No words are required; most Marines caught sleeping are ashamed, knowing they have sinned. Self-correction is always preferred to forced correction. However, a second offense by the same individual requires additional instruction; wake him and explain in no uncertain terms, "Look asshole, while others are sleeping, you are responsible for their lives. When you sleep on watch, you fail them. I am ashamed of you." Not waiting for a response, I would turn my back and walk away. Third offense by the same individual; remove his rifle before grabbing him by the throat and forcing him to the ground, squeezing so tight he can't breathe. When he wakes, he is without oxygen, unable to speak. I then order him to do push-ups while explaining that he can't remain a squad member because he can't be trusted.

I had command of only one man during my entire tour in Vietnam that reached the third time of sleeping on watch, and he did it on three consecutive nights. You see, one way to deal with fear is to fall asleep – you won't be scared then. That's what he is doing.

Completing our turn in the defensive positions and returning to the squad size tents, I conceive a test to see if this Marine replacement is fixable. Motivated by my memory of how Sergeant Jefferson's squad had been devastated by a sapper attack and then overrun by charging infantry, I told the offending Marine he has to make a choice. "Option number one; tell the company commander that you have been asleep on watch three consecutive nights. Option number two; fill your backpack with sand, put on all your field gear, helmet, rifle, and cartridge belt complete with ammo and two quarts of water, and stand at parade rest in front of this tent until I tell you to stand down." He replied, "I will take option two."

After saddling up with his sand-filled pack, rifle, and field gear, I position him in front of our squad-size tent, facing another line of tents separated by a dirt road thirty yards wide where everyone can see him. I draw a line in front and behind his feet before presenting him with an ultimatum. "If you cross either line front or back, you will be sent to the captain who will most likely send you to a brig." Now I hear myself saying some of the exact words stated to me as I stood in front of a captain when I was a new guy in Vietnam. "I will not let you kill my Marines because of your incompetence and immaturity." I went on to say, "If you want to be a member of this squad, you will not move, you will stand here, and you will consider how you failed everyone by sleeping on watch three successive nights. You will take the heat, and you will withstand the pain until I order you to stand down. Do you understand"? His reply, "Yes."

I left him standing for approximately four hours. During that period, unbeknown to him, a corpsman was assigned to monitor him continuously. No senior noncommissioned officer or commissioned officer witnessing his opportunity for reflection interfered as this Marine stood at parade rest in front of our squad's tent facing the dirt street. Late in the afternoon, with the sun still high, I approached this young Marine and asked if he knew why he could never sleep on watch again? The exhausted replacement answered the question perfectly. Standing just a few feet to his front, I could see the hatred for me as he spoke. This man's eyes revealed that he is on the verge of attack. I order him to stand down and return to our squad. He made the transition!

Several days later, our company reassigned some replacement Marines to distribute them within its platoons and squads. Perfect opportunity for the Marine who has recently endured a brutal lesson of personal responsibility to volunteer to serve under another squad leader. I overheard a conversation between him and another replacement discussing why he did not volunteer to get out from under my supervision.

"Hey man, this is your chance to get away from Corporal Mezick and start fresh." His answer, I will never forget. "I hate him, and I want never to see him again. I am not asking for reassignment because I believe that son of a bitch will get me home."

CHAPTER FIVE

Loc Dien Village

Combined Action Company / Combined Action Platoon

Counterinsurgency Warfare / Counterguerrilla Warfare

After returning from field operations in Quang Tri Province to the Marine Combat Base in Phu Bai, many of the First Battalion Fourth Marines officers and senior noncommissioned officers are reassigned. Most are sent to the Fourth Marines Battalion Headquarters to assist in planning future operations. After seven months of serving in a line company, these leaders are valuable as advisors and tacticians.

Unbeknownst to me, my duty assignment is also about to change, bringing with it a major transition: a huge transformation, a new unit, and a unique opportunity to lead Marines using counterguerrilla warfare tactics[32]. I am about to become a member of an all-volunteer Combined

---

[32] **Guerrilla warfare** is a form of irregular warfare in which small groups of combatants, such as paramilitary personnel, armed civilians, or irregulars, use military tactics including ambushes, sabotage, raids, petty warfare, hit-and-run tactics, and mobility, to fight a larger and less-mobile traditional military. Wikipedia **Counterguerrilla warfare** - The most effective counter to guerilla warfare is a secure and content civilian populace. Guerilla fighters recruit from and receive supplies from the local population. If that local population has no driving reason to actively participate in resisting government or occupation forces, the base of support for more radical elements will dry up. "Jake Amsler, studied History at American Military University" **Countergency-Warfare** is the use of all elements of a nation's power—including not only combined-arms operations but also psychological, political, economic, intelligence, and diplomatic operations—to defeat an insurgency. https://www.benning. army.mil/MSSP/Counterinsurgency/

Action Company, CAC[33]. A program that combined Marines and local Vietnamese forces called Popular Forces, PFs, lived and fought together in Vietnam's villages. The official statement declared PFs to be men too old, too weak, or suffering from some disorder, preventing them from being drafted into the regular Vietnamese Army. However, I never worked with even one PF who fell into those categories. They were all of military-age and physically fit.

Every Marine desiring to serve in a CAC unit in 1966 had to first volunteer with the following prerequisites: a minimum of four months of combat experience, a recommendation from the leadership of their parent unit, and an attitude compatible with living and fighting with the Vietnamese. A CAC unit consisted of a squad of thirteen hand-picked Marines led by a sergeant E-5 or a corporal E-4, a U.S. Navy hospital corpsman, and a platoon of thirty PFs[34] led by a Vietnamese sergeant under the command of a village chief.

Counterguerrilla warfare tactics were the mainstay of CAC Operations. Think of the war in reverse, using small unit guerrilla warfare tactics to combat guerrilla warfare. Yes, we used their tactics against them to fight for village control and, most importantly, support the people who inhabited the villages. Win the people – Win the War! A must-know about the Vietnam War; the Viet Cong could not function in South Vietnam without its population's support. Let me repeat that last statement. The Viet Cong could not function in South Vietnam without its population's support.

Guerrilla warfare and insurgent warfare were not new to the U.S. Marine Corps. The so-called Banana Wars in Panama, Cuba, Veracruz, Haiti,

---

[33] **CAC, for Combined Action Company was changed to CAP**, for "Combined Action Platoons". From a purely military standpoint, the units were of platoon, not company, strength. In addition, "cac" is a Vietnamese word for the male generative organ, and the motto included the phrase "suc manh", which means strength. https://en.wikipedia.org/wiki/Search_and_destroy

[34] **The number of PFs** physically present in a Combined Action Platoon constantly varied from fifteen to twenty. Most patrols and ambushes consisted of five Marines and five PFs.

Santo Domingo, and Nicaragua, mostly taking place during the early 1900s, provided the Marine Corps with guerrilla warfare experiences later consolidated into a manual. This report, called the "Strategy and Tactics of Small Wars," written in 1921, was the foundational information for the "Small Wars Manual," written in 1935. The major challenge of implementing Counterinsurgent and Counterguerrilla Warfare was its divergence from a war of attrition, the strategy of wearing down the enemy to the point of collapse through continuous losses of personnel, equipment, and supplies. That was General Westmoreland's predominant stratagem to win the Vietnam War.

To best understand a CAC unit's mission using counterinsurgent and counterguerrilla warfare tactics, it is beneficial to read Mao Tse-Tung's words, the Chinese communist revolutionary and great spokesman for guerilla tactics. He declared that the most critical ingredient of a successful war of national liberation is the control of the people. In his words, "The people are the sea in which the partisan fish swim." He instructed that their support need not be given voluntarily to be effective. Terrorism, he proclaimed, was an effective tool to gain this vital necessity if the people are not voluntarily providing it. If the peasants didn't volunteer their cooperation, then control them with applied violence and punishment, including torture and assassination.

The CAC units' strategy was to defeat the Vietnamese Communists by living and fighting alongside the peasants, the very people the VC so desperately depended on to survive. Unlike infantry units who forced the VC out of the villages with sweep and destroy missions and then left, Combined Action Platoons didn't leave; they fought and lived in the villages.

The CAC units' primary mission was to defeat the VC at the village level by providing security for the peasants and protecting the local village leaders. Vital to our mission was the prevention of VC tax collection paid in the form of rice. We ambushed the tax agents, and whenever we discovered caches of collected rice, it was redistributed to the peasants. We also attempted to gather intelligence about enemy forces and provide our large combat bases with an early alarm system.

A Combined Action Platoon's success was directly proportional to its ability to diminish VC control of the villages with counterguerrilla warfare tactics. We killed and humiliated them in their home territory with never-ending patrols and ambushes, protected the village government's leaders, and defended the village rice harvest. We endeavored to win the peasants' confidence by making their lives more secure, providing medical services and civic action programs. The VC diligently worked to maintain or regain control of the villages by killing and humiliating us or anyone working or cooperating with a combined action platoon.

Serving as a squad leader in a Combined Action Platoon was the perfect solution to the challenge of finding an assignment where I would lead at a higher level without the supervision of officers and senior noncommissioned officers.

Many of the pivotal events that will forever change our lives occur when our timelines of existence intersect with opportunities offered by fate. I believe, "We become what we think about;" opportunity will eventually meet preparation.

I entered the complex world of counterguerrilla and counterinsurgent warfare when I became a Combined Action Platoon member. I would eventually become an expert in the application of counterguerrilla warfare tactics. However, this skill set was marginalized by my lack of comprehension of the extent to which insurgent warfare's political elements coexisted within the South Vietnamese Government's entire structure.

Why Volunteer?

So, how did I get reassigned from a squad leader in a line company to a squad leader in a Counterguerrilla Warfare unit? The short answer, I volunteered.

Sergeant Costa approaches me by walking down a dirt road that separated squad-size tents within the Phu Bai Marine Combat Base's confines. He informs me that he and I are to become members of a Combined Action Company, generally referred to as CAC. He boldly announces, "Don't worry, I've already got you accepted. All you have to do is show up tonight and interview with the captain in charge of all the CAC units." I reply, "CAC Unit! What the hell is a CAC Unit"? Costa answers, "A squad of thirteen Marines and one Corpsman who live in a village working with a platoon of Vietnamese Popular Force fighters to provide security." I asked, "Why the hell would I think it's a good idea to separate myself from a 150-man line company to live in a village with a squad of Marines and a platoon of so-called Vietnamese fighters. It sounds like a static position poorly defended with no help. Not to mention you and I don't speak Vietnamese. Think that might be a problem?" Costa replies, "No officers; squad leaders decide where the squad goes and how long it stays. We will no longer be a pin on a map where officers determine our destinies. Combined Action Marines are top-notch grunts operating in the enemy's backyard." I respond immediately, "I'm in! How do I find this captain for the interview?"

I don't know exactly what I am volunteering for, but I am eager to join a unit using counterguerrilla warfare tactics run by enlisted men. I have enormous respect for Marine officers who lead from the front and inspire those in their command by example. However, large battalion and company size operations result in platoon and squad assignments that order grunts to walk forward until they come under fire. You only survive those types of operations because fate determines that someone else gets wounded or killed before you do. Thus, the expression, "Pin on a Map." You have no control; you are the pin. By contrast, an independent squad utilizing counterguerrilla warfare tactics is all about how much you know and how well you can adapt. The bottom line, you have a considerable level of control and are no longer just a pin on a map blindly walking into enemy fields of fire.

Yes, indeed, a CAC squad is mostly without support, ambushing, and patrolling in contested areas. However, these integrated units offer an opportunity for the squad leader to function as a platoon leader. A squad of hand-picked Marines armed with enhanced firepower making its own decisions is in stark contrast to grunts' everyday life. I truly desire to lead at the next level, to determine as much as possible how, where, and when my command will fight.

Just a few hours after speaking with Sergeant Costa, I take my position in a line of Marines waiting to be interviewed by the company commander of all the Combined Action Platoons in Thua Thien Province. When my turn comes, I enter the captain's quarters, taking a seat as directed near his desk. Asked a few "Plain Jane" questions, I answer with a few "Plain Jane" replies. Not much energy from the captain, who seems to be more interested in the document he is reading. I hope it contains a favorable recommendation from my platoon commander, Lieutenant Garner. After several more minutes of our tedious exchange, he looks up and says, "Welcome aboard!" Returning to Bravo Company, I give notice of my transfer to a Combined Action Company[35].

The next afternoon I report to my new unit's headquarters and immediately attempt to locate Sergeant Costa; he is not in the area. I will never see him again. That evening I have a meal in the mess hall where I find a place to sit among several new Marine replacements. I can readily recognize them as new replacements by their crisp uniforms and healthy body weight.

Several minutes later, a Marine just back from a Force Recon operation sits down among us. You know he is a Recon Marine and freshly out of the field because he smells like Vietnam and still has camouflage paint on his face. This man eats like a hungry animal, never looking up. He devours his meal in record time and then looks across the table at a new guy's dinner. Growling like a tiger, he smashes his fork into the other Marine's steak and drags it to his plate. The Marine who lost his steak gets up and gets another one after again waiting in line. He considered

---

[35] **If you were selected** for the all-volunteer Combined Action Company your parent unit could not prevent you from leaving.

this approach much better than defending his dinner from the gentleman across the table. I think he made a wise decision.

There is nothing to do but go to sleep after leaving the mess hall. I was awakened about 0200, 2:00 a.m., and told to report with my rifle and cartridge belt to the command post. A jeep is waiting for me with a driver sitting behind the wheel, ready and eager to depart. A U.S. hand grenade had struck a Popular Force man, and we are his medical evacuation. My instructions, "Kill anyone that tries to stop the jeep between here and the village." I chamber a round in my M14 rifle and reply, "You drive, I shoot. Let's go!"

The PF was dead with many little puncture wounds from the grenade. A U.S. M26 hand grenade contains a pre-notched fragmentation coil that lies along the inside of the grenade's body producing about 1,000 small fragments when detonated. This man is mortally wounded, with most of his internal organs punctured. We nor anyone else can save this man. There is nothing to do but return to Phu Bai, leaving the dead PF to his family for burial.

The following morning, I am transported to my new home, Loc Dien Village, where dual CAC squads occupy an old French compound about a quarter-mile south of the Truoi River Bridge. A company of Marines forced the VC out of the village in anticipation of our arrival. We are soon to be alone, a CAC unit 9 miles south of the Marine Combat Base at Phu Bai.

Before going any further, a question comes to mind, what about CAC training? Surely, I will be instructed with a mission statement, some language skills, and basic knowledge about the country's religions, especially the Buddhist religion, with its many holidays and beliefs. No, none – zero instructions of any kind. Why not?

My best guess, the counterinsurgency program, as it expands, is taking a precious resource from the line companies, combat-experienced Marines. Not all the battalion commanders think highly of the Combined Action Company's attempt to win the Vietnamese people's hearts and minds. Some, maybe a majority, feel if we grab these people by the balls and squeeze, their hearts and minds will follow. However, they do see the value of an early warning of enemy buildup in Phu Bai's vicinity and the importance of protecting the bridges so vital to the main transportation route of South Vietnam, Route 1. As a result, CAC Marines find themselves caught between competing war strategies within the U.S. Marine Corps. I would have significantly benefited from an introduction to the Vietnamese language, customs, and religions, but such training for me was not to be.

The refinement of ambushes comes from experience. The downside of hands-on learning the fine details of close contact ambushes is that the learning curve comes with dead and wounded Marines and PFs. Perhaps, at this time in the war, the Marine Corps only knows how to teach the basics of an ambush, and the realities of close contact combat will have to be learned by experience. Well, we soon evolved to become ambush experts, but that transformation comes with a deadly price.

Village Market

Transferring out of Bravo Company, First Battalion, Fourth Marines to become a counterinsurgent warfare unit member creates a strong sense of adventure and an equally strong sense of insecurity. I feel as though I am on the edge of a cliff with a strong wind pushing me ever closer to the edge. Surrounded by Marines, some new to counterinsurgent warfare, and a few transferred from other CAC Villages, I am once again alone, not knowing anyone. Due to my rank of corporal, I will soon be assigned a leadership position. I need to do much better than I did in Chu Lia when I found myself with an identical leadership challenge and at first made a total mess of it.

Our new CAC Squad's sergeant begins an orientation process by providing us with topographic maps that define our tactical area of responsibility. Then, the sergeant, another corporal, and I are given a helicopter ride to observe our Village's hamlets and quickly learn how the maze of trails and rice paddy dikes are interconnected. Looking down from the low flying aircraft, I soon realize how difficult it is to transfer the mental vision of the land I created from studying the maps to observing the same ground and its features from a low flying helicopter. When we ask the pilot to fly over the same area once again so we can adjust to this observational challenge, he says, "No, too dangerous." He claims repeated flyovers will create excessive exposure to small arms fire and rocket-propelled grenades. So, the aerial orientation of our tactical area of responsibility is a great idea but not as effective as you might think.

During the first week of our arrival, several CAC members are invited to attend a Vietnamese special event at the Loc Dien Village outdoor market hosting vendors selling food and crafts. The idea is to reduce the tension caused by the Marine presence in the Village. We are instructed not to take our rifles, smile at everyone, and use some of our Vietnamese money to purchase a handicraft or anything else we think will spread goodwill.

Wow, that sounds like fun. The outdoor market is my first attempt at being an ambassador for the United States of America. It is also the first time in over seven months that I do not have my M14 rifle in my hands when I leave a secure area. It feels bizarre, but if walking through the village market without a rifle is normal for CAC Marines, I will do as instructed.

Strolling amongst the vendors displaying their wares at the market, I become genuinely interested, and the Vietnamese seem to enjoy my sincere attention. Our small group becomes separated from one another, or I become split from the group. I get so interested in the market; I don't keep up with the other Marines. When I discover that I am alone, I immediately realize the danger posed by my exposure and that I must return to our secure area as soon as possible.

Loc Dien Village Market

I begin briskly walking, selecting a trail that will surely lead away from the market and back to our compound. Now, the reality of no rifle and being by myself in an unfamiliar VC contested Vietnamese Village creates incredible stress. Especially as my selected route is not the one I think it is. Imagine how insecure I feel. It is like kayaking toward an unknown waterfall when you suddenly begin to hear the roar of falling water.

The marketplace is soon a distant memory. I approach the hamlet's outer limits and become surrounded by rice paddies as I walk on a maze of dikes. My travel route selection leads me to a different hamlet and an intersection of several additional dikes and trails. I am lost! I have no idea which one or if any travel options before me lead back to our secure area.

As I stand contemplating my choice of directions, I am soon surrounded by a group of ten or so Vietnamese villagers. They immediately realize that I am lost and in need of assistance. A loud and vigorous conversation breaks out among them. A robust-looking man approaches, attempting to grab my arm but stops when his eyes meet mine. I am not about to let him apprehend me. My tense body and deadly stare convey a readiness to fight to my death before allowing capture. More intense conversation erupts among the villagers. Now, an older man with several long whiskers protruding from his chin directs me with arm and hand movements to select the dike directly to my right. I smile, thank him, and leave immediately.

The dike leads to a trail and then directly to our compound about a mile away. I could have become a prisoner of war if it were not for the elderly gentlemen providing the desperately needed directions.

Once again, fate has decided that I will live! Several weeks later, a captured Marine with his arms tied to a bamboo pole behind his back was paraded through hamlet after hamlet and publicly beaten before he died. That might very well have been my fate had it had not been for the elderly Vietnamese man that undoubtedly saved my life.

Speaking with the sergeant in charge, I share my experience and underscore the danger of being too relaxed. I ask him to instruct the Marines serving in our CAC unit to never leave the compound without their firearms arms for any reason. He does, lesson learned, that is the first and last time any of us ever went anywhere beyond our immediate area without military arms and maintaining discipline.

I realize that we are all experiencing a steep and challenging learning curve; everything and everyone is, at first, a mystery. Our sergeant in charge is just as challenged as the rest of us. Our lives now depend on how well we can understand our environment and the villagers' social complexities. The VC comprehend everything about the people because they are the people. Our presence gives new meaning to the word foreigner as we differ from the village residents in almost every way possible. Our ultimate objective of liberating Loc Dien Village from VC control depends on the Vietnamese; we can help them, but we can't become them.

Call for Mortar Support – Fear Comprehension

My decision to volunteer to serve in a distant Vietnamese village staffed by just a squad of Marines and a platoon of Vietnamese local forces is motivated primarily by one overwhelming desire. That is to remove me from officers' and senior noncommissioned officers' direct command. After serving half a year in a line company, I desperately want more control. However, having an officer with you has some benefits I never adequately appreciated until I perform the duties usually carried out by the officer in charge.

Leading a daytime patrol, I notice some commotion about one hundred yards to our front. A group of ten or so Vietnamese men are running on a rice paddy dike leading away from Loc Dien Village, heading for a VC-controlled hamlet beyond our tactical area of responsibility. Before we can engage, we are required to see a weapon. Now we are confronted with a huge problem faced by every American who served in Vietnam, especially those operating in a CAC squad. The villagers, the VC, and the PFs all dress alike, making identification difficult. The PFs with us shout, "VC – VC," and a Marine bellows out, "I see a weapon - hell, they all got weapons." We immediately begin exchanging small arms fire with the running VC. I call for mortar support from the weapons platoon that is still temporarily assigned to our compound.

Here comes a transition of leadership. The weapons crew need map coordinates to determine the required aiming adjustments for their mortars. As the patrol leader, it falls on me to determine the correct map location to direct the fire mission. If I am wrong, I may very well kill my men and myself. Confronted with this responsibility, I wish an officer was here to provide the map coordinates. Careful what you ask for – you might get it. I called in what I determine to be the correct coordinates and request high explosive rounds. We all hunker down as we hear the very distinctive sounds of mortar rounds leaving their tubes. The requested ordinance is on its way. Where will the mortar rounds strike? Have I read the map correctly? Have I just killed us? The shells hit the dike behind the VC. I request a fire mission adjustment that adds fifty yards to the first strike and then fire for effect. The weapons crew soon sends a barrage of 81 mm mortar rounds to my determined coordinates.

No, we don't go out and check the results of our fire mission. The dike leads to a VC-controlled hamlet out of our tactical area of responsibility. Get stupid and write a check your five Marines and five PFs can't cash, and you will kill everyone in your command. The difference between counterguerrilla warfare tactics and company and battalion engagement tactics is avoiding overt and obvious offense. When infantry squads need help, they call on their platoon and company to assist them. Counterguerrilla warfare teams are primarily on their own with minimal reserves. CAC units can't deploy air and artillery support in populated areas most of the time because collateral damage defeats the entire strategy of winning the local population's hearts and minds.

Our brief fight does gain us respect from the villagers who have been under VC domination for years. The tough guys who have been demanding that the villagers support them with food, labor, and conscripts are looking weak and very beatable as they run from the hamlet they once controlled. Our job is to bloody the noses of the VC every time we cross paths. Running the VC out of the village is an excellent first step. I performed well.

Fear Comprehension

I am about to share a different type of transition that is embarrassing and difficult to reveal.

One week before the Marines supporting our two CAC squads departs, my squad is assigned a night ambush in Loc Dien Village. We prepare ourselves to leave the compound by checking one another for anything that will make unwanted noise. In this death game, the hunter often becomes the hunted as this blood sport is played with automatic rifles and grenades.

The night is dark and cold with a gusty wind, unusual for late spring in Vietnam. A Marine from the line company on perimeter watch adjacent to our exit point from the compound tells us how thankful he is not going with us. He whispers, "Man, you guys are walking into the mouth of the lion. Quite frankly, I'm scared shitless on this side of the wall!"

The Marine on watch infects every one of us by saying what we are all feeling. This "Shit is Scary!" You do not become a counterguerrilla warfare Marine overnight. Eventually, you develop a new reference point, but that adjustment requires exposure and real-time experience. It doesn't happen all at once. This night, my squad of Marines and PFs are unstable, and I can feel it.

How do I respond to my squad's insecurity? I lead them only one-quarter of the way to the assigned ambush site and set up a defensive position because I feel fear. Was it their fear, or was it my fear that convinced me to change the squad's mission from offense to defense? I made a huge mistake, and I am still troubled by it today. I should have provided an example of professional leadership by advancing to the ambush site and channeling our distributed fear into operational proficiency. I did not perform well that night. I neglected to provide leadership. I failed those men, and the next day two of them told me to what extent they were disappointed.

My lack of leadership motivated me further to discover the raw reality of fear. A more profound comprehension of fear allows me to control my anxiety and eventually comprehend fear well enough to use it as a weapon against the enemy. Fear in combat is unavoidable. However, managing and understanding its emotional power is an incredible leadership tool.

I promised myself that I would never perform so poorly again. Once again, I stop praying for my life to be spared and ask God to please allow me to die fighting and not die a coward. This lack of fortitude and judgment can never happen again, and it never did!

As a Marine leader in combat, I don't have the privilege of personal considerations, neglecting my command's responsibilities. Therefore, I begin an in-depth exploration of fear that challenges and serves me for the rest of my life. I have often spoken of fear in my writings, and I will continue to as we proceed. War is many things, often different for those who are experiencing the same situation. However, everyone who has known war has, known fear.

Water Buffalo – Dead Marine

The commanding sergeant of the dual CAC team serving in Loc Diem's village leads a daytime patrol through the surrounding rice paddies. Our mission on this beautiful day is to learn the maze of trails and the connecting rice paddy dikes that provide the only solid ground for walking in late June. The dikes are confusing in the light of day, but they are extremely difficult to navigate at night, especially in low-hanging fog. We need to learn alternate routes to prevent the creation of a predictable schedule inviting an enemy ambush.

My position in the patrol is about two-thirds to the column's rear as we walk one man behind the other, separated by several yards. The surrounding paddies are under several inches of water; the earth below is a deep, leg-sucking, muddy muck.

A water buffalo off to our right front stands in the paddies staring at our patrol as we walk by. These animals are enormous, standing five to six feet tall and weighing anywhere from 1,500 to 2,600 pounds at maturity. Due to their vast height and weight, they are ideal for working the rice paddies' deep muck aided by their large hooves and flexible foot joints. Small Vietnamese children routinely guide the animals by gently pulling on a large ring inserted into the buffalo's nose.

Water Buffalo become aggressive in the presence of
meat-eating Americans.

Water buffalo don't like Americans; our scent is different because of
the large amount of meat in our diets. One thing for sure, our presence
upsets them. As we approach, the buffalo begins to snort and paw the
paddy muck with his front feet before it charges the Marines walking to
the front of our column.

From my position towards the rear of the column, I can see none of
this—the roar of four or five M14 rifles firing in fully automatic mode
shatter the day. I direct the Marines behind me and directly to my front
to jump into the rice paddy, form a frontal assault line, and run to the
point of contact to enter the fight.

We find at the front of the patrol a dead water buffalo and a seriously
wounded Marine. When the buffalo charged, the Marines had no choice

but to kill the animal. You can't outrun a water buffalo, especially in a flooded rice paddy. One of the fired bullets has ricocheted off the dike's hard surface and struck the fallen Marine in his eye before entering his brain.

The corpsman immediately begins a series of chest compressions and mouth-to-mouth resuscitation as several bamboo poles are fetched from the rice paddy and fashioned into a crude stretcher. Then, after only a few yards of transport, the stretcher breaks, the wounded man crashes to the ground, where he continues to breathe for a few moments before he dies.

Witnessing the last breath of a strapping young man in the prime of his life is emotionally challenging. The dead cannot be reborn.

We set up a perimeter facing out in all directions to resist anyone who will take advantage of our situation. Yes, the VC will be delighted to attack if they find us in disarray. There is no time for grief or personal reflection, not now; stay strong; things can get a lot worse. The dead Marine is transported to our compound by a military vehicle called a mule[36].

We know that one member of our squad who was in the path of the charging buffalo fired the bullet that ricocheted off the trail. We are all perfectly at peace, not knowing or wanting to know precisely which one of us fired the killing round.

To our amazement and disappointment, the Marine Corps' legal department sees this accidental loss of life differently. To protect the Marine who did fire the fateful round, he must be identified and found innocent of murder. A team of military investigators accompanied by a security team arrives at our compound to determine precisely what happened and who fired the killing round.

---

[36] **Mule** - The U.S. Military M274 Truck, Platform, Utility, 1/2 Ton, 4X4 or "Carrier, Light Weapons, Infantry, 1/2 ton, 4x4", also known as the "Mule", "Military Mule", or "Mechanical Mule", is a 4-wheel drive, gasoline-powered truck/tractor type vehicle that can carry up to 1/2 tons off-road. It was introduced in 1956 and used until the 1980s. U.S. Military M274 Truck, Platform, Utility 1/2 Ton, 4X4 | Military Wiki | Fandom (wikia.org)

First, we all must provide a statement during a one-on-one interview with a Judge Advocate General Marine, JAG[37], Officer. When I report that I directed my section of the column to jump into the rice paddies and charge the point of contact, the officer's jaw drops. This Marine lives in a different world, the legal world of JAG personnel.

I explained that if we had been attacked and took cover in our present location, we would have been destroyed trying to fight the enemy from his predetermined bullseye. The only way to survive was to close with the attacker, grab him by the belt buckle, and remove his range of fire by closing the distance between him and us. Get off the bullseye.

When you come under fire at close range, this response is called immediate action and must be taught because it directly opposes the natural desire to get down immediately where you are standing. It only works for close contact, but close-up contact is the norm for counterguerrilla warfare.

Following individual statements provided to the JAG officers, the Marines who fired at the buffalo are escorted by a security team to the accident's location and slowly reenacted their every move.

The detailed investigation produces the answer revealing which of us killed our fellow Marine. I still don't know how that was determined, but I wasn't privy to the depositions or the reenactment.

The result of establishing blame is devastating for the Marine responsible for the fateful round. The young man who died was his close friend, and they are both in the closing month of their thirteenth-month tours. He is visibly dispirited and never recovers from a deep state of depression before rotating back to the states.

For me, losing a Marine to friendly fire is more emotionally draining than losing one to hostile fire. After Sergeant Jefferson was killed in Chu Lia, I swore I would never again allow myself to become too close to anyone.

---

[37] Judge Advocate General's Corps, also known as JAG or JAG Corps, refers to the legal branch or specialty of a military concerned with military justice and military law. Officers serving in a JAG Corps are typically called Judge Advocates. https://jag.fandom.com/wiki/Judge_Advocate_General%27s_Corps

You only have so many times that you can sustain that emotional fragility and sadness before you begin making poor decisions.

I mentally shift gears concerning emotional swings and their unavoidable weaknesses to gain the stability I need as a leader. I teach myself to be a bit distant, not allowing anyone to get too close. I have, to this day, been unable to unshift those emotional gears. I have been a bit of a loner ever since. I enjoy the company of others, but no one gets beyond an emotional boundary with me. When I returned from Vietnam, I had to work hard, especially with my wife and baby daughter, to allow them to enter my emotional fortress.

Some experiences that a young man in combat will encounter will make him strong and mature. Others will have to be tolerated and managed because they are of little use or downright dangerous in a nonmilitary, peaceful society.

Promotion – Critical Analysis

The sergeant in charge of our dual squad CAC platoon will soon rotate back to the states. He selects me to replace him until a sergeant E-5 is available for the assignment. The number of Marines serving in the dual CAC unit and its distant location mandates that a sergeant be in command. I am now a corporal E-4 with a three-month suspended bust on my record. Not exactly a glowing or competitive resume on paper. However, promotions during the Vietnam War were based chiefly on performance rather than a perfect record regarding disciplinary actions.

My new assignment created an additional level of challenge, the responsibility of total unit command. First comes the planning of patrol routes and the selection of ambush sites. Then, perimeter defense 24/7 and village leadership coordination. Our unit's success depends on how well we coordinate our efforts with the village chief, the village elders, and the sergeant of the PFs. I am encouraged to earn the Vietnamese people's respect and confidence by studying every aspect of their lives.

I soon become aware of how three competing governments manipulate the peasant's lives. Why all this Vietnamese outreach? It is just this simple; "Win the people-Win the war!"

I previously complained about becoming a CAC unit member with no instruction of the Vietnamese language or the customs and religions that dominate village life. Well, the time spent with the sergeant is as close as I will come to a formal school[38]. What he knows about commanding a Combined Action Platoon he shares by verbal instruction and example. However, what he doesn't know or cares not to share is left for me to learn independently.

I select patrol and ambush sites for both squads, attempting to keep a Marine presence in all the village's hamlets. I mix up travel routes, times of departures, and duration times to not create a routine. I help coordinate a laundry service staffed by a family living just outside our compound who wash our clothes-each man paying when he receives his cleaned trousers and shirts. The laundry service goes a long way to create a positive relationship with the villagers. The money we pay for our laundry circulates throughout the entire village as payment for all sorts of goods and services.

The water buffalo killed after attacking our patrol was immediately butchered and eaten[39] by the villagers. The family who owned the animal received full payment from the U.S. government. That gesture showed how we treated accidental Vietnamese losses for which we were responsible. It demonstrated the considerable contrast between

---

[38] **CAC School;** The earliest CAP-specific training was non-existent to rudimentary at best, but it soon became somewhat more formalized, with Marine volunteers being trained in the Combined Action School at Da Nang. Classes included re-familiarization with military topics including weapons (both US and VC / NVA), land navigation, scouting and patrolling, but also classes in Vietnamese language, culture, and history in an attempt to give the Marines some insight into their hosts' culture. The classes were taught mainly by Marines, but some (such as Vietnamese language) were taught by Vietnamese personnel. USMC CAC Oscar - Combined Action Program History (google.com)

[39] **Red meat -** was basically absent from the local diet and considered a rare treat.

us and the VC. Every culture has a sense of fair and just treatment, and every culture knows when that sense of fair and appropriate treatment is violated.

Shortly after assuming my new leadership assignment, we receive information from the locals about the approximate schedule of an upcoming VC-mandated propaganda lecture to be held in the village schoolhouse. The leadership in North Vietnam instituted a South Vietnam program that used teaching teams to explain the communist doctrine and motivate South Vietnam residents to meet the needs of the north's combat forces who would liberate their country.

In my opinion, during my tour in Vietnam, the success of communist influence at the village level was never understood or respected by U.S. forces. The North Vietnamese built an entire resistance to foreign control of their country by brainwashing the local population with communist propaganda lectures and applied violence. Yes, our counterguerrilla operations are productive in fighting the VC for physical presence in the village. However, due to our inability to speak Vietnamese fluently and our limited knowledge of Vietnamese history and culture, we can't comprehend the propaganda teams' immense influence and their use of embedded communist agents in every village.

Suspecting that the propaganda team will arrive the night before their scheduled presentation, I plan an ambush to intercept them at what I believe to be their most likely point of entry. When I share the plan's details with the sergeant in charge of both CAC squads, he congratulates me before making only one change. I planned to lead the ambush personally. Instead, he says, "No way. You are now the leader of the entire two squad CAC unit, not just the leader of one ambush. Everyone depends on you to command every aspect of our deployment here. You have two squads to carry out the ambushes and patrols; start thinking more at the command level and less at the execution level." I objected. I was overruled.

The corporal who receives my orders to conduct the ambush determines how he will deploy his squad's firepower at the assigned ambush site. My orders tell him where to go and how long to stay. All other decisions are his to make. The duration of the ambush is all night ending just before daybreak.

The ambush's long duration increases the probability of enemy contact but requires two men to a position, one sleeping while the other is on watch. While the standard for line company ambushes, this alternation of watch and sleep seriously reduces offensive efficiency, half the available firepower is asleep and wakes up to a firefight.

The night of the ambush, a team of Marines and PFs slowly and silently maneuver their way to the assigned destination and set up in two-man positions. The ambush site provides little concealing cover, but the absence of moonlight and wind favors the attackers.

Hours later, several VC walk directly into the zone of intended fire. At the lead position, a PF fires his Thompson 45 caliber submachine gun directly into the legs and lower abdomen of a VC, who promptly falls. The VC is wounded but full of fight and immediately throws a grenade, killing a Marine. Shortly after that, another PF is wounded by VC small arms fire.

The corpsman assigned to the ambush wakes up to all hell breaking out to hear a Vietnamese man pleading for help. He responds in the dark, providing morphine to the wounded individual, not realizing his patient is the VC who killed the Marine. At daybreak, everyone recognizes who the corpsman has treated. He soon succumbs to his wounds, leaving the results of the ambush one dead VC, one dead Marine, and one wounded PF. The dead Marine and injured PF are evacuated to a field hospital, and the dead VC is brought back to the compound.

Later that morning, a major, not our company commander, arrives and holds a critique of the entire situation. He dismounts from his jeep and walks directly over to us as we gathered around the dead VC lying at our feet. He immediately asks, "Who was in charge of the ambush"? When the corporal who had command began to speak, the major interrupted and handed him a short stick and told him to draw a representation in the dirt of how he had deployed his men and weapons. After showing exactly how he positioned his squad's firepower, the major asks a riveting question.

"What are the results of your ambush"? The corporal answers, "One dead Marine, one wounded PF, and one dead VC." Now addressing all of us, the major asks, "Are you satisfied with the results"? Not waiting for an answer, he immediately returns to his jeep and is driven away. We are left to look at one another and the dirt drawing.

The officer offered no advice, nor did he criticize the tactics used. However, he did leave us with the vital task of evaluating and performing a critical analysis of every aspect of the ambush. Learning "The Art of Critical Analysis" is essential to my transition to becoming a leader of Marines in combat. The ability to correctly analyze what happened during a mission not hindered by politics, bias or personal gain enables change. The ability to accurately perform such an analysis of a present or past situation is a talent of immense importance! Those who learned "The Art of Critical Analysis" could use that talent for the rest of their lives.

This ambush yielded valuable lessons. First, all future ambushes planned or led by me will not have two men alternating sleep and watch. Shorter duration ambushes with everyone awake and alert is far more effective. Second, ambushes require maximum deadly force to be delivered, and that force must continue without pause to prevent the enemy from recovering and counterattacking. Third, the attackers must move through the kill zone, firing their weapons, never letting up on the pressure. A wounded enemy a few yards away is our worst nightmare.

We now realize how critical it is to shoot our weapons accurately at night to deliver a wound that kills immediately. Striking your opponent with bullets on both sides of his chest, especially from an M14 rifle or a 45-caliber submachine gun, will provide the desired results. Looking over the sights of a rifle at night will cause you to shoot high. Too long, a burst from an M14 firing fully automatic will cause the rounds to climb up and away from the point of aim. Wounding the enemy at close range will undoubtedly lead to casualties on your side. Getting to the ambush site and deploying your people to deliver maximum fire on the enemy is what we learned in Marine infantry training. However, what happens immediately after the first fired round defines who lives and who dies.

I determine that I will not allow my position as the overall leader to prevent me from going on operations, especially if I planned an ambush with a high degree of enemy contact. When the sergeant rotated back to the states, and I was totally in charge, I put myself back into the rotation of ambushes and patrols. That leadership adjustment provides an opportunity for the other corporals to take a turn in assuming the responsibilities of unit command. This decision is prudent, as it builds depth at all command positions and further creates confidence in the command structure from bottom to top and top to bottom. The closer you are to the enemy, the better you will lead!

I further learned the incredible value of "Critical Analysis" by searching only for truth, entering the world of action and reaction, accepting the conclusions provided by critical thinking no matter how painful or humiliating that reality may be. As a result, I begin seeing and comprehending the world as it is, not as I wished it were.

I have come to realize an inescapable fact; leaders, especially in combat, are always directly or indirectly responsible for the success or failure of their command. When Marines die following your orders, a piece of you dies as well.

Time to Train – Time to Refine

Motivated by the unfortunate outcomes of a recent ambush and the major's question, "Are you satisfied with the results"? We immediately begin as a unit to study and improve every aspect of our performance. Small counterguerrilla warfare units working independently in VC contested Vietnam villages must perform as a highly efficient team.

There is much to learn and perfect. Our lives depend on our development of close contact combat skills. Most important is to learn what to do when the shooting starts. How do we win an up-close firefight without taking casualties? We define and then create solutions and procedures in answer to a host of questions.

We teach ourselves to move silently at night and let the wind and ambient light determine how often we stop and listen. When we pause, every other Marine and PF in the column looks in alternate directions for signs of movement or sound uncommon to the environment. Again moving, the Marine looking to the rear of our patrol is quietly notified. Experience provides the answer of how and who will walk the point[40] position of a patrol. As a unit, we learn to step in and through water without making noise and how to release a foot stuck in rice paddy muck and not create that sucking sound as air and water enter below a rising boot. We practice how to react to an attack from different types of cover at various distances by creating immediate action drills. From now on, the PFs will wait for a Marine to initiate our ambushes. Determining when to fire our weapons is just as important as how well we place rounds into the enemy's heart, lungs, or brain to prevent a close encounter counterattack from a slowing dying combatant. To determine where to position automatic rifles and claymore mines, we envision how we would naturally respond and take cover under fire if attacked by our ambush. Experience demonstrates that the element of surprise, overwhelming pressure, and instilling fear in the enemy are the foundational elements of a successful ambush. The accurate application of controlled, relentless, and unforgiving violence prevents friendly casualties.

Every CAC Marine is taught how to safely place claymore mines to avoid injury from their back blasts, or heaven forbid, the devastation that will result from positioning them backward. We practice the application of firepower aggression while maintaining firepower discipline. We hold after-mission discussions to improve how and when to engage or not engage the enemy when confronted with an unanticipated situation. If overpowered by a more significant force, we consider how to protect a wounded Marine. We discuss how to control fear within ourselves and

---

[40] **Point** - The point position of a patrol as the name implies was the most forward position and thus the most dangerous. We rotated this position among the Marines, often running a dual point shared by a Marine and PF. The PFs also rotated the point position among their men. This system of rotation allowed everyone to learn the skills and responsibilities of the point position and distributed its inherent danger.

how to maximize the enemy's fear. Everyone is made aware of how important it is to avoid killing or wounding the villagers. We train how to use the assortment of weapons available to us effectively. Under what conditions are an M 79 rocket-propelled grenade launcher effective, and under what conditions is it effectively useless?

Just as we study the enemy and perfect our performance, the enemy analyses us perfecting their performance. Like the first quarter of a football game or the first few rounds of a professional boxing match, one opponent learning the other's strengths and weaknesses. It is inevitable; they are discovering how and where we patrol and ambush. I suspect they receive information from some of the villagers and PFs working with us. I realize this is a civil war and many families have members on competing sides. Everything becomes more complicated as we learn one another's abilities. Our world is one of counterguerrilla warfare, a deadly contest between opposing sides fighting for control of the people who inhabit this troubled land.

Gesture of Appreciation

Our relationship with the villagers becomes closer when the company of Marines with its attached mortar support leaves the village of Loc Dien. The locals can then see our vulnerability in manpower and exposure. However, they seem to appreciate our presence even more. As a gesture of appreciation, the village chief, with the village elders' blessing, shows respect for our two dead Marines and the wounded PF by inviting us to a banquet.

This culinary gesture purported to be comparable to Thanksgiving dinner is a bit different. Imagine the disappointment of fantasizing about turkey, with all the trimmings, to sit down to a banquet of rice and rice only. The selection before us consists of seven large dishes of rice, each prepared differently. The PFs are delighted and select heartily from each serving plate. We, of course, do the same and show sincere gratitude for the festive meal. The rice wine they serve is extraordinarily potent; its fumes will burst into flames if exposed to a lit match.

Fate

Fate is an unavoidable subject of contemplation for everyone who has experienced combat. So it is natural to ponder the mystery of how some combatants repeatedly escape injury while others seem to have the misfortune to be in the wrong place at the wrong time through no fault of their own. Lance Corporal Briar is a perfect example of a man chosen by fate, time after time, to survive when the same exposure kills or wounds others.

One of our squads proceeding to an ambush site in the village of Loc Dien is attacked with a burst of AK 47 automatic rifle fire. Lance Corporal Briar, the Marine walking point, is hit, but the bullets don't enter his body. Instead, the fired rounds strike several ammo pouches that each hold a magazine containing eighteen 7.62 mm caliber rounds[41]. Every other bullet in the magazine is a tracer that has a small pyrotechnic charge in its base. The energy from the received bullets striking the tracers causes multiple explosions within several of Briar's magazines. Reasonably, Lance Corporal Briar should be seriously wounded or killed. But, to everyone's amazement, he escapes all injuries. His body is fine. However, his mental state is in high gear, but he soon regains complete composure.

The next time Lance Corporal Briar rotates to the point position, leading a night patrol, his squad is again attacked. That assault begins with a thrown concussion grenade that lands at Briar's feet. The explosion throws him onto his back. Briar is now suffering from a concussion – completely dizzy and unable to participate in the firefight surrounding him. The next day, Briar is given a day of rest as he was suffering from a headache. Otherwise, he is ok.

As if all this is not enough to prove that some men are mysteriously protected, I discover that Lance Corporal Briar had been shot before his

---

[41] **Magazine Capacity** - The M 14 rifle magazine holds 20 rounds of ammunition but were normally loaded with 18 rounds to make sure the spring at the bottom of the magazine would not become over compressed and would push the rounds to the top of magazine to be chambered during automatic rifle fire.

present assignment, receiving a flesh wound to his left thigh. He spent a couple of weeks aboard a U.S. Navy hospital ship positioned just off the coast of Vietnam and then returned to duty.

No one, especially Briar, knows why he is selected to survive multiple catastrophic events. However, his squad removes him from the rotation to the point position. Call it superstition or an obvious fact; when this Marine walks point, all hell breaks out.

PFs Refuse the Ambush Site

The Vietnamese sergeant of our Popular Force platoon, the Trung Si, receives information that the Viet Cong are about to hold a mandatory propaganda session at the village schoolhouse. To prevent VC retaliation, information about the Viet Cong rarely comes from one identifiable source. However, our Popular Force sergeant, who boldly shares his discovery, is unafraid of reprisal. He is committed to the South Vietnamese Government and protects his village with genuine passion and disdain for the VC and their leaders in the North.

We realize our CAC platoon must prevent the scheduled propaganda meeting from occurring. The question before us is how to do it? Somehow, we need to thwart the compulsory brainwashing session without endangering the villagers. In addition to the apparent fact, the VC require the schoolhouse to hold their meeting; we also realize they may know we know of their intentions. Typically, the propaganda sessions are held after the day's work, taking place in the late afternoon and ending well before dark. To avoid our attempt to disrupt the meeting, we predict that they will change the standard starting time by beginning early in the morning. Based on our best guesstimate, I put together a plan to ambush the VC propaganda team.

The night before the scheduled meeting, I plan a diversionary ambush that leaves the compound shortly after dark and returns well after midnight. Just as the returning team enters the compound, the main ambush intended to disrupt the meeting leaves. The duplicity is designed to confuse anyone reporting to the VC the departure and return times of our nightly ambushes.

I realize that if some of the villagers and PFs provide us with information about the VC, others provide information about us to the VC.

We proceed with great caution en route to the ambush site, often stopping to listen, and then silently advance with two men walking point, one Marine and one PF. Approaching our destination, the point PF stops and refuses to continue. He is afraid, and worse yet, he begins to speak to another PF as they huddled together. Their fear is contaminating the entire team. Leaving my position in the middle of the column, I approach the point position and quietly ask, "What's going on"? The Marine sharing the point position shrugs his shoulders to say, "I have no idea."

The problem is fear of what might happen, not fear of what is happening. This fear is contagious, especially among the PFs. Remembering my utter failure, the last time I led an ambush team suffering from pervasive fear and how poorly I had reacted, I will not allow that lack of leadership to occur again.

To resolve the situation, I grab the PF assigned to the point position by the collar and pull him forward. Now, he and I are the double point as we proceed to the ambush site. His fear may have been motivated by the fact that our ambush location is close to where a PF was recently wounded and a Marine killed. I deploy our team at an intersection of a trail and a rice paddy dike that provide access to the schoolhouse from two directions. The junction creates probable enemy approaches into our intended fields of fire but gives inadequate concealment to us. We will have to depend on the darkness of the night and our absolute silence to prevent being prematurely discovered by an approaching enemy.

After positioning the ambush team to create a kill zone covering the intersection of the rice paddy dike and the walking trail, I deploy Claymore mines to discharge directly in line with both sides of the rice paddy dike and the far side of the trail. When the enemy comes under fire, I predict that anyone not hit will take cover along the low natural terrain adjacent to the trail, and paddy dike, effectively lining themselves up in a row. The blast from the Claymores will decimate that alignment with a secondary strike.

One Marine and one PF cover our rear exposure in case of the awful possibility the VC are already in the village and will attack us from the rear. Sitting quietly in the dark, I feel the team regaining composure as we wait with our rifle safeties off and with the Claymore mines' firing devices in easy reach. We stay at the ready for five hours, hoping to intercept the propaganda team.

At first light, many villagers uncharacteristically show up to attend the meeting we have prevented. Big success! We stopped the VC mind-altering pep rally scheduled to take place as predicted. I suspect our ambush had been discovered either by the villagers sympathetic to the VC or detected by the advancing VC themselves. That night we gained confidence with the villagers and our PFs, who are now proud of themselves.

How impactful we were to the villagers by preventing the propaganda meeting is made clear to me when invited to have dinner with the family that performed our laundry service. No security risk, their home is practically in our compound. To my surprise, they report just about everything that happened the night of the ambush. The entire family is favorably impressed when somehow, they learn that the PFs who refused to proceed to the ambush site were convinced to change their minds and later performed well. They could have only known the details of our ambush from the PFs reporting their view of that night's events.

Dinner with the family consists of rice mixed with a bit of fish. The beverage consumed at the end of the meal is room temperature tea made with unprocessed river water. After everyone finished the main course – I alone am presented a small green leaf beautifully wrapped around a prize inside. I unwrap the leaf as instructed, exposing a one-inch square, jelly-like object covered with white sugar powder. Everyone looks delighted and urges me to eat the offered treat. Of course, I do, thinking for sure it is candy. I am wrong. When I crush the dessert with my teeth, it explodes in my mouth, unleashing a foul-tasting bitter fluid. I swallow as fast as possible to prevent the natural impulse of spitting it out, hoping I will not vomit immediately. I inquire as best I can to determine what I have just eaten. They reply with great delight, "Buffalo Eye!" Have I eaten the eye of a buffalo, or is it simply the name given to their desert? I will never know, but I can report with certainty that I got sick, extremely sick—my second case of dysentery.

I am beginning to understand the Vietnamese people as never before. Serving in a line company for over six months, I became annoyed with their lack of patriotism and poor battlefield performance. I felt little or no empathy for their suffering. My attitude changed after being entangled in their everyday lives, living with them in their villages, fighting with them, attempting to learn their language, and sometimes hearing the screams of a mother delivering a baby while lying on a wooden bed. Those experiences bring to light the Vietnamese people's humanity, and in my opinion, their God-given right to live and prosper in peace.

I discover that only a thin line separates my inherent human capacity for violence from my innate human capacity for compassion.

Shotgun – Visiting Correspondents

The armory at the Marine Combat Base in Phu Bai sent us an effective close contact weapon. A full choke, 12 gauge, Remington 870 pump shotgun holding five rounds of military 00 buckshot. This weapon is lethal at close range, and close range, twenty-five yards or less, is standard for counterguerrilla ambushes in Vietnam. A VC shot in the face demonstrated the shotgun's ability to destroy human flesh.

However, the weapon has several major problems. When you shoot the shotgun at night, it gives away your position by illuminating you with a bright ball of fire, leaving its muzzle. You might as well put a flashing bullseye on your forehead in the middle of a firefight. We discover the shotgun has other problems, poor safety mechanism, plus a hair-trigger. Now that's a bad combination. The safety mechanism is a mechanical device designed to prevent unwanted firearm discharges by restricting trigger movement. A hair-trigger will discharge a firearm with only the slightest pressure applied to it.

Sitting in a chair in the sergeant's quarters of our compound, I inadvertently strike the cement floor with the butt of the shotgun; it discharges, sending nine pellets of 00 buckshot through the tin roof, creating a torn and fragmented hole. We sent the 12 gauge back to Phu Bai requesting that the armory add a flash suppressor and address the trigger and safety sensitivities.

To impress guests that occasionally visit our compound, we hung Lance Corporal Briar's cartridge belt with its mangled magazine pouches from the ceiling. Yeah, we hung it adjacent to the fragmented hole created by the accidental discharge of the 12-gauge shotgun. Our display hugely impresses a team of reporters who visit. You can readily see by the facial expressions they are confused or downright in disbelief that one of our Marines was wearing the cartridge belt when attacked with a burst of bullets from an AK 47 rifle. To add to their lack of confidence in our report, we share that the Marine wearing the cartridge belt was unharmed.

The visiting correspondents who make their living reporting and writing about the war are invited to accompany us on an ambush that evening. After declining our invitation, they leave our compound that afternoon, well before dark. I doubt they submitted a story to their publications about Corporal Briar's incredible tale of fate. That's okay; we didn't write a story about them either.

The weight of leadership

Leaders make decisions; others follow. Most everyone accepts that statement, but few of us understand how onerous those decisions can be on the leaders making them. Leadership decisions made in combat will inspire you or haunt you for the rest of your life. The transitions of young men will come to a sudden halt if their leader makes poor decisions. Marines in your command will immediately follow your orders.

One of our squads during an after-mission debriefing provided a perfect example of the weight of leadership decisions. After leading a night ambush, a corporal shared how he was confronted with a decision to attack aggressively or remain silent, letting the enemy walk by.

The corporal deployed his squad at the edge of a hamlet under cover of trees and brush adjacent to a trail bordering a massive expanse of rice paddies. The trail is wide and well used. Five Marines and five PFs spaced about three yards apart cover a kill zone to their front approximately thirty yards wide. When the enemy walks in front of their firepower, they will attack at close range.

About 0200 hours, 2:00 am, the ambush team hears a great deal of talking and sees the lights of cigarettes as VC and North Vietnamese troops walk directly into their preplanned kill zone. The leadership question is when to initiate the ambush? When should the corporal in charge command his team to begin the attack? This level of detail was never mentioned during Marine infantry training. The squad leader has the enemy exactly where he wants them, right in front of the ambush's total firepower. Is it time to start shooting? No, not exactly! The squad is deployed to ambush a small group of three to six tax agents.

Yes, they have the enemy exactly in their kill zone, but they also have another one hundred or so behind them. Suppose a small unit attacks a large column walking one behind another. In that case, the ambush must be designed and deployed to strike a long column, hit it hard with a primary attack followed by a secondary attack, focused on where the enemy will immediately take cover, and then disengage. Get the hell out of there before you get flanked by the column of troops, not under fire. Flanking actions attack the edge of a formation where it has limited ability to defend itself. The tactic of rolling up your enemy's flank has been around for thousands of years; think biblical times.

What did the leader do? What were his orders? He gave no orders of any kind. The ambush team sat motionless, not making a sound, and let that one-hundred-plus enemy unit walk by at ten to fifteen yards. Good decision, yes! One cough, or one sound of any kind, would have given away their position, resulting in certain death for the entire CAC team.

Welcome to the world of counterguerrilla warfare, where the enemy is often the dominant force. What was needed that night was an artillery strike or airstrike to be called on the long column after they left the village. However, the Marines are too far away for artillery support, and air support was not immediately available to CAC units in 1966. So we were on our own, just five Marines and five PFs. The war in reverse.

Back at the compound, the corporal's after mission debriefing educated us all as we imagined the challenge of having so many men that want to kill you walk in front of you, just a few yards away. The enemy's route, time of movement, and travel direction were reported to Phu Bai's leadership. If VC and North Vietnamese troops used this route regularly, we could arrange for them to be attacked by Huey helicopters armed with high capacity rapid-fire machine guns. We tried multiple times to intercept this large force ourselves by returning to the discovered travel route to strike them. Expecting to engage a large force, we planned the ambush to attack a long column, using the tactic of maximum violence applied for a short period, followed by a secondary strike, both using many claymore mines. Using classic guerrilla warfare tactics, we planned to disengage after hitting them twice and then melt into the darkness of the night. The challenge was not knowing when or if they would ever use that route again. Indeed, there was no set schedule for us to take advantage of, and we never did catch an enemy force of that size, not during my command of the unit.

Report of a PF being forcibly choked

Our dual CAC squad receives a surprise visit from a headquarters team comprised of several officers and an excellent interpreter. They speak with most of the team and many of the PFs working with us. Essentially, this is an evaluation of our progress to measure how effective we are in pacifying the former VC-controlled village. After interviewing our CAC team, they request we take them for a walk in the nearby hamlet. They often stop to speak with anyone they can engage in conversation. I suspect that this is a hands-on inspection to study the effectiveness of the "Win the Hearts and Minds of the Vietnamese People" program.

The villagers' response was better than I anticipated, judging by facial expressions and the interpreter's reports. The headquarters team seems pleased.

That is until we are just about to return to the compound when a PF reports to one of the officers that I forcibly choked him on an ambush. The officer is outraged and immediately asks me if I choked the PF as described? I report, "Yes, he was asleep on an ambush when he was supposed to be awake. That lack of discipline can and will result in other members of the team, including him, getting killed." The officer declared the PFs were to be treated in the same manner as all the Marines in my command. I reply, "Yes, Sir, I agree."

One of the Marines in the area, but far enough away to hear none of our conversations, is called over. I ask him the following question, "When you fell asleep on an ambush last month, how did I wake you"? He answered immediately, "I woke up with you choking me." The officer told the interpreter to explain to the complaining PF that everyone receives equal treatment.

I have accepted the responsibility of commanding the entire two-squad CAC team conducting counterguerrilla warfare operations with a platoon of PFs. The demands of my new leadership position require me to make decisions about death. My youth and carefree attitude are gone, never to return as I obtain an unnatural maturity level for a young man, just twenty-one years old. I am not here to make friends; my mission is to provide security for Loc Dien Village and kill as many VC as possible by leading, motivating, and educating the men under my command. My promise to myself is to get as many of these Marines home to their families as possible. I can't control everything – men sleeping on watch, I could manage, and I did!

Leadership Dilemma Who's Who

Leadership decisions in combat, knowing what to do, when to do it, and acting upon that knowledge will often determine who lives and who dies. In my opinion, great leaders are born with a natural ability to lead.

However, even born leaders need to be trained not to make historical mistakes. I believe the best leadership training stands on a foundation of leadership education, example, and experience. Teaching someone to lead who is not a natural leader is extremely difficult. What you learn from instruction and example provides leadership tools but does not ensure effective leadership decisions. You can't successfully train leadership by only having potential leaders read books and observe quality leadership examples. The ability to accurately comprehend the consequences of past, present, and future decisions is a gift denied to many aspiring leaders.

Knowing what to do is only half the required skill set. The ability to inspire those in your command to follow you because you earned their respect is equally important. I believe the ability to lead must be in your blood, a component of your genetic inheritance.

The pervasive insurgent influence waged by the VC, the political component of the war, created standing agreements with many of the village chiefs and peasants that define the treatment of one another's families, the amount of rice tax paid to the VC, and God knows what else. The language barrier, Vietnamese political customs, religion, and traditions all make the Vietnam War's political component just about impossible for us Marines. At a bare minimum, we know the VC strongly influence the Popular Force working with us. We can never totally trust the Vietnamese we work with until they prove themselves in a firefight.

An ever-present problem in a Combined Action Platoon is identifying the enemy during daylight hours. A curfew goes into effect at night. Anyone out and about is considered the enemy and becomes an unrestricted target. During the day, determining who is a friend and who is a foe is not so straightforward. The VC, PFs, and local villagers all dress the same. You are often dependent during daylight hours on your PFs to tell you who are enemies and who are not. Some of the PFs are connected on both sides of the conflict that divides their country, causing us never to trust them. Many Vietnamese hamlets often contain parents' homes with sons and daughters on opposing sides.

My squad, during a daylight patrol, experienced the identification dilemma. The hamlets' trails are mostly crowned with tree leaves and other vegetation creating a tunnel effect that seriously reduces visibility. Even on bright and sunny days, you can't see well. Furthermore, the trails are rarely straight and often crisscrossed with others. One moment no one is there. The next moment an entire force can be standing a few yards away.

Tunnel effect bright sunlight on the outside, dark on the inside

Early one morning of a bright and beautiful day, my patrol abruptly encounters an all- Vietnamese patrol at the intersection of two trails. I instantly bring my M14 rifle to a firing position to start shooting when a PF steps directly to my front and frantically screams, "NO VC - NO VC," as he points to the red scarfs they all have tied around their necks.

This unit is an independent Government of South Vietnam military force called Biet Kichs; think special forces, better yet, commandos, Vietnamese style. You got it; the red scarfs mean good guys. I was one second away from starting a shoot-out at point-blank range with a friendly force. Had it not been for the PF's interference, I would have created a situation of death and total confusion, a state of chaos known in WW II as "FUBAR" fucked up beyond all recognition. Well, that day's example of the difficulty of determining who is enemy and who is friend should have been a non-event, just one more learning experience, except it laid the foundation for another chance encounter with an all-Vietnamese unit.

Several days later, after completing a two-hour daytime patrol, my squad and I are immediately approached by two members of an intelligence team from the Phu Bai Marine Combat Base. They ask if we have seen or heard of an enemy force during our patrol. After reporting we have not, we are ordered to return to the village schoolhouse and proceed to a rice paddy dike that leads to a known VC-controlled hamlet out of our tactical area of responsibility. We are then to walk the dike heading south towards the hamlet for approximately one-quarter of a mile before returning.

Without a break, we march back to the designated dike that leads to the VC-controlled hamlet. We don't know why we are being sent to walk the dike, but it must make sense if the order came from Phu Bai Headquarters.

After walking the dike for about one-quarter of a mile, we take a short break before returning using the same, and by the way, the only dike that connects the two hamlets. On either side of the dike are enormous expanses of rice paddies. My patrol consists of five Marines and five PFs, all walking behind the other, separated by several yards. Looking straight ahead from my center position in the column, I see someone walking towards us. The PF walking the point position of our patrol is relaxed and not at all alarmed. Most of the Marines and PFs don't see the advancing Vietnamese man as they are staring at the man's back in front of them. These men have been walking for over four hours during the hottest part of the day, enduring temperatures exceeding one hundred degrees Fahrenheit.

As the Vietnamese man approaches, I realize that he is the first man in a long line of Vietnamese. The two columns politely pass on the narrow rice paddy dike. The other unit has at least a two-to-one manpower advantage as they are now behind us, alongside us, and to the front of us: no red scarfs. These guys look like VC because they are VC, or at least I think so. Well, if they are, why are they not shooting at us? Why are the PFs not reporting VC - VC? No one is making eye contact, not with me.

So, there we are, the ten of us spread out in a column one behind the other, passing what I determine to be a VC unit that has two huge advantages. Tactical position and a larger number of combatants, at least two to one. Here is the dilemma for both sides. It is difficult to shoot anyone except the person directly across from you when you are that close to one another – think of a firefight between two columns passing one another in a narrow hallway.

What to do – what order to give? Once the two columns pass, I can spread my team out in the rice paddies and direct fire on their column. Yeah, the column that is still in a straight line on the dike. Whoa, If I can kill them because of our new position, they can attack us because of our new position. There is no cover in the rice paddies, just muck and short stalks of rice standing barely above the shallow water. No, the order to break our present position must wait until I hear the other side breaking their current position. As the two patrols walk the dike in opposite directions, I listen for sounds of them flanking.

When the distance between us increases, I laugh loudly – in return one, and only one man from the other unit also laughs loudly. Two leaders from opposing sides just acknowledged a mutual understanding of a situation that would have been too costly to either side. Think of mutual confusion.

I suspect as we initially approached one another, they were also confused about our identity. Our point man is a PF dressed just like them coming from their VC-controlled hamlet. The next man is a Marine, but not dressed like regular line company Marines; we wear no helmets and carry various weapons. At a distance, we look more like a VC patrol than we do a Marine patrol. Reaching the village schoolhouse, I immediately ask the PFs if the unit we just passed were VC. I receive not one but three different answers, "No, yes, and not sure." Well, that means VC, at least it does to me.

Returning to the compound, the two members from Battalion Intelligence who had knowingly sent my squad into a VC-held area without telling us what to expect approach. They knew from received information that a VC unit would be in the hamlet. That was why my squad was directed to patrol the same area twice.

Those Marines or their chain of command went one step beyond their expertise. They did a great job with the intelligence information, but they knew little about close contact firefights. For them, if we crossed paths with the enemy, we would surely kill all the bad guys, and none of us would be injured. Had they told us what was going on, we, the Marines doing the killing, would have made an aggressive battle plan.

Successful Counterguerrilla Warfare leadership requires those in command to understand the fine points of close contact combat. How quickly combatants die after being struck by high-velocity projectiles is directly proportional to where their bodies are struck. Knowing when one man can successfully kill another without committing suicide is essential in determining when and how to attack your opponent.

For many of the planners and leaders at Battalion Headquarters, their job stops when they provide information to others who will engage the enemy. For us, the men at that point of contact, our job is not over; it is just beginning. That's where and when the killing starts.

R&R – New Village

After several months of serving as the dual CAC squad leader, later named Hotel 8, deployed at an old French compound about a quarter-mile south of the Truoi River Bridge in Loc Dien Village, I am replaced by a sergeant E –5.

I spent less than a week working with the new sergeant before being notified that I will be going on R&R, a five-day vacation providing "Rest and Relaxation." Up to this point in my thirteenth-month tour, I have not given R&R much consideration. Quite frankly, I have forgotten that this incredible escape from continuous stress is available. I have now been in country for over nine months, never missing a day of duty[42].

By the way, I was not asked if I wanted to go on R&R, nor was I asked where I would like to go. Kuala Lumpur, Malaysia, was selected for me, as was the date of departure. So, off I go. I was given a khaki uniform, a shower, and a shave before boarding a civilian four-engine propeller airplane. The flight required about five hours to fly from Da Nang Vietnam to Kuala Lumpur, Malaysia, approximately a thousand miles.

A Lance Corporal was assigned the seat next to me. He said hello and was silent for over two hours. The last thing either of us wanted to do was talk about the war, and quite frankly, neither of us had much desire for small talk. We were both deep in private thoughts. Shortly after our pilot announced that we would soon be landing, my seating companion, after another long period of silence, asked, "What are you going to do with your time? You know your time for the next five days"? My reply. "Get laid – eat a fine steak – drink some whiskey. Then, get laid – eat a fine steak – drink some whiskey and repeat that sequence until they send me back to Nam." He responded, "Can I come with you"? I said, "Yeah, hell yeah, you can!" We shook hands and exchanged names; his name was Mike. We were inseparable for the next five days.

After landing, we boarded a reserved bus and were welcomed to Kuala Lumpur, Malaysia, by a Marine in civilian clothes. As the bus pulled away from the airport, our greeter explained the policies we must follow during our stay in Kula Lumpur. "First, you can't wear military uniforms in this city. We are on our way to a clothing store where arrangements have been made for you to purchase civilian clothes. Then we will proceed to your hotel. To ensure that you are alive and well, you must check in with the hotel desk every forty-eight hours in person or by phone. In addition, you must check in with the hotel desk in person once every seventy-two

---

[42] **Missing days of duty** - Marines that requested to be sent to safer areas for any reason other than a serious wound or collapsing from sickness were considered "Non-Hackers". No Marine desired that label! Oh no. Marines do not quit; they slow down, they fall, but they don't stay down. The word quit had been removed from our vocabularies during recruit training.

hours. When you register at the hotel, you may sign up for dinner with an American family that has generously offered their hospitality to any Marine serving in Vietnam. To accept an invitation, you need to schedule a day and time. That's it, stay out of trouble, enjoy yourself, do whatever you want!"

After registering at the hotel desk, a porter escorted Mike and me to our assigned rooms. I tipped the man for his assistance and requested that he send a woman to each of our rooms. He replied that it was now after 1:00 a.m. and too late for such arrangements. I told him that I understood our request's difficulty and suggested he will be handsomely rewarded if he got creative and provided the desired companionship. Fifteen minutes later, he put us in a cab.

The cab driver takes us to an apartment building, where we are greeted by a middle-aged woman who escorts us upstairs. She opens two apartment room doors, and after financial arrangements, we are invited to stay the night with whoever presently occupies the rooms. I don't care too much about the women's particulars on the other side of the door. I had not touched a woman in over nine months. I am mentally and physically on fire. To my delight, my partner-to-be is a beautiful woman who speaks English. Whatever I paid for her services was not enough! She and I spent hours trying to dampen my passion. After several encounters, I found a hand fan and worked vigorously to move cool air over her now sweaty body. She was most appreciative.

Early the next morning, Mike and I are invited to a group breakfast with all the women who shared the apartment building. My sleeping partner speaks of our previous night with amusement. Everyone enjoys a great laugh when she reports how I fanned her. Yes, she was tipped well, probably not enough!

After accepting the offered invitation to become dinner guests, we took a cab to the sponsoring family's home. A surgeon and his wife treated us like royalty as we enjoyed a fantastic meal, followed by a warm and pleasant after-dinner conversation. Leaving their beautiful home, we were thanked for our service and driven back to town.

Our host, without inquiring, clearly knew how we intended to spend the rest of the evening. He took us to a bar where you could leave with an escort if you paid the owner of the bar what he estimated she would earn as a barmaid that night and then paid for her escort services. No problem – we pay. Taking the escorts back to our hotel, we spent an hour or so dancing in the ballroom before retiring to our rooms.

Early the following afternoon, I am awakened by a loud knock. Upon opening the door, I am greeted by a lady who gently pushes me back to the bed with a soft hand and a beautiful smile. The porter has sent her. She immediately removes all her clothes and suggests that after sex, she would act as my tour guide showing all the city's sights. Ok, why not. The four of us, including Mike and his new tour guide, walk the streets like tourists. After spending the day and early evening together, we parted ways with our guides.

The hotel porter stopped by later that evening as Mike and I enjoyed a drink in the hotel bar before retiring for the night. After we thanked him for providing the tour guides, he suggests the best is yet to come. Arrangements had been made for Mike and me to spend tomorrow afternoon with the best massage providers in the city. He was correct! We spent the next afternoon and early evening with women who had devoted a lifetime studying pressure touch and sex.

On the morning of the sixth day, we flew back to Vietnam, arriving at Da Nang Air Base late that afternoon. That night Mike and I went to the enlisted man's club, an outdoor area arranged under a canopy furnished with an assortment of picnic tables. It wasn't easy to share a table with a group of Marines who were happy beyond belief after completing their 13-month tours. These Marines are about to depart for home and unite with their families. Mike and I are going back to war. I never saw Mike again, but I can guarantee he and I will never forget the five days we spent together on R&R.

The stress relief provided by my week of vacation was fantastic. However, after returning to Loc Dien Village, I discovered that R&R is also a bit counterproductive. The environment I just left was free from fear and death. However, the experience broke my frame of mind. I always felt sorry for the guys who managed to meet their families in Hawaii. Most of them returned to duty sad and mentally challenged. Short-lived visits with loved ones or experiencing an R&R like the one I just returned from could be emotionally devastating.

Several days after returning to duty, I receive a surprise visit. The company commander and the company first sergeant enter the room as I sit at a table mapping out the patrol and ambush for the next day. I am instructed to gather all my gear and load it into a waiting jeep. No one explains where I am going or why I am going there, not a word. We head north on Route #1. After crossing a bridge over the Song Nong River, we stop in front of a concrete archway that leads to a courtyard. A squad of seasoned "Hardcore looking Marines" assembles, standing at parade rest, forming a line facing me. One of them takes my gear to the sergeant's quarters as I get out of the jeep and meet my new squad. The company commander and first sergeant immediately drive away, leaving me standing in front of my new CAC squad. Looking at them, I say, "Looks like I'm in charge." One of them mumbles, "No shit." That's how my new command begins; no briefing of any kind; they never even asked if I wanted the assignment!

CHAPTER SIX

Loc Bon Village

New Command

My new assignment's home base is an old French compound on the north side of the Song Nong River Bridge, straddling Highway 1 in the village of Loc Bon. Originally designated as CAC IV, it was later renamed Alpha 3 and, later yet, Hotel 1, before becoming the 1st platoon assigned to the 5th company of the 3rd Combined Action Group, 3-5-1. The alphanumeric references to the villages changed as the Marine Corps Combined Action Program expanded throughout the I Corps Tactical Zone[43] of Vietnam.

First and foremost, the Marines serving in the village of Loc Bon are hardcore experienced young men who know how to fight a war without external support. Trust me, leading hand-picked Marines who all have previous combat experience is a privilege denied to most officers and non-commissioned officers. As the squad leader, I never have to contend with personnel problems involving drug use, racial tensions, or poor attitudes reflecting anti-war demonstrations in U.S. cities. We are white, brown, and black[44].

---

[43] **The I Corps Tactical Zone** was a corps of the Army of the Republic of Vietnam (ARVN), the army of the nation state of South Vietnam that existed from 1955 to 1975. It was one of four corps of the ARVN. This was the northernmost region of South Vietnam, bordering North Vietnam at the Vietnamese Demilitarized Zone (DMZ). These five provinces are Quảng Trị Province, (Khe Sanh, Đông Hà, Quảng Trị City), Thừa Thiên-Huế Province, (Phu Bai, Huế City), Quảng Nam Province, (Đà Nẵng, Hội An), Quảng Tín Province, (Tam Kỳ, Chu Lai) and Quảng Ngãi Province, (Quảng Ngãi). I Corps (South Vietnam) - Wikipedia

[44] **The civil rights movement in the U.S.** that began in the 1950s saw major progress with the passage in 1964 and 1965 of major civil rights legislation. Forced change directed by federal law created a state of turmoil in the United States, especially in the southern states. Most of the racial tension and division of the time was eliminated during Marine Boot Camp. Everyone was treated the same by white and black drill sergeants. Marines serving in Vietnam accepted one another's total presence – We needed and depended on one another.

No one judges another by his race. Everyone judges others by their ability to work within the unit.

As an independent counterguerrilla / counterinsurgent force comprised of thirteen Marines and a Navy Corpsman working with a platoon of Vietnamese Popular Forces in a remote village, our deployment is not an environment where talking about the politics of war takes place. World leaders have failed to settle the dispute of who and how South Vietnam will be governed. Without a political solution, bullets and bombs will determine the outcome, not diplomacy. We are fighting and dying in a country called Vietnam because we are ordered to, which is enough for us.

Most of the squad are young, between eighteen and twenty-two years old, with high school education. None of us have ever served in rear areas, enjoying a large, fortified base's relative safety and security. During the later months of 1966, every member serving in a Combined Action Platoon are volunteers, men of the bush, with at least four months of combat experience.

I insist on just a few rules: no more than two beers a day[45], no drugs, no sleeping on perimeter watch or, heaven forbid, on an ambush, no sex with the villagers, especially unmarried young women; more on that subject later. The last rule, no one man anything! We must always work as a team; it is never acceptable for one man to go anywhere out of the compound for any reason by himself. If just one member of a CAP squad stops following orders or starts having a secret life, his activities will endanger our entire unit. Therefore, maintaining an environment of strict conduct concerning the squad's work and the squad's play falls on my shoulders. My solution to this leadership challenge is to create a code of conduct built upon peer pressure. Essentially, one Marine approaching another who is breaking the code of conduct and demanding that the Marine

---

[45] **We could buy beer** from a Vietnamese self-made vendor called, Boxie, pronounced "Bac-Si" the Vietnamese word for doctor. His home was within our compound. He was the village medical expert. During the war with the French, Bac-Si served with the Viet Minh as what the Marines call a corpsman and the Army call a medic.

make an immediate change in attitude or performance. That undefined code within the squad worked well.

I was sent to the village of Loc Bon to lead, not to become one of the guys. I realize, for all practical purposes, we are alone. During the later months of 1966, no external help is routinely available to us, not the kind that will make much difference.

The undeniable weakness of the early CAC and CAP units is their static defensive positions. We leave and return to the same compound every day and night. The exact locations of the fortifications protecting our compound are known to everyone, including the VC. Allowing the squad to relax too much at any time, especially during the day, may well cost everyone their life. The antidote is to keep the team engaged, pursue, and kill the VC, take control of the village, involve everyone in planning ambushes and patrols, training, and cross-training with live-fire practice.

My "Golden Rule" never suffer the loss of one of our team members for one of theirs. I will never forget the officer's question presented at an after-action debriefing, "Are you satisfied with the results"? The pain of that question became a determining factor in how and when I committed my command. No fair fights: counterguerrilla warfare is not a sporting event. Whenever possible, we will attack the enemy on our terms, having a tactical advantage. If I can catch the VC sleeping, I will kill them all before they awaken.

The leadership of a small, counterinsurgent warfare unit, independently deployed, without the benefit of a strict military environment created by the presence of officers and senior noncommissioned officers, is achieved by earning respect. I lead daytime patrols and nighttime ambushes on the same schedule that I order everyone else. Being assigned to this unit as their leader seems natural. I bring to my new squad the lessons learned from over nine months of combat experience. I have continuously transitioned from the new guy trying to find himself to a seasoned noncommissioned officer. My confidence and ability to lead men in counterguerrilla warfare are now well established.

Something else has happened. I am addicted to adrenaline. Yeah, I feel amazingly comfortable on the edge of life. It is hard to explain how firing an automatic weapon or an M 79 grenade launcher at another human being can be exciting, but trust me, it is. I should feel more comfortable behind the fighting positions that defend our compound. I don't. I find myself preferring the inherent insecurity and suspense inevitably created by leading patrols and ambushes. I have come to accept and enjoy the hyper mental state created from the fight or flight hormone rush. I exploit the superhuman sensation of experiencing an incredible state of alertness as I carefully place one foot in front of another, gently walking to an ambush site.

I suspect what is so difficult for some to understand about the adrenaline rush resulting from trying to kill another human being in a war is that they don't realize a human being is trying to kill you. Counterguerrilla warfare is essentially a high-stakes competition where the loser dies. I receive one and only one bit of feedback from the sergeant who preceded me, "The village chief is a Communist. Do not share future patrol routes and locations of ambushes. He will give it all to the VC."

Meet the Village Chief

After taking command of my new Combined Action Platoon, I am soon greeted by the village chief and the platoon sergeant of the Popular forces with courtesy and respect. I return their friendly gestures as we begin what is to become a contentious relationship.

The village chief suggests that he and the PFs lead an ambush this evening so I can see how well his team supports the Marines in his village. Of course, I accept, hoping this night will become the foundation of a sincere relationship with the village leadership and, most importantly, with the PFs. They will constitute fifty percent of the manpower of every future ambush and patrol.

We leave our compound in the evening shortly after 2030 hours, 8:30 pm, with the PFs leading the way. The Vietnamese sergeant chooses to position all five of his PFs in the front of the column, with all five of us Marines following in the back as we walk single file to an ambush site he has selected. Tonight, this ambush is their show, so I don't suggest what I consider to be a far better distribution of men and weapons. When we arrive, I am stunned at how close we are to our fortified compound, less than two hundred yards away. Too close, in my opinion, for a high probability of a successful ambush. However, I am impressed with how well the PFs move in close quarters, barely producing a sound. Smaller men move with efficiency and balance, especially in challenging terrain. Not one of these Vietnamese men is taller than 5'5", and I guess their body weight not to exceed 110 pounds.

In war, if you are strong enough to carry and operate the tools of war, it is of little or no advantage to be tall and overly muscular. The Vietnam War combatants are not swinging swords or clubs as they go about killing one another. Modern firearms supported with high-capacity magazines have seriously reduced the advantage of brute strength and physical prowess. A slight squeeze on the trigger of any firearm used in the Vietnam War will create the energy required to kill. However, modern firearms can't replace physical endurance, a well-working nervous system, and a warrior's heart and mind. These attributes are yet to be determined in the PFs that move so quietly.

The duration of the village chief's ambush is less than 45 minutes. Considering the ambush site's proximity to our fortified compound, the distribution of the Marines and PFs, and the ambush's short duration, this entire activity is a charade, all for show. The village chief's attempt to create a relationship of mutual trust and cooperation has failed. He demonstrates with his "Pretend Ambush" how little regard he has for me as a leader.

Several days later, to everyone's surprise, the Village Chief is transported to Hue City for interrogation after being arrested by the South Vietnamese Government and officially accused of being a VC undercover agent. The sergeant who preceded me had started the very laborious process of removing an active Vietnamese Village Chief. First, he reported the offender to the US military command, and they, in turn, notified the Vietnamese political authority. The charge of being a VC agent created multiple administrative procedures within the Vietnamese government. The fate of the Village Chief of Loc Bon will ultimately be determined by Vietnamese officials who were notorious for corruption and their often false sense of allegiance to the South Vietnamese Government.

The next evening after coordinating with artillery harassment fire from the Marine Combat Base in Phu Bai, I lead my first ambush as the squad leader of Loc Bon. The Marines and PFs are intermingled, forming a column of Marine-PF-Marine-PF. I didn't share the ambush's chosen location or departure time with the PFs or Marines. The PFs, or I should more accurately report some of the PFs, are upset by their lack of advance notice. A trail leading to the village from the mountains to the West offered a likely enemy approach. We stayed four hours, entirely alert, rifle safeties off, not a sound from anyone. Those procedures became the foundation of all future ambushes.

Working with my new squad, I soon realize that the individual Marines and PFs serving in Loc Bon village are even better than I first believed. However, I also become aware that the working relationship between the Marines and PFs is a bit contentious. Not as close a relationship as you would expect for a team working together for over a year. Was the lack of harmony our fault?

Are we unable to truly accept the PFs, or have the VC figured a way to keep the PFs from further integrating with the Marines? We live in the same fortified compound, but we have separate eating, sleeping, and resting quarters. To build a superior fighting force, we all need to live together, gain mutual respect, and somehow reset the Village Chief's atmosphere of deception. The positive experience of leading my first CAC unit in the Village of Loc Diem had demonstrated how well the village leadership, the PFs, and the Marines can work together and how effective that relationship can be. The Village of Loc Diem was also affected by VC counterinsurgent penetration into the village government and its residents. However, I sensed much stronger cooperation here in the village of Loc Bon.

The village chief has a trial in Hue city and is found innocent of all charges. Yet, to our amazement, within three weeks of being arrested, he returns to Loc Bon village and assumes his previous functions, including his double-agent role. I now know he is unquestionably working against our efforts, and I need to marginalize his influence. He may have been found innocent by corrupt Vietnamese politicians, but he is guilty as charged as far as we Marines are concerned. Do the PF rank and file see this situation as acceptable? If we foreigners can quickly determine his true allegiance, they, the PFs, must also know that their Village Chief is a double agent. Is there a vigorous power struggle within the village? Are all the villagers and PFs cooperating with the VC?

I begin involving the squad in daily discussions. We learn from each other by cross-training one another's areas of expertise. We practice the proper firing of our M14 automatic rifles[46]. First and foremost, we learn the shooting skills of firing short bursts by letting off the trigger causing the muzzle to return to its aiming point. Everyone's life depends on how accurately everyone else shoots, especially important at night and critical at close range. A wounded enemy, just a few yards from you, is deadly! That fact can't be overstated. We must learn to kill, not wound the enemy. How well we shoot, how well we understand the safe deployment of grenades, the must-knows of an M-60 machine gun (its loading, firing, cleaning, and barrel changing), the rules and realities of a claymore mine, and much more will determine who lives.

Our task is to learn and master what we know we will need to know to better adapt to the inevitable, unpredictable challenges we are not prepared for. Marines under fire perform exactly as they are trained. My job is to create a learning environment and instill confidence by getting everyone out into the bush. Yes, I seriously reduce the VC's influence by having the squad spend more time out of the fortified compound, patrolling and ambushing in and about the village's hamlets.

---

[46] **Shooting skills -** In the Marine infantry squad, one man out of four had an M14 rifle capable of firing fully automatic. In a CAC / CAP squad, every Marine's M14 was capable of firing fully automatic.

To influence and encourage the villagers to support the South Vietnamese Government, we must first be accepted by the local population, especially the village elders. We take every precaution not to harm the villagers or sink the boats they depend on to harvest fish and travel the waterways. Destroying the villager's homes during a firefight or with supporting arms will undo years of mutual trust. Realizing how vital their water buffalo are to rice production, we take every precaution not to injure them. We endeavor to learn their language, customs, and religious beliefs to prevent us from unintentionally disrespecting them. Our hospital corpsman significantly improves our relationship with the villagers of Loc Bon by regularly providing medical services. Our body's defenses become accustomed to tolerating the bacteria in the local food and water as we occasionally share meals.

One of my first tasks as the new squad leader is to determine how we will protect our village compound if attacked? I soon realize that Loc Bon is vulnerable to a well-organized assault even though defended with fortified fighting positions providing interlocking fire supported by an M-60 machine gun, claymore mines, and laws. Our compound's unavoidable weakness is that the defensive fighting positions are static, and everyone knows their exact locations. In my opinion, if a large VC unit attempts to overrun the few defenders of Loc Bon, they will succeed[47].

The North Vietnamese know a great deal about village control. For at least a century, they have been employing insurgent warfare against the French, Japanese, French once again, and then Americans. We are competing for village control in a foreign country, with an exceedingly difficult language, strange customs, and a harsh climate. Our presence in Loc Bon is an irritant, not yet a key obstacle to the communist leaders. The tactic of living among the people, actively fighting to support the local government, and improving the living conditions with more efficient farming methods and health services will eventually win the war where bullets and bombs will not. The problem for the United States citizens is

---

[47] **Cap Villages Attacked** - Several combined action platoons in the I Corp Tactical Area of Vietnam were successfully attacked during the summer and fall of 1966.

that winning the war from within will take many years and a substantial commitment of blood and cash.

As the squad leader of Loc Bon, my challenge is teaching and motivating others how and when to fight. My goal is to help everyone grasp the fine line that separates our application of unbridled violence without losing all compassion for the Vietnamese villagers who we are trying to persuade and protect. I meet that challenge and accomplish that mission to the best of my ability by example.

Captain's Ambush- Learn the Trails – M14 Rifle – Bac-Si

During the second week of my deployment to the village of Loc Bon, I am notified that Captain Broderick, the officer in charge of all the CAP squads in the Phu Bai area, will command a dual ambush team, one from Loc Bon and the other from the village to the north, Thu Tanh.

Positioned on high ground facing the distant villages, both teams form a long line with our backs to the mountains behind us. The plan's logic is to intercept any VC tax agents working in either of the villages. We intend to ambush them as they return to their daytime sanctuary. Several hours pass before my squad receives a tense and somewhat confusing radio message from the other squad. "VC are walking parallel to the rear of the ambush." They are behind us. The whispered radio report from the other squad is not clear or concise; the best I can piece together is that VC are to our rear.

Trying to make sense of the situation, I leave my position with the main force and low walk in a stooped and crouched manner to the Marine, providing rear security. I immediately see three VC carrying what appears to be AK-47 rifles. The Marine providing rear security is armed with an M14 automatic rifle, and I have an M-79 grenade launcher. I order that on the count of three, we both fire on the VC. Wait! I am about to start a firefight with the rear-guard Marine and myself in the middle. The present situation is just this; three VC are walking, one behind the other with several yards between them. They are to our front, and the entire ambush team is behind us. We are in the middle!

Once we start the fight, the rest of the squad will be shooting towards us as they come under attack from the three VC. Second consideration! The M-79 grenade launcher doesn't arm when it leaves its muzzle. The fired 40 mm projectile will not explode until it has traveled 30 yards and then contacts an object that opposes its forward motion. The enemy is about 30 yards away, so I am not sure if I fire a round that it will detonate at their distance from us. Another limitation is the M-79 grenade launcher can only fire once before reloading. Under the influence of these considerations, I "low walk, like a waddling duck," back to the primary ambush team and order everyone to reverse direction and then "duck walk" back to the rear security position. Now, all the firepower is positioned to attack the enemy, with no one in the middle blocking anyone's fire. We arrive in force, too late. The trio of VC has safely walked out of sight, totally unaware of our presence.

During the debriefing later that night, Captain Broderick seemed pleased with my decisions. Just because you plan well and execute the plan ideally doesn't guarantee that you will catch anything in your snare. Ambush locations are always selected where we think the enemy will be at a time and place in the future, the best guess. Our selected ambush location that night was accurate, within thirty yards, but the ambush's firepower was facing the wrong direction.

The day after Captain Broderick's ambush, I focus on learning our squad's assigned tactical area of responsibility, better known as our "TAOR." Planning patrols and ambushes around and in every hamlet, we soon learn to navigate the highly traveled trails and then, the less frequently used footpaths, the shortcuts. By discovering the villagers' major and minor travel routes, we also expose the main and minor travel routes used by the VC. Want to catch a VC? Think like a VC. Learn how and where they live. Understand what they do in our village at night and where they rest during the day? We strive to discover their entire routine of life and then exploit that knowledge to our advantage. Thinking like a VC would be much easier if the PFs who work with us were more proactive in sharing what they know. They do provide some information and often perform well. However, I become confident that the sergeant of the PFs under the village chief's control is preventing more cooperation between willing PFs and Marines.

What about our strengths and weaknesses? The M14 automatic rifle is our principal weapon. When we carry this rifle with a full magazine, we are constantly supporting a 10.7-pound weight. We reverse the rifle sling to support it with an over-the-shoulder carry, allowing the rifle to hang just above the hip. This configuration reduces the constant muscle strain on our arms from the loaded rifle's weight and allows a forward-firing position. But the rifle slung over the shoulder produces an accuracy problem. Trust me; no one shoots accurately from the hip. If surprised by the sudden appearance of the enemy, you are better off to shoot at the ground, at his feet, startling him and gaining the time necessary to bring the rifle to your shoulder.

To prove the inaccuracy of shooting from the hip, I have the men walk parallel to a standing cardboard C-ration case box measuring about two and a half feet tall and one and a half feet wide. On my command, they quickly turn 90 degrees and fire from the hip. Their accuracy is poor, allowing the enemy time to counter-attack. Then I repeat the demonstration with a shoulder-mounted rifle. Again, on my command, as each Marine walks parallel to the C-ration box, I order them to turn 90 degrees and fire from the shoulder. The box crumbles after being struck by multiple bullets.

New replacements to my squad are asked during an initial interview how long they can hold an M14 rifle firing fully automatic without letting off the trigger. The correct answer? Never squeeze the trigger longer than necessary for a three-to-four round burst. With that type of response, I move on to the next subject. Occasionally, the replacement will report that he can hold a long burst – Yeah, firing twenty continuous rounds from his automatic M14 rifle is no problem due to his superior arm strength. Hearing such an absurd report, I immediately take him to the bridge crossing the Song Nong River, throw a C-ration cardboard case box into the water and have him fire his continuous twenty-round burst as I safely step back and away. The rounds striking the water provide conclusive evidence of inaccuracy as his fired bullets continuously walk up the river, away from the floating box. Then, returning to the squad leader's quarters and continuing the "new guy" interview, I announce, "Now that we have proven that you are incompetent in your ability to fire an M14 rifle in fully automatic mode, let's begin to fix this condition. Everyone's life in this squad now depends on your ability to master your M14 rifle, shooting it, cleaning it, and properly servicing its magazines and ammunition."

To some, all this focus on shooting properly may sound a bit much or downright excessive. To those folks, I suggest that if they can find one alive, talk to a Marine or soldier that has been in a firefight and his weapon malfunctioned, or he could not shoot accurately enough to compete with the enemy.

My relationship with the Village Chief of Loc Bon after returning from his Hue trial is one of mutual mistrust. He rarely speaks to me. The previous attempt to have him removed from his village leadership position through official Vietnamese channels has failed. Now he knows that all us Marines are painfully aware that he is a VC-installed village chief. This man is kind of like having a rattlesnake under your bed, dangerous but just out of reach. I plan to seriously reduce his credibility by creating a solid relationship with the PFs and the villagers built on hard work and mutual respect.

One Vietnamese man, the village medic named Bac-Si, seems to share my goal of working around the Village Chief's influence. Bac-Si's home is within our fortified compound with an open carport type of structure attached. Positioned under the open carport are picnic tables that provide a meeting place for the PFs, villagers, and Marines to share a soda or an occasional beer. Bac-Si's makeshift refreshment inn creates a low-key environment providing an opportunity for Marines and PFs to learn the other's language.

I see in Bac-Si, the antidote to the poisonous leadership of the VC-installed and politically protected village chief. Sitting alone with Bac-Si and doing my best to gain his confidence as I struggle with the Vietnamese language, I begin to understand how to communicate with few words. I experience how people of different languages, customs, and histories can share thoughts through some mysterious energy exchange.

Natural Talent to Kill

A close contact ambush is an eruption of deadly force intended to kill opponents at close range. When correctly performed, an ambush is an execution of your adversaries, not a firefight.

Some Marines are naturally talented at firing their weapons at precisely the right time, allowing the enemy to expose themselves to the ambush's total firepower. The correct time to initiate an ambush is more demanding than you may realize because you do not shoot when you first see the enemy. Silently, you wait and allow your adversary, most often armed with an automatic rifle capable of shooting your body full of bullets in less than one second, to walk closer and closer to your position. Ideally, when the enemy has fully advanced into the ambush's preplanned kill zone, everyone fires accurately to assassinate the approaching combatants immediately. We all learn ambush skills of ever-increasing complexity by experience. However, some Marines naturally process unteachable attributes that enable them to perform flawlessly in the face of death.

Very few can answer with confidence how well they will respond to the challenge of approaching death because so very few are tested with such a challenge. Ideally, the ambush leader will initiate the ambush by discharging his weapon first or commanding everyone to start firing. The other members of the ambush team have only to wait for the leader to make that decision. However, that ideal condition is more often the exception than the norm because the VC rarely walk into an ambush precisely as you plan and predict. Instead, they generally approach from an angle. That unpredictability of an approaching enemy requires that every member of the ambush team be ready and capable to perform as the "lead fire," that is, the one member who will determine when everyone else will begin shooting. All the Marines mentally prepare themselves for this challenge, but no one knows how well they will perform until tested!

Controlling your fear as armed VC approach closer and closer to your position and determining when, if at all, to initiate the ambush is a huge personal challenge. But there is another embedded, unique challenge within that challenge. **Are you capable of committing cold-blooded murder?** The controlling factors of aggression are different for members of an ambush because you are about to kill someone who is not presently shooting. Returning fire at someone that is shooting at you, well, that's a natural response. It's self-defense. That type of violence is accepted by almost everyone worldwide. However, when fate selects you and only you as the "lead fire" of an ambush, you are not, at that time, in an active firefight. No one is shooting at you. Looking down the barrel of your M14 rifle at an unsuspecting human being, you wait for the correct angle of fire to present itself so you can commit murder. Well, that's what civilians call taking a life, but none of that matters to you at this pivotal moment. You must mentally override your customary respect for human life and squeeze the trigger. The lives of the human beings that you genuinely care about, that is, the life of every other member of the ambush team, are then depending on you to kill an unaware human being who is not presently performing any act of aggression.

Cold-blooded murder is forbidden by the laws and morals of just about everyone worldwide. Most Marines do not possess the entire set of skills or the correct mental processing to perform as the "lead fire" of a close contact ambush. That is, until they witness the disastrous results of poor timing, under aggression, or over aggression. Dead and wounded Marines are often the result of an incomplete ambush skill set! The exchange of deadly force in a close contact ambush doesn't allow for error. The cost of such an education is often paid in the currency of life, the lives of Marines, and PFs.

Some Marines possess this set of skills, naturally. They only require a refinement soon learned by practical experience and critical analysis. The bottom line, the "natural" seems to focus on the task at hand entirely. He can control all the adrenaline rushing through his body, using it to contemplate all the variables, of the equations, of death. Then, he accepts the answer and executes it with precision and timing. How can anyone be so naturally good at murder? My best guess - genetic inheritance. Trust me; you don't know much about your inherited capacity for violence until you are thrust into a violent environment.

All the Marines of Loc Bon have previously been in combat and know what it is like to fight for their lives. However, several were, in my opinion, "naturals." Lance Corporal Ramos demonstrated his natural and learned skills when fate selected him as the "lead fire."

I plan an ambush site adjacent to a trail that connects the mountains in the west to the village of Loc Bon. An ambush team consisting of five Maines and five PFs silently arrive at the designated location shortly after 22:00 hours, 10:00 p.m. After patiently waiting several hours, three VC approach Lance Corporal Ramos' position. Like it or not, he is in the lead fire position. Due to his physical location to the approaching VC, he must determine when to initiate the ambush. Less than a minute later, the other members of the ambush team see the approaching VC. Everyone is waiting for Ramos to fire; he doesn't. The VC advance closer. Ramos does not shoot. The VC continue to approach. Whoa. Is Ramos asleep? No, he allows the VC to expose themselves to the intended kill zone's full impact. Then and only then does he initiate the ambush by firing short bursts from his M14 automatic rifle. The other Marines and PFs open fire. The VC die without a fight. A perfect ambush.

Those of us in the village compound, the other Marines and PFs who have performed an ambush the night before, hear the automatic rifle fire, lots of it. Knowing that Marines in my command are fighting for their lives, carrying out an ambush that I designed and ordered, I rush out and jump on top of a bunker and scream as loud as humanly possible, "Kill them! Kill them! Goddamn it, kill them!" They can't hear me, but I feel an unexplainable and barely controllable direct connection to the men of my squad.

Within minutes, we received a radio report from the ambush team that three VC were down and no Marines or PFs had been killed or wounded. I lead a patrol to the ambush site, where we secure the immediate area by setting up a defensive perimeter and assess the situation. The question before us is what to do with the dead VC and the captured AK-47 rifles? Most of us have briefly held this weapon, and we all know its distinctive sound, but I have never fired one. Several of us take turns shooting the captured rifles. Oh, my God! We are immediately impressed. This weapon is easy to shoot in a fully automatic mode of fire. It creates much less recoil and inherent upward muzzle climbing than an M14 fired in fully automatic mode. The AK-47 has another advantage; its magazine holds 30 rounds, ten more per magazine than the M14.

The PFs tell us that the dead VC are tax agents. They were en route to the village of Loc Bon to instruct selected families on how much rice they have to pay to the Viet Cong. Non-compliance with their demands is not an option. If the rice taxes are not paid, the offender will be punished up to and including public execution.

The first step in convincing Loc Bon's population to resist the VC is to show them that their adversaries can be beaten. There is no better way to convey that message than for the peasants to see the dead VC publicly displayed. So, that's what we do with the bodies and the captured weapons. We lay the bodies and rifles adjacent to Route 1, the major north-south highway that passes right through the center of our Loc Bon compound.

Several of us Marines and PFs sit on the steps of a concrete building directly in front of the displayed VC to control the scene. Almost everyone in the vehicles who pass our gruesome display takes a quick look, and several vehicles pull off the road, and the driver and passengers get out for a closer inspection. One of those closer inspections creates a scene of bewilderment and downright disbelief.

A very polished Army officer, one of the most impressive I have ever seen (think tall, muscular, manly) decked out in a perfectly clean and pressed field uniform, gets out of his jeep, walks to, and stands over the dead VC. This ultimate figure of an officer poses as his driver takes his picture repeatedly, making sure at least one photograph will be to his liking. This officer is taking credit for having killed the displayed VC. He is unashamedly stealing the courage of other men. He never once acknowledges us, the Marines that sit two yards away in our highly worn and soiled field utilities. "Mr. Perfect" never once looks at the men who are fighting this war and producing the subject matter for his much-desired photos.

The jeep drives off, leaving us staring at one another until one of our group asked, "What the fuck was that"? No one has an answer to the questions of who, what, or why concerning the officer's photoshoot. However, regardless of his perfect image, we all agree that any man who will conduct himself in such a fashion is a poor representative of a commissioned officer in the U.S. Military.

After several hours of publicly displaying the dead VC, the sergeant of the PFs requests we release the bodies to the women standing directly behind him. The PF sergeant reports that one of the dead VC is from the village of Loc Bon. The other two are not from this area. If the other two VC are not from this area, why are the other women here to claim the bodies? I let this question go unanswered, realizing that only the Vietnamese component of our team can determine that personal connection. We are powerless as foreigners with limited Vietnamese language skills to determine which villagers actively support the VC. The Village Chief and the sergeant of the PFs are not powerless to make that determination, but they are silent on such matters.

Essentially, there is much we do not know about what is going on in the village of Loc Bon. For example, what is the actual relationship between the villagers and the VC? Why are the Vietnamese leaders not aggressively doing their job[48]? The Marines serving in the village well understand the military components of counterguerrilla warfare. However, we are utterly inept at realizing that the village's control is mainly affected by the political impact of insurgent warfare.

---

[48] **Vietnamese not doing their job** - I was to learn many years later, an astonishing fact reported by Bernard B. Fall in his last book, "Last Reflections on a War" that the communists had killed over 10,000 thousand village chiefs in a country that had over 16,000 hamlets". Many of the original village chiefs who supported the South Vietnamese Government had been assassinated and replaced with communist village chiefs' years before U.S. troop involvement in South Vietnam.

We agree to release the bodies and respectfully help the women remove them. The captured weapons are sent to Phu Bai[49].

I have mastered the "art of the ambush" and learned to recognize the men with natural talents for close contact warfare and provide them with leadership opportunities.

Two undeniable facts have become public knowledge. First, the Marines and PFs serving in Loc Bon's village perform ambushes and patrols successfully and professionally. The other undeniable fact is that the Village Chief and the sergeant of the PFs do not allow the villagers to share information about the VC. Defending the village and its local government is our task. Discovering and sharing in-depth knowledge and personal connections between the VC and the village families is their task. The village chief and the PF sergeant are taking the 'combined' out of the Combined Action Platoon by controlling the extent that the PFs and the villagers can cooperate with the Marines serving in the village of Loc Bon.

Taunting – M79 Grenade Launcher – Biet Kichs – Sergeant Baker

Our most recent ambush and public display of the dead VC and their weapons created the intended effect. We unquestionably demonstrated our ability to defend the village of Loc Bon and show the VC's vulnerability. Soon the local VC leadership created a public display to undermine our progress and show Loc Bon's residents that they control the village.

Several nights after a successful ambush, I am abruptly awakened from a deep sleep about 0200 hours, 2:00 am, by one of the Marines performing perimeter watch. I hear a distant voice repeatedly calling my name, "Corporal Mezick, Corporal Mezick wake up, wake up." Jumping up

---

[49] **No automatic weapon** - could become the property of the man responsible for its capture. Non-automatic, pistols or rifles, could be held in the rear area until that man rotated back to the U.S.

from my cot, only half awake, I struggle to become fully aware of my surroundings. I take several steps in a dreamlike state of consciousness to gather my senses to comprehend his agitated and fearful report. He explains VC are directly outside the compound and are daring us to come out and fight. Leaving the sergeant's quarters and entering the courtyard of our compound, I immediately hear the challenge. From the darkness of a moonless night, one individual is taunting us in broken English and Vietnamese, "Marine come and fight, Marine Lai day chien dau!" Phonetic pronunciation: (Marine Lie Di Che n dow)

My instructions to everyone, "Relax." If they want to fight so badly, they are certainly welcome to breach our compound's defensive positions. I suspect they only hope we are naïve enough to walk outside our fortified positions and directly into their preplanned fields of fire. We do not respond verbally or walk into what I consider a death trap. The taunting continues intermittently for over an hour with repeated invitations to come out and fight. We ignore their challenges to leave our compound and fight them on their terms. Not my style. They still don't understand that we are using the same guerrilla warfare tactics as they are. We are striking them on our terms when we have the advantages of surprise and selected fields of fire. There is no wisdom in walking into a known trap designed to kill you. Knowing when to fight is just as important as how well you fight.

The next morning the villagers report that the VC had installed chest-high booby traps on every exit trail from our compound. They removed them before daylight. Think of a fisherman pulling in an empty net. In this case, no Marines were destroyed by walking into their booby trap tripwires. The deadly explosives are meant to kill or seriously wound us Marines, not the villagers. The VC don't want to harm the villagers unintentionally because they are dependent on the local population to support them with food and recruits. The intended effect of calling us out to fight was to humiliate us in the villagers' eyes and reestablish their dominance. The VC are very proficient in performing the political components of insurgent warfare. I suspect their efforts didn't achieve their desired goals because they never taunted us again. We asked the PFs working with us where the VC went after they left Loc Bon? No one could or would answer that question. We receive no information about them from the village chief or the sergeant of the PFs.

Eventually, I realize that a status quo exists in my second Combined Action Platoon, CAP , more deeply than it had in my first CAP village. Yes, there is a complex coexistence between the VC and the Vietnamese villagers. Unfortunately, though, the challenge of comprehending this delicate balance of power is tricky in the village of Loc Bon as the Village Chief covertly and sometimes overtly works to isolate us. Even the Marines joining the Combined Action Program later in its development who attended a school in Da Nang designed to help Marines integrate with Vietnamese villagers are hampered by their limited Vietnamese language skills and their inadequate understanding of Vietnamese culture.

Our opportunity to interact with the local population is limited to the PFs and the Vietnamese living in our compound. Our interactions with the villagers outside our compound vary. Some are friendly, some watch us with caution, and others are openly resentful of our presence. The more I understand the VC's political tactics, the more I realize that only the Vietnamese people can oppose that type of influence. You can't walk into someone else's home and settle their family's dispute. You can just settle things down to help them resolve their disagreement.

The Blooper Vest of Loc Bon

The Village of Loc Bon has two features that separate it from other CAP units. One is "The Blooper Vest," and the other is a unique South Vietnamese military unit called "Biet Kichs."

A squad leader serving in a Marine infantry platoon and a squad leader of a CAP squad typically carry the M79 grenade launcher. A single-shot, break-open, shoulder-fired weapon. It is breech-loaded and fires a 40 x 46-mm grenade that is easy to load and fire. The wisdom supporting the squad leader carrying the M79 during the Vietnam War is just this; the standard infantry squad consists of three four-man fire teams armed with rifles. The squad leader commands typically from a position directly behind or in his squad's middle, allowing him to see and control all three fire teams. Depending on the target's distance, the M79's muzzle is generally pointed up and above shoulder height, allowing it to fire over the other Marines' heads.

The M79 is most effective as the squad's supporting weapon for several reasons. First, its fire rate is too slow to be effective in a close contact firefight because, as previously mentioned, the M79 must be reloaded after every shot. Think of a single shot, break-open shotgun. It works the same way. Reason number two, close contact fighting with an M-79, is not good. The fired grenade will not explode until it travels approximately 30 yards and then strikes a hard service. Yeah, until it is armed, by the fired projectile traveling 30 yards or more, it shoots a 40 mm slug. On the upside, as a support weapon, the M-79 enables the squad to drop grenades on the enemy at distances far beyond, throwing grenades by hand. It works very well within the range of one hundred to one hundred fifty yards, where the distance to the target can be estimated well. The effective maximum range is out to four hundred yards if you can somehow estimate so long a distance. Let there be no doubt the M79 Grenade Launcher significantly increases a rifle squads' firepower by providing the capabilities of a very portable, small mortar.

I especially miss carrying my M14 rifle. I understand the weapon's capabilities, strengths, and weaknesses. I take care of my M14 rifle, and my M14 rifle - takes care of me. Just the sound of its magazine locking into its receiver, and then, after releasing the operating arm, the sound of the bolt chambering a round fills me with immense confidence.

Like it or not, someone needs to bring the squad's M79, and that someone is mostly me. I soon discover that carrying the ammunition for the M79 is challenging. Each 40mm grenade weighs about half a pound. The issued cloth bandolier used to carry the ammunition only holds six M79 rounds. No one wants to get in a firefight and run out of ammo. My solution is to have a Vietnamese tailor construct a vest out of heavy canvas complete with pouches that each snuggly hold one 40mm M79 grenade. The pouches are attached in rows on the front of the vest from top to bottom. The total number of rounds, a bunch! I name it the "Moon Vest." My logic, I will not run out of ammunition, and if I get hit, all the rounds will explode and most likely deposit me on the moon. The squad eventually named it "Sergeant Mezick's Blooper Vest," referring to the bloop sound that an M-79 makes as a 40mm projectile leaves its barrel.

I came to love my personally tailored vest and enjoy the powerful sense of confidence it creates by enabling me to carry extra ammunition. However, because most of our ambushes are under 30 yards from the intended kill zone, I still prefer to take my M14 rifle. The M-79 and the blooper vest are always used during daytime patrols and night ambushes designed to engage the enemy at a distance that will enable the fired grenade to arm and explode on impact. No, I never needed to use all the rounds carried in the vest during a firefight, which is precisely why I had the vest made.

The Biet Kichs of Loc Bon

The other unusual feature in the village of Loc Bon is that it is an occasional base camp for a unique South Vietnamese military unit called Biet Kichs. The Biet Kichs, as far as we understood, were paid, and equipped by the government of South Vietnam, think commandos, who were not under the control of the GVN regular army. Their uniforms are dark utilities that fit so well; they must have been tailored for each man. The Biet Kichs are seasoned troops, young but not too young, carrying an assortment of weapons supplied by the U.S. Government. Well, that's what we believe. They are unique in appearance and attitude, conducting themselves like "Cock Roosters." To me, they appear to be just itching for a fight with somebody, yea, anybody. I can't help but think of them as mercenaries working for the highest bidder.

The Biet Kichs of Loc Bon

Rumors regarding the warfare tactics employed by the Biet Kichs, if true, are illegal for any branch of the United States military serving in Vietnam. An example of one of their reported, but not verified by us; tactics was to punish village curfew violators by extreme example. Villagers are not permitted to walk the trails and rice paddy dikes after dark. Anyone out and about after darkness is considered a VC and an unrestricted target. The villagers understandably dislike the imposed curfew and often violate it. While conducting a night patrol, a curfew violator was encountered by the Biet Kichs. To set an example, they shot him in the arm with a 45-caliber pistol.

Quite frankly, no one knows just what the Biet Kichs in our base camp do on their operations except for one Marine, Sergeant Baker. The one and only American assigned to this otherwise Vietnamese unit.

His responsibility is to coordinate their movements with Phu Bai artillery harassment fire. Yes, you read it correctly. One American is working with an otherwise Vietnamese unit unrestricted by standard engagement rules, conducting missions not discussed outside of their unit. I never understood their chain of command or from whom they received their operational orders.

Sergeant Baker is a different kind of guy. He transformed from an average Combined Action Platoon leader into someone who volunteered to be embedded, and I mean entirely inserted in an otherwise wholly foreign special force unit. Sergeant Baker is not their leader, but one of them accepted and respected. He is also their link to US fire support and medevacs. When in our village, Baker rests with the Biet Kichs before they leave again, for God only knows where to do God only knows what. He is relatively quiet and never speaks of his life or missions with the Biet Kichs. Be that as it may, there was one exception: he and I had a real conversation.

After returning to our compound with my ambush team at about 0100 hours, 1:00 in the morning, I find Sergeant Baker waiting to speak with me. A half bottle of Vietnamese white wine sits in front of him on the picnic table under Bac-Si's pavilion. Pouring me a drink, he discloses that he needs to privately speak with someone he thinks will understand his present predicament. I don't know why he feels I will appreciate the pending personal crisis he is about to share. Nevertheless, I consider it a compliment to be taken into the confidence of a man I genuinely respect. He explains that he is just a few days away from completing his third continuous tour in Vietnam. He went on to say that the rules controlling repeated tours forbid anyone from doing four continuous tours. Therefore, he will have to return to the United States for at least six months.

Then he began to explain his predicament by declaring his deep fear of going home due to the anger he feels for his former wife and best friend. My reply, "Whoa! What happened between the three of you"? When he answers my question, his voice becomes intense and forceful. "During my first thirteen-month tour in Vietnam, my wife wrote and announced that she and my best friend were in love and spending all the money sent to her from my paycheck each month[50]. The bitch wrote how much she enjoyed being fucked by my best friend. Her letter described how the two of them were buying pots and pans and furniture with my money. I could not stop her from receiving her monthly allotment until I was legally divorced." I exclaimed, "Oh shit, how do you get a divorce in Vietnam"? He replied, "When I showed the JAG officers in Phu Bai her signed letter, they completed the required paperwork in record time. As a result, I received the fastest divorce possible, which took about two months. Then, my monthly payments to her stopped. I was mad and wanted to punish them both with an ass-kicking they would never forget. By the time my first 13-month tour was over, I had thought better of going home, thinking another six months in the Nam would help me forget all this shit. So, I re-upped for another tour, taking the mandatory 30-day leave, but not in the United States. When that six-month tour was over, I re-upped for another six months. Now I must go back to the States."

He then stops talking and sits motionless. His expression is very grave and sad. I wait for him to continue speaking but soon realize he is done. I ask, "Why is going home such an ordeal? The past is the past, and you will soon find another woman? Look, she has done you a big favor by showing you who she is upfront. Better now than ten years and a couple of kids later." He broke his silence with one sentence, "I am sure that I will kill them both if I go home."

Sergeant Baker left Vietnam several days later and began the return trip to his hometown. I don't know what happened to him, his former wife, or his best friend after his arrival. I hope for everyone's sake that they had left town with no forwarding address.

---

[50] **Mandatory Pay Allotment** - At the time his wife wrote the letter, Baker was a Corporal E-4 with under four years of service in the Marine Corps. That rank and time of service mandated by military law that your wife would receive a monthly allotment of your pay. You could not override that mandate unless divorced.

The night the VC taunted us was a vivid educational experience. Their show of dominance by publicly daring us to come out of our compound and walk into their prepositioned bobby traps was a striking example of how the VC combined insurgent and guerrilla warfare components to control the peasants.

The creation of the Blooper Vest was also a change. A transition into a man who now considers the act of wrapping himself in a bomb to be preferable to running out of ammunition in a firefight.

The heart-to-heart talk with Sergeant Baker is a transition of caution! I realize the war experience can alter your mind so that a viable solution to a domestic problem is to murder your offenders. Will Sergeant Baker's mental state become mine in the future? Baker and I live in an environment where taking another human being's life is considered acceptable and normal. What constrains you after returning home where taking the life of another human being is murder?

The Light Across the River - Being Followed

The nightly ambushes have become non-productive. Regardless of how I vary the departure times, duration times, and locations, our repeated attempts to ambush the VC working in Loc Bon village have become unsuccessful. Why? What changed?

The VC seem to know how to work around us. Eventually, we discover that someone within the South Vietnamese Regional Forces deployed on the south side of the Song Nong River announces our departure times. When calling the PFs from their sleeping quarters to join the nightly ambush team, we notice a light will come on from the other side of the river. The light announces that we are leaving the compound. I never discover who is reporting our departure times. We may have sounded the alarm ourselves.

Every night shortly before the ambush team leaves, we call for the five PFs that are to join us with a loud request in Vietnamese, "Nghĩa quân tôi muốn đi phục kích." which translates to, "PF, I want to go on an ambush."

If the PFs are taking too long to join us, we repeat the request adding that we want to go right now using a louder and more resounding voice, "Nghĩa quân tôi muốn đi phục kích Ngay bây giờ," which translates to, "I want to go on an ambush right now."

To be sure, when our nightly ambush teams leave our compound, their departure times are somehow being announced to a VC light operator on the south side of the Song Nong River. Upon receiving notice that a squad of Marines and PFs is leaving, the light operator flashes an alert to a VC team on the river's north side. Regardless of which direction we choose, a VC team will follow us to and from our ambush site. After we return, the VC have freedom of movement throughout the entire village, knowing that we rarely conduct two ambushes in one night. Most of the time, they are safe until our daytime patrol reenters the village the next day.

We can tell by the sound of barking dogs we are being followed. There are lots of dogs in the hamlets, so hearing a dog barking occasionally is normal. Dogs are the same worldwide. The closer you get to their owners, the more aggressive they become. We suspect our followers are stalking us by walking through the Vietnamese homes' front yards adjacent to the trails to avoid being seen. Following us in such a manner does provide the VC with concealment, but it also causes the dogs to bark more frequently. If our followers think we won't notice the dog barking has changed in intensity and duration, they are wrong. What we don't know is how to make the VC stop following us.

I take the bold step of confiding in the only Vietnamese villager I think I can trust, Bac-Si. Sitting alone with him, I describe how a signal light from the south side of the river reveals our departure times. He knowingly smiles; his facial expression conveys a message – "Good, you caught on." I went on to say that we suspect the increased dog barking in the village means we are being followed. After nodding his head as a sign of agreement, he slowly speaks as he moves small objects on a table to help me understand his solution. He suggests that we move and set up in a different location after spending an hour or so in our first ambush site.

Realizing Bac-Si's suggestion of multiple ambush sites will cause the VC who trail us to move more often and thus increase our opportunity to detect them, I put this tactic into practice the following night. After spending about two hours at the first ambush site, I move the ten-man team to our next site staying about forty-five minutes. Leaving the second ambush site and moving towards the third, I choose a departure trail that leads to an abrupt turn of about 70 degrees. After the ambush team completely walks through the trail turn, we become invisible to anyone behind us. You can't see around a corner. We hear the dogs barking as our followers advance. One of the PFs touches my arm and whispers, "VC!" Now we have a tactical advantage. We know that as the VC walk towards us, they are unaware of our present location. Perfect opportunity to deploy what the military calls a hasty ambush designed to engage an unsuspecting enemy by immediately setting up a kill zone.

On the far side of the trail's turn, I stop our forward movement, turn everyone 90 degrees to their right, and silently back the team off the trail about 10 yards. The intended kill zone is close; from our rifles' muzzles to the center of the advancing VC's chests will be less than thirty feet. Our only cover is the darkness of night.

Within two minutes, a PF prematurely initiates the ambush with his 45-caliber Thompson machine gun. He should have waited and let all the approaching VC walk completely into our kill zone, where the full effect of our firepower will strike them. To make matters worse, when he fires his Thompson machine gun at the advancing VC, he misses! Now we have lost the element of surprise. One of the Marines, the former police officer, fires a burst of bullets from his M14 rifle into the lead VC's chest killing him instantly.

Everyone stops shooting after the initial burst of fire. Most of the ambush team never sees the approaching VC but blindly fires to their immediate front to create shock and fear within the enemy. VC almost always travel in groups of three. That means we most likely have a deadly force directly to our front, only a few yards away, hiding in the vicinity of their recently killed comrade. We need to keep any surviving VC under pressure by continuing the attack. The VC will recover from the ambush's initial shock and counterattack at point-blank range given enough time.

I command everyone to continue firing. However, the team doesn't shoot with the intensity required to prevent a counterattack and then silence. I mumble to myself, "Aw shit," as I stand up so I can fire over the heads of the PFs and Marines that are kneeling in a line to my front. I realize that as I stand, I become the most obvious target to the enemy. I command, "FIRE! FIRE," as I spray bullets into the cover facing us. Following my example, all Marines and PFs fire their weapons with enough intensity to terrify anyone considering a counterattack. All those red tracer bullets and the enormous sound from the Marines and PFs all firing together give the impression that we are a much larger force.

We can't see well in the darkness of the night, but I feel sure there are VC within a few yards of us. We need to pressure them, fill them with overwhelming fear, and prevent a counterattack. Next command, "Ceasefire." Next command, "Laugh." Next command, "Advance online."

We swept into and through the ambush's kill zone. The Marine to my right shouts, "VC! VC!" I see someone running away directly to my left front, heading straight into the doorway of a villager's home. He isn't carrying a weapon. Shooting at him will put rounds into the bamboo and grass structure where a man, his wife, and several children sleep. I chose to shoot into the trail, keeping fear and pressure on the unarmed VC but not killing the very people we are trying to protect. The running VC escapes by using the small yards of other village homes as cover to conceal himself. We can hear his progress by the sounds of barking dogs as he runs from one yard to the next. We continue to flush out any remaining VC by searching the immediate areas to our front and sides.

After satisfying ourselves that there are no more VC in the surrounding area, we set about the task of transporting the dead VC back to our compound. Not an easy task without the aid of a vehicle. A nearby home has used bamboo poles to support an entrance cover over its front door. We remove one of the poles and use it to support the dead VC's weight by tying his arms and knees to it with belts removed from our camouflaged utilities. Two men shoulder the pole with the body hanging directly below. We need to move immediately because our present location is now known to everyone due to our rifle fire. I assign two men to walk point side-by-side. The rear of our squad is protected by two men walking side-by-side backward. The rest of the squad guards our flanks by walking sideways, with every other man pointing his rifle to either the right or left flank. We encounter no resistance as we return.

Entering our compound, the villagers, PFs, and Marines gather around. Walking over to the PF who had missed with his Thompson submachine gun, I raise his hand and declare him a mighty warrior as I announce that he killed the VC. Well, he grins from ear to ear. Later that month, he is transported to Hue, treated to an honorary dinner, and presented with a bravery medal. The recognition he receives for killing the VC will make things difficult for him to work as a VC agent in the future. I never accepted his actions of prematurely initiating the ambush and his inaccurate shooting as anything other than attempting to help the VC escape. All of us Marines know which one of us has killed the VC. Shifting the recognition to a marginal PF, I believe is working both sides of the war is equivalent to killing two VC. Everyone is cool with it.

Captain Broderick, our commanding officer, is delighted that we have no Marines or PFs killed or wounded in the ambush. I am also pleased. However, I realize that we all narrowly escaped the death and destruction of a counterattack. My assessment of success in counterguerrilla warfare is redefined to the following results: Marines 100 percent alive - enemy 100 percent dead.

We publicly display the dead VC and his submachine gun for all to witness. His body is claimed the next day by a relative from another village.

Captured VC Weapons

Later the same afternoon, the PFs report something amazing. A villager has discovered a pulled US M26 hand grenade pin lying on the ground directly to the front of the previous night's ambush site. The recently found pin is not from our grenades; we didn't throw any. However, it is a pin from a US-issued grenade. It is not unheard of for the VC to be armed with US weapons stolen or purchased on the Vietnamese black market. This grenade pin was pulled and dropped by the VC that we flushed as we advanced after laughing. The VC who ran away was not unarmed; he held a US M26 hand grenade. He pulled the pin and was about to throw the grenade but lost his nerve when we advanced towards him in the dark. The grip of his hand held in place a spring-pressured spoon. If he lost his grip, the grenade would have exploded in the next three to five seconds. The family sleeping in the home that the VC ran to was spared injury twice that night. Once from being struck by my bullets smashing through the front door of their home, if I had shot him on their doorstep and again by the armed grenade, that would have exploded.

Everything changed the moment the PF prematurely initiated the attack. The squad adapted their tactics to the situation before them, with actions decided in real-time. The bottom line, we killed the enemy, protected the villagers, and sustained no casualties. The mistake that could have gotten us all killed was that the PF shot too soon, not to mention he missed!

Due to our limited ability to speak and comprehend the Vietnamese language, instructing the PFs to always wait for the Marines to initiate ambushes is mostly a failure. Their immediate chain of command is their Vietnamese PF sergeant, not us. So, even if they understand our explanations, requests, or instructions, that doesn't mean they will comply. Likewise, teaching the PFs to shoot their assortment of US-supplied M1 carbines and 45 caliber machine guns accurately is difficult because they don't have enough ammunition for live fire practice.

We reluctantly become aware that some PFs are not interested in any change within the delicate balance of power between the villagers, the village government, and the VC. The Vietnamese are first and foremost committed to the survival of their families and themselves. Vietnam is their home; we Marines are visiting.

The logic of why the squad laughed while advancing through the ambush's kill zone had nothing to do with being happy; it had everything to do with instilling fear in the enemy that I believed was about to counterattack. During Operation Oregon, I learned the incredible effect of laughter to release fear in those laughing while instilling fear in those hearing the laughter.

Fear has been and always will be an ever-present inseparable component of war. Successful leadership of men in combat requires leaders to understand their fear, the fear of those in their command, and the enemy's fear. Once understood, fear can be employed as a potent psychological weapon.

I displayed my comprehension of counterguerrilla warfare tactics by skillfully utilizing the elements of opportunity, aggression, and counterattack prevention. Up-close combat leadership skills come after experiencing face-to-face firefights that eventually enable you to foresee what to expect before it happens. However, I also realize the indisputable truth of close contact combat; that is, ultimately, everyone dies.

Leadership Challenges

Many leadership challenges of the Vietnam War had little to do with how well you led men in combat. The environment within a Combined Action Platoon is the responsibility of the non-commissioned officer in charge. Without unit cohesion, a Combined Action Platoon can destroy itself from within. Reading men by observing their physical and mental presence is essential to successful leadership, especially true for leaders of small counterinsurgent squads deployed in distant Vietnamese villages. Sergeants and corporals are often tasked with problems quite different from war tactics or general military procedures.

The Marines serving in the village of Loc Bon have copious amounts of in-depth talent. Most of these Marines are capable of leading patrols and ambushes, and if required, several can lead the entire Combined Action Platoon. Some are graduates of a counterinsurgency warfare school located in Da Nang. The school's two-week program is a huge step forward for the attending Marines to learn the Vietnamese language and customs of the villagers they will soon be living with. The future CAP Marines attending the school are also taught small unit tactics, booby traps, map reading, and the procedures for coordinating supporting fire. Most importantly, an attempt is made to impart a sense of mission defining the goals of fighting the Vietnam War from within the Vietnamese population.

The CAP squad serving in the Village of Loc Bon in 1966 has several non-combat leadership challenges within the team. I discover one member is in love with a Vietnamese woman who lives in our compound. The woman has a family but no permanent man in her home. The performance of the Marine involved is rock solid in every other respect. I learn he has extended his 13-month tour by six months, primarily because of her. Their relationship seems to be accepted by the squad, the PFs, and the village elders. So, how do I handle this long-standing situation as a leader? I leave it alone. The affair between the Marine and the husbandless mother is long-established well before I came to the village. Everyone knows, and no one cares, even though we have a rule, no sex with the villagers. The Marine is not a security risk because he is not sneaking around with secret activities.

However, a more serious challenge arises when one squad member has sex with the most beautiful, young, unmarried woman in the village. The affair is dangerous and unacceptable. Young Vietnamese men did not marry until they could provide for their wives and future families. They need land to grow rice, a water buffalo to work the rice paddies, and a home for the bride. Any young Vietnamese man striving to acquire this level of independence will be broken-hearted if he discovers that the love of his life is sleeping with a Marine. He will be angry and seek revenge. Sex with women of the village will create enemies among us that know everything about us.

Serving as the squad leader in my first CAP squad, I received a warning about a deadly incident in another village. An exploding grenade killed a CAP Marine and a young Vietnamese woman as they were copulating. Their attacker was thought to be a young Vietnamese man with a broken heart.

Marine officers commanding platoons and companies of infantry will have no problem responding to those in their command engaging in sex with the Vietnamese. They would set an example for everyone with disciplinary action. Not so easy here. Unlike regular grunts with little exposure to the Vietnamese female population, CAP Marines live with Vietnam's women. They interact with them every day. Remember, these men are young, and their sex drive is powerful. Young Vietnamese women with beautiful long black hair dancing over their pure white Áo dàis (owl dies), a tight-fitting silk tunic worn over trousers, creates a strong sense of desire. Sex with the Vietnamese is forbidden by order of our superiors, punishable by loss of rank. To be sure, the disciplinary action will be especially harsh for the leader that allows such conduct.

My solution to this challenge is to provide the men with a sexual release that doesn't endanger their lives. Sex with women of the village, particularly unmarried women, is dangerous for the individual and the unit. Bac-Si, once again, comes to my rescue. He offers to bring Vietnamese prostitutes to the village occasionally. A room adjacent to his carport/refreshment area will provide the required privacy. The Vietnamese considered prostitution a profession having no objection if the Marines were respectful, paying, and treating the prostitutes properly.

What about venereal disease? Any sexually transmitted disease is a severe risk and one of the main reasons the brass has forbidden sex with the Vietnamese. I weighed the dangers of contracting a venereal disease with the potential repercussions of sleeping with young unmarried women within our compound; both endanger the CAP team's safety and our mission.

My solution select option one with conditions: Bac-Si is responsible for selecting healthy women. One case of any venereal disease will terminate his new source of income. The prostitutes must come during daylight hours and be gone by four in the afternoon. The men desiring their services will not all gather at one time, creating a security risk. The entire experience must be low-key, drawing little attention.

My military career and rank are seriously at risk for conceiving such a solution. If a villager or anyone from our CAP unit reports my decision, I will be toast. Well, I'm not trying to get promoted or elected. The prostitutes provide a real-world solution to a real-world problem.

Another leadership challenge is a Marine sleeping on watch. He is new to the squad and going through what everyone calls the "new guy period." That is, learning your job and, most importantly, being accepted by the other Marines. Our CAP unit's new member fell asleep while manning a defensive position in the village compound. First offense, I let him know

I had observed him sleeping by clearing my throat to awaken him. There were no words, only a low volume noise to revive him; he has received his one free bite. The following week, the same man is again asleep on watch. I wake him and explain how dangerous his sleeping offense is to himself and the other squad members. I scream, "While you are on watch, others are asleep, depending on you to protect them." I asked if he wanted to be sent back to the Marine Combat Base in Phu Bai? "Your conduct is dangerous, and I would rather give the other Marines more work than to endanger them from your incompetence." He replied, "I'm ashamed, and I most definitely want to continue as a member of the squad." I respond, "Tomorrow, you will get an opportunity to demonstrate your sincerity."

The following day, I ordered him to start cutting vegetation growing to the rear of the squad's Quonset hut. He asked, "How long?" I answered, "Until I tell you to stop. I expect the entire area to be weed-free." He went to work. Several hours later, the captain's jeep pulled to a stop in front of the archway to our compound. I met him at the entrance. He was visiting his CAP squads to ensure we understood and complied with the battalion commander's order to clean all the ammunition for our M-60 machine gun[51]. Standing in front of the tall captain, my height of 5 feet 9 inches, allows him a clear view to observe the highly motivated Marine cutting weeds behind us. Before leaving, the captain inquires as to why the Marine is performing a rather unnecessary task? I tell him, "Sir, the man who is landscaping our rear area is participating in a personal reality workshop."

The captain left without further comment. He is not an officer who questions his squad leader's methods of discipline. He realizes full well the noncommissioned officers in charge of his CAP squads shoulder the responsibility of command. To my knowledge, the Marine who cut weeds so well never slept on watch again.

---

[51] **M-60 machine gun ammunition** - If you didn't clean belt fed ammunition, the humid climate in Vietnam, caused corrosion and the rounds may not properly feed through the weapon.

We had other internal challenges, but nothing serious. Peer pressure within the unit is very effective. Breaking a few rules are often laughed off by some men. However, endangering the lives of others in your squad with irresponsible conduct is never a laughing matter. My challenge is to create an environment of high standards and not make rules that don't make sense. We are all in this together. We work, play, and die together—no hidden exceptions.

Assassination Attempt

The VC have a standing bounty for captured or dead CAP Marines. The most significant bounties are for squad leaders and Marines that speak the Vietnamese language well. We all know of the bounty and joke about how little is offered for our respective heads.

I soon realize just how much the VC leadership is offended by our successful ambushes and public display of their dead comrades. For example, the battalion commander from Phu Bai (a colonel who served in the battle of Guadalcanal during WWII as a PFC) has issued an order demanding that every Marine shave daily. Later, he visited our compound to check for compliance. Witnessing a Marine with several days of beard growth, he demands an explanation. Before the unshaven Marine can speak, I interrupt. I tell the colonel that he has a skin condition aggravated by shaving. The colonel responds by saying, "Bullshit, have him shave every day."

Setting an example for the squad, I shave every morning at the same location using water in an inverted helmet and a small mirror hanging from a support beam outside of the sergeant's quarters. Big mistake! One beautiful morning, a bullet cracked the air just above my head. The rifle shot came from across the Song Nong River. A PF then squatting low to the ground let me know that the fired bullet was meant to kill me. The shot was taken at a range of just over 300 yards (very doable for a marksman). Once again, fate selected me to live. I immediately stop any activity that occurs at the same time and in the same place day after day.

The attempt to assassinate me is taken very lightly by the village chief, who makes no effort to identify the shooter. I suspect the village chief ordered the attempt on my life. He is under pressure from the VC to eliminate the Loc Bon Combined Action Platoon Marine leader. Our successes are his failures. I now believe that the VC have demanded that he, the village chief, find an internal solution to their problem. Yes, now I think the village chief of Lac Bon ordered my assassination.

I gained the ability to recognize internal threats and provide solutions that worked. I became a leader who led ever more by example; bullets to prostitutes – our lives were interdependent.

I transitioned to become aware that success itself is a danger. With success comes admiration and respect from those supporting you. From those opposing you, success creates anger and a desire for revenge. Continued success within the Village of Loc Bon requires me to strive for a level of abnormal maturity for a twenty-one-year-old man. Everyone is looking at me. I need to advance the attributes of leadership. Never have I been so aware; never have I been so alive; never have I been so lonely.

Request Assassination Order

The village chief of Loc Bon becomes more aggressive in his efforts to minimize any progress of encouraging the local population to support the South Vietnamese Government. He makes every effort to position us Marines between the VC and the villagers as though it is our war. He never blatantly confronts me or any other Marine living in his village, but his opposition has become obvious.

One of his tactics of resistance exposes my incompetence in speaking the Vietnamese language. The chief invites several Marines and PFs to a public outdoor gathering (think village meeting). I naively believe he is trying to show the villagers a level of cooperation between the local government, the PFs, and the Marines.

Standing on a raised platform, the village chief speaks to many villagers with much excitement and enthusiasm when he abruptly pauses and invites me to talk to the gathering. I foolishly accept, totally unprepared. Much of my Vietnamese language skills are just crude expressions learned by working with the PFs. The crowd is quite amused when I attempt to tell them how we are here to protect and help them. Translated, I said, "I like you very much. You are pretty. I will protect you. I no bullshit you!"

To make matters worse, as I am speaking, a loud noise arises from the back of the gathering that resembles a gunshot. My reflexes take control of my actions, and I quickly draw my 45-caliber pistol. Yes, I make a complete fool of myself. The villagers have a great laugh. Score one for the village chief; he has just undone three months of positive image building in a single setting. Unfortunately, everything we are trying to accomplish with Loc Bon's residents is being minimized by a VC operative who is also the village chief of Loc Bon.

Shortly after being publicly embarrassed by the Village Chief, Captain Broderick visits. He comes to the village to ask for a progress report of our efforts to win over the local government. Explaining that I believe the village chief is responsible for the recent assassination attempt on my life, I request permission to neutralize him once and for all. The captain reminds me that the South Vietnamese Government officials in Hue have already arrested him, tried him, and declared him innocent of all charges of being a VC operative.

The captain went on to say, "It would be sad if a Marine had an accidental discharge, you know if the village chief could be lured out to check the defensive positions of the compound one night and someone shot him." I replied, "Killing the village chief will be no different than killing any other VC. I will kill this man, but I need an official order to protect myself from the charge of unlawful killing." The captain replied that he could not issue such an order, "Assassination, regardless of how warranted, is illegal and will be prosecuted as murder."

The captain and I both realize that another solution, one within the law governing our actions, is required. The village chief went about his business as a VC operative unharmed by the U.S. government or its agents. Politicians worldwide are often above the laws that govern their subjects. Vietnam was no exception.

Most Powerful Compliment I Ever Received

The village compound receives a visitor, a Kit Carson Scout, who belongs to a unique program initially created by the U.S. Marine Corps. The scouts are prior Viet Cong or North Vietnamese soldiers who have defected and were recruited to work with Marine infantry units as intelligence scouts. Paid by the U.S. and treated as staff non-commissioned officers with a nominal rank (not official) of staff sergeant. (Wikipedia) Most of them switched their allegiance due to the medical treatment they received from the Americans after being severely wounded or suffering from malaria.

Not just any soldier that changed sides is accepted to serve as a Kit Carson Scout. They are first interviewed and then meticulously vetted to make sure they aren't double agents. The scouts were initially trained by the Viet Cong or the North Vietnamese Army and have fought against American and South Vietnamese forces. They understand in detail the military tactics as well as the political influence deployed against U.S. Forces. Very often, they walk among the enemy, going unnoticed in a crowd.

Our guest is low-key and requests to speak with me privately. I receive him in the sergeant's quarters, where we begin a long-detailed conversation about everything I can think to ask about the North Vietnamese and the Viet Cong. This man is educated and speaks English exceptionally well. The North Vietnamese have killed his family (wife and four children). He said, "Without proper cause." Whatever the Hell that means. He is enraged by their loss and is seeking unlimited revenge. The passion in my guest's voice and physical presence is undeniable; the man is on fire.

The Kit Carson Scout is armed with a beautiful pearl-handled 45-caliber pistol presented to him by the battalion commander for outstanding service to the Marine Corps. I asked, and he answered with in-depth knowledge question after question about the tactics, structure, and the nature of the North Vietnamese and the Viet Cong. This man is a professor of small unit counterguerrilla operations. Regardless of how well he performs as a scout, I thought his talents and knowledge could be best utilized by spending a few weeks with each CAP Platoon.

After an hour of conversation, he proposes a small unit assault mission beyond my previous CAP's tactical area of responsibility. "The VC are on low land adjacent to the east side of the Truoi River. I asked, "How can you be so sure of their presence"? "Because I walked among them several days ago." He went on to suggest that my squad would join forces with the two-squad CAP, later designated Hotel 8, located about one-quarter mile south of the Truoi River Bridge along highway one. We, the attackers, would land by chopper and surprise the enemy just before daybreak.

Feeling complimented by his request and realizing that he has been evaluating me, I accept his basic plan during our conversation. Only cautioning the approaching choppers' sound will alert the enemy. He agrees and asks for a solution. I suggest that one reinforced squad could use boats to reach the objective in darkness securing a landing zone protecting the choppers from unopposed ground fire. Both units would then join force and strike the VC.

I heard nothing more of our proposed plan for a week or so before receiving orders that my squad and a few men from my previous CAP squad would constitute the advanced landing unit using Vietnamese boats to cross the river in darkness. That may sound easy, but one of the uncontrollable risks is that we had no way of knowing if Vietnamese fishermen would be working the river the night of our crossing. If they detect us traversing the river, they will certainly sound the alarm. Coming under fire in Vietnamese boats means certain death. The choppers will have to land soon after we secure the LZ, and then the attack must begin immediately.

I am transported by jeep to the two-squad CAP, where I had briefly served as the NCO in charge of both squads and the platoon of PFs defending the village of Loc Dien. I brief the leaders and request three volunteers to join my team for the river crossing. For security reasons, the plan will not be presented to all the CAP Marines of either village until shortly before the operation.

Briefing the leaders, I explain the attack will consist of my squad from the village of Loc Bon crossing the river in Vietnamese boats and securing a helicopter landing zone for the two squads from the village of Loc Dien. Once on the ground, the two teams will join forces and attack. I ask for three volunteers. A black Marine who had served with me when I was the squad leader of Loc Dien raised his hand with several other Marines and volunteered to join my squad. Walking out of the briefing room, I ask him if he understands his just volunteered mission's inherent risks. His reply, I will never forget, by far, the most impactful compliment I have ever received. "This entire operation sounds undoable to me. But, if your river crossing is not successful, everyone on those choppers is dead. So, I'm sure if it all goes to Hell, you will die fighting. I will be pleased to die fighting next to you!"

The operation never takes place. I suspect the request for choppers and Vietnamese boats is denied as the operation is deemed too dangerous for men and aircraft.

The transitions of change are becoming scary. Within the last weeks, I have asked my commanding official to order me to assassinate the village chief of Loc Bon. I have also inspired men to volunteer to take a boat ride into Hell. I am no longer sure of who I am.

Defend A Captured VC Rice Cache

Late in the afternoon of a September cloudy and drizzly day, the Combined Action Platoon serving in Loc Bon's village receives a high priority coded message. Based on a daily changing phrase of keywords, called simple substitution, the sensitive transmission is secure. The decoded message orders me to lead a squad of Marines and PFs to a location defined by encoded map coordinates. Upon arrival, I am to take command of all personnel on-site. Uncharacteristically our ordered destination is beyond our tactical area of responsibility heading east into a flood plain dominated by acres and acres of submerged rice paddies. We don't know why we are being sent or what we should do when we get there.

I protect our only topographical map from falling rain by wrapping it in clear plastic as I use it to navigate towards the Song An CUU River that flows south from Hue city, heading towards Cầu Hai Bay (Cow Hi-Bay). The drizzly rain of the early afternoon changes to a steady downpour. We work our way across a maze of rice paddy dikes that provide the only land above the rising water.

Arriving at the assigned destination, we meet the CAP squad stationed in the village directly north of ours. Everyone has gathered around a large concrete building two stories high positioned on a circle of dry ground no more significant than sixty yards in diameter. The interior of the building is filled from top to bottom with rice. The other CAP squad has discovered a Viet Cong rice cache! The VC need a central storage point for all the rice they have extorted from the local population. Taking possession of their vast food cache is undoubtedly going to upset them.

Shortly after arriving, I send a message to our CAP commander in Phu Bai that our squad from Loc Bon is on the scene with five Marines and five PFs. My orders: protect the rice until the morning when, it will be moved by helicopter to a secure location. Headquarters suspects that a VC force of unknown strength is in the immediate area and intends to move the rice using the Song An CUU River as a highway.

I immediately inspect the surrounding terrain in which our guys are establishing defensive fighting positions. I become concerned. Flooded rice paddies surround the rice cache in its waterproof concrete building. Think island. Only a few rice paddies, dikes, and a small yard around the building are above water. The colossal defensive problem is that most of us can't dig fighting positions because the water table is too high. Without a means of getting our bodies below ground level, we are exposed to shrapnel and bullets. Some men can make a small trench to lay in, but most of us are entirely unprotected, just laying on our stomachs. Everyone forced to fight while lying in water built crude platforms by stacking mounds of rice paddy mud and muck to support their firearms. Once a firefight starts, our casualties are going to be high.

The VC will need to take the rice back tonight if they have any chance to recover it. The two CAP squads, totaling ten Marines and 10 PFs, stand between them and their food.

The rain falls with more intensity; it feels like buckets of liquid being poured over you. The wind picks up as total darkness engulfs us. The entire area gets weird, as though telling us to leave before it is too late. Contacting my commanding officer in Phu Bia, "Sir, after careful reflection, I consider the rice cache to be undefendable against an organized attack. I am requesting permission to blow holes in the roof of the building and expose the rice to the monsoon rains." The captain replies, "Request denied you are to hold your present position and defend the rice. I report, "Yes, Sir. We will be here in the morning, one way or another."

Within twenty minutes, Captain Broderick radioed me, " Phu Bai artillery is assigned to support you with pre-planned fire missions. On request, your unit will receive artillery support at pre-determined locations. Immediately call for illumination rounds at fire mission A, thru fire mission C to check for accuracy, adjust if required."

The firing data used to aim the artillery is determined by the artillery battery in Phu Bai from map coordinates surrounding our defensive positions that define exactly where we need the artillery shells. That's an enormous comfort; trying to accurately read a map in the pouring rain with a small light is difficult, especially when attacked. Requesting artillery support with incorrect map coordinates may kill us all with friendly fire.

It gets dark quickly; the wind begins to blow in gusts, further increasing the rain's intensity. Our ability to see and hear anyone approaching is minimal. I figure the VC will attack soon because after they destroy us, they will have a chore to move their rice cache, requiring many laborers and boats. All this will take time. The prevailing weather and visibility neutralize air support for us. In the Fall of 1966, there is no night vision equipment available to us or our supporting aircraft. By today's standards, the Vietnam War was low-tech. The incredible advances in electronics providing high-tech weapons are only a fantasy in late 1966. Tonight, the fight will be an up-close slug match with our assigned artillery as our only outside assistance against the VC's mortars, rocket-propelled grenades, and small arms.

Well, it didn't take long. About an hour after darkness, our lines are probed with small arms fire. The VC want to learn the exact locations of our defensive positions and determine how serious we are about holding the captured rice. They fail to understand that Marines don't get to pick their orders; they only follow them. We follow orders because the foundation of Marine training is and always will be to follow orders. Just that simple! We're not going anywhere. They are in for a fight.

I call for illumination rounds to be fired over our position, temporarily replacing the night's darkness with eerier slowing descending lights supported by parachutes. The light reflecting off the water comforts us with fantastic visibility exposing anyone advancing towards our position. Now, all we must do is shoot well. When the parachutes supporting the illumination rounds descend, their light fades, and we can't see beyond a few yards. The sound of gusty wind and falling rain drastically reduces our ability to hear. Without the intermittent illumination, we can't detect the approaching enemy until they stand immediately before us.

The spooky standoff between the CAP squads and VC is defined by the sounds of small arms fire and contrasting periods of illumination and darkness. The combination of occasional illumination and flooded mucky rice paddies make a mass attack by the VC difficult. However, as the night advances, time is on our side. Finally, after several hours, the VC realize they can't regain possession of their rice without a prolonged fight with a determined force supported by artillery.

As we hunker down in the mud and pouring rain, the night passes slowly, not knowing if the VC will punish us with a mortar attack. Daybreak comes gradually, but finally, it comes. Oh my God, it is magnificent! The rain stops, and the sun comes out, warming our souls. Never have I more appreciated the sun's gift of light and warmth.

Now, things get bizarre. The other CAP squad leader begins firing his M-79 grenade launcher into the adjacent rice paddy for no apparent reason.

He soon wounds one of his own PFs with shrapnel from his fired rounds. A water buffalo that has quietly spent the night in his small flimsy-built fenced-in area now becomes enraged and bursts through the fence and charges a group of Marines and PFs. One of my Marines shoots and kills the buffalo with a burst of his M14. A round ricochets off the ground and hits a Marine from the other squad in the butt (flesh wound). I will never forget his response as he grabs the throbbing wound. "You just shot me!"

All of this happens just as a helicopter carrying several officers from Phu Bai Combat Base arrives at the scene. One of the officers asks me how the PF and the Marine were wounded. I tell him, "Ask the Sergeant in charge of the other CAP Squad." I then ordered my squad to leave promptly. We just walk off and return to our sparsely defended village compound. God only knows what sequence of events was told to the officers by the remaining Marines and PFs.

I am one of the world's worst politicians. As the non-commissioned officer in charge (even though I was a Corporal, I was in charge), I should have given a complete account of all events. Well, that would have been terrible for the Sergeant of the other CAP Squad. I genuinely don't care what he reports. As far as I am concerned, mission accomplished. The discovered rice cache is protected from use by the enemy, and my guys are all alive!

Back in our village, we return to our routine of patrols, ambushes, and med calls. Eventually, everyone settles down and gets some needed rest. We hear nothing further about the rice mission.

A week or so later, Captain Broderick arrives and directs me to walk with him to a private area. "Congratulations, you've been promoted to sergeant E5!" I will never forget his words, "You can't spend a medal. And, besides, I've had to move you once because you were not a sergeant." He is referring to my first CAP assignment in the village of Loc Dien. A corporal E4 was insufficient to permanently lead that unit because it contained two CAP squads, requiring an E5 or above to be the non-commissioned officer in charge. Not to mention, I have been awarded a

$50.00 fine and a three-month suspended bust to lance corporal E3 during my first three weeks in Vietnam.

The captain is impressed with our CAP platoon serving in the village of Loc Bon. Pleased that we helped protect the discovered VC rice cache and the outstanding results of our ambushes and patrols. He suggests we gather all the Marines and present the other promotions he is holding. Great news until I learn the name of one of the men, about to be promoted to corporal E4. The Marine under consideration is not ready to assume the responsibilities of a non-commissioned officer serving in a Combined Action Platoon. Therefore, I object to his promotion. The captain seems disappointed but says that he will honor my request. I don't know how he handled the promotions after I left the CAP unit. You see, these men had already been promoted; they didn't know it yet.

I had just stepped on a great day for the squad with lots of promotions and everyone publicly respected for defending the rice cache, as well as the outstanding accomplishments of our ambushes and patrols.

So, why am I now such a hardass? Bottom line. I cared about these men, including our PFs. I felt strongly that one of the promotions would most likely cost someone their life. We are fighting a war. I would undoubtedly make the same decision today. I believe that all the men, including the man I objected to being promoted, eventually received their promotions. None of them knew that I delayed them.

What have I transitioned to while serving as a Marine non-commissioned office in combat for over a year? What kind of leader am I? My best answer: an old, seasoned man in a young man's body! My youth is forever over! I have become extremely serious and awakened a keen sense of comprehension that I previously didn't know I possessed. I have developed the ability to understand, in fine detail, the tactics of counterguerrilla warfare. I also realize I have a natural tendency for independence. Being off and away from the group as its leader feels normal. I enjoy not getting too close to anyone. I would spend the rest of my life striving for substance, character, and respect, often at the expense of not developing more effective social skills. I now realize a successful life stands on a foundation of people skills. We all need each other.

Cycle of Rice
Dinner with a Vietnamese Family

I have come to appreciate the rice cycle further; planting to harvest rice is the overwhelming focus of Vietnamese life. Our efforts in the village of Loc Bon to bring stability and a sense of belonging to and becoming a member of a democratic South Vietnam Government will require many rice cycles. Progress measured by the attitudes and loyalties of the inhabitants is slow but changing steadily. The bottom line, we are improving the security and well-being of their environment. We don't tell them how to live or how to govern themselves. Our success depends on Vietnam's people, creating a sense of loyalty to the South Vietnam Government. Patriotism to one's country first requires an existing country that you feel is yours. One that allows you to prosper and one you feel obligated to defend. In recent history, Vietnam has been controlled by foreign countries for over one hundred years, so defining patriotism is difficult. We are not Vietnamese, nor will we stay here as individuals. For South Vietnam to become an independent nation, our influence and efforts will need to continue for decades.

One obvious sign of our acceptance by the villagers living within our compound is how often we are regularly invited into their homes to share a meal. After months of living with the Vietnamese, our body's immune systems have adjusted to tolerate the local bacteria allowing us to eat the native foods without becoming ill. Without refrigeration, the flesh of fish caught early in the morning and sold at the open market in the afternoon from woven baskets were in a state of decay. Bacteria are ever-present. Water required to cook and prepare hot tea comes from the river without any processing to remove pollutants.

After six months of living with the Vietnamese, my body has adapted to their food, and I have learned their dinner customs. Yes, their customs and habits are often bizarre at first. What is different? Just about everything! The food generally has a strong and unpleasant smell. You most likely would not select any of it from a menu for its taste, smell, or visual presentation. Men get the most significant amounts of fish mixed with rice. Women receive the next largest portions and the children the smallest. After the meal, everyone rinses their mouth by swishing warm tea over their teeth and spitting the recovered food particles on the dirt floor[52]. As guests, we Marines can never allow ourselves to reject the customs of Vietnamese daily life. Once befriended, rejecting their traditions or food is considered an insult. Misconduct in their homes is not only unacceptable; it is dangerous. We can never forget how vulnerable and exposed ten Marines are living in a Vietnamese village. I have become accustomed to all the circumstances that may occur during dinner with a Vietnamese family. I think I have seen it all.

Bac Si, my good friend, my Vietnamese adviser, invites me to share an afternoon dinner with his family. Of course, I immediately accept his generous offer of hospitality. However, I don't know if his invitation is an act of friendship or another test of my trustworthiness. Yes, much can be determined by closely observing a dinner guest in any culture. Nevertheless, I sense something is about to happen between us. I hope he will share more information about the actual relationship between the Vietnamese living in the village of Loc Bon and the VC.

During dinner, Bac Si's bare-bottomed baby boy has a bowel movement. The Vietnamese pheasants do not use diapers of any type. No one seems alarmed as the mother supports the child at the hips allowing the infant to bend forward with its bottom facing out as it expels its runny bowels on the dirt floor. Everyone immediately begins to say the same words, "Cuie Cuie Cuie." To my surprise, the family dog springs to its feet before rushing to the supported baby to begin licking the infant's bottom. After the child is licked clean, the dog consumes all fecal matter remaining on the floor. Everyone smiles and continues the meal.

---

[52] **Researchers believe that antimicrobial molecules called "catechins" found in green tea** have the potential to kill bacteria associated with tooth decay and gum disease. As a result, green tea has the potential to prevent tooth loss and other oral health problems. www.nvwelldental.com › https://nvwelldental.com/4-benefits-of-green-tea-for-your-dental-health/

The smell of the bowel movement and the proximity of fecal matter to my food is extremely difficult to endure as it adds to the strange odor of the rice and soupy fish meal. Somehow, I continue to sit at the table, smile, and go on with the meal as though nothing has happened. My relationship with this family is one of mutual respect and interdependence. I have accepted their culture and customs.

However, I am confident the CAP Marines' relationship with the PFs needs to be more harmonious. Working together on ambushes and patrols is not enough to truly integrate the team. I now think we must eat the same foods and sleep in the same rooms, although neither the Marines nor the PFs desires total integration. For all of us to come together as one fighting force, it will require a boot camp that forces Marines and PFs to experience and share every aspect of life without options. An environment where we do everything together. One of the problems with such a solution is that we Marines will have to change much of what we call normal.

The overwhelming problems are language and control. How do you make Marines out of men from another country and culture who you can't effectively speak with and who you don't have complete control of? Regardless of the difficulty, we need to work harder to reach a level of overall acceptance between the PFs and the Marines to pierce the Vietnamese people's cultural veil. The PFs working with us can provide much more information about the VC if we can bridge the social divide that separates us. The school in Da Nang for the CAP Marines needs an extensive counterpart for the PFs.

Living and fighting with the Vietnamese have a profound effect on my view of the Vietnam War. I begin to see the PFs and other villagers as people, not Vietnamese people or gooks, just people. Yes, they are quite different in language, culture, and prosperity, but they have the same aspirations for their families as we do. Humans have much in common, regardless of language, skin color, or place of birth.

The villagers of Vietnam don't realize their country is ground zero for a much larger conflict than that of a divided Vietnam. The superpowers of the world are in a cold war, and Vietnam is a flashpoint. **Fear of all-out**

nuclear war with its potential to destroy humanity is an ever-present reality dictating the strategies of the Vietnam War.

Aggressive actions by the United States, the Soviet Union, or China are all restricted by the concept of assured mutual destruction. The people of Vietnam are fighting a war within a war. In my opinion, world leaders don't care about the people of North or South Vietnam; they are considered collateral damage. Most of us Marines will go home after our thirteen-month tours. The Vietnamese villagers will focus on the cycle of rice, planting to harvest.

State of Mind - Writing Poetry

The transitions of change are apparent in all the Marines serving in the village of Loc Bon. We can never totally relax mentally or physically. The pressure of never-ending patrols and ambushes is accumulative. Nevertheless, we all seem to change in our ways. Some Marines mature quickly into leaders learning to be measured in response to pressure and danger. Others become quick to anger and are resentful of the Vietnamese. A few seem more relaxed and appeared to enjoy the entire experience, always volunteering to walk point or lead night ambushes. Everyone's Vietnamese language skills improve, but several Marines become very proficient in their ability to speak with the villagers. Indisputably, everyone changes.

War, especially close contact warfare, will most definitely produce transformation. Your body and mind are challenged. The body, if not permanently damaged or disfigured, will restore itself. The mind is the challenge. The adrenaline surge of combat somehow imprints everything experienced into the deep crevices of your brain. Those potent memories will never altogether leave you. The residual emotions of combat will have to be managed, controlled, and channeled. Living in a hostile environment, one in which others desire to kill you, creates acute stress. After being bitten by a dog, it's natural to feel tension in the presence of other dogs. Well, after fighting for your life, it's natural to feel anxiety every time you see, hear, or smell anything that reminds you of the experience.

You now have a new source of energy that can empower or destroy you. Somehow you need to take the energy and release it positively—no running away from your mind. You must deal with this ever-present energy, channel it somehow because it's there. Easy to say. Difficult to accomplish. If you're not careful, the rest of society will see you as different. Some men never speak of their experiences seeking to be just like everyone else. Problem: you are no longer just like everyone else. Unreleased energy formed by powerful memories of combat can build to a dangerous potential causing erratic behavior! Suicide. Quick to anger. Broken relationships. Car crashes. Excessive everything, especially drinking and drugs. The residual energy must be personally confronted. But amazingly, this same mental energy, properly channeled, can propel you into a phenomenally successful life standing on a foundation of pride and accomplishment.

During the last two weeks of my deployment, a vivid example of my changed mindset came about in a strange and unprecedented manner, poetry! Yeah, that's what I said, poetry. One of the squad's ambushes and patrol leaders recounted his experience of a recent firefight with the VC during an ambush he led. He shared his incredible strong emotions with me, resulting from his additional responsibilities of leading Marines in close combat for the first time. He created within me an emotional wave when he reported that under the pressure of leadership during the exchange with the VC, he kept thinking, "What would Sergeant Mezick do"?

He went on to ask me to stop writing the letter I was composing on Bac Si's picnic table and write several lines of poetry. "Do what?" This man was either a college graduate or a college dropout who had studied English literature. Before this conversation, I hadn't known he'd ever attended college. I replied, "I have no idea how to write poetry. Listen, that's not my world." He calmly pushed a fresh sheet of paper in front of me and said, "Write what you feel inside, what you think about the most." Well, I'm sure what I wrote was not poetry, but it was a vivid portal in which to expose the mindset of a twenty-one-year-old Sergeant serving as a Combined Action Platoon leader in the twelfth month of his thirteen-month tour in Vietnam.

Don't Shy Away

What is death? No, don't shy away. Answer me. Why do some fear it? Does it not come to all? What lies behind those glassy eyes and cold limbs? Why can some smile while others lie with the face of horror? No, don't shy. Face the inevitable. Ha, you found the solution. You are obviously dead.

Fear

What is fear? We all have it. Some crumble from it, and some thrive with it. How can this be? Are not all men the same? Doesn't your chest tighten and your stomach throb as mine? Hasn't your life flashed through your brain in a second? Haven't you reached for a comforting thought and found none? Yes? Then you are a man among men. Lift your head with pride and guide those near you. They know not, fear.

I have transitioned to a mindset that has achieved some abnormal comprehension of death and fear. Humans are the only species that know they will die in the future.

Coming to some level of peace with the comprehension of death, fear, and sex at an early age is a huge advantage in life. Your mind is unburdened with those considerations allowing you to use all your mental resources to focus on whatever else you decide to think about.

Departure

My thirteen-month tour is about to come to an end. I have done my best not to dwell on my time "In Country" by constantly counting the days left before I will return home. Nothing positive comes from calculating time; the trick is to get into your work entirely. I don't announce to my squad that I am about to leave. It doesn't matter; everyone knows approximately how long everyone else has been "In Country." I am not due to leave until November 25th and write my wife to expect me home in mid-December.

Well, all this departure business comes crashing down when I am asked to join my captain, the company first sergeant, Bac Si, and the Vietnamese leader of the Biet Kichs, who are all standing next to the road across from Bac Si's pavilion. I approach the waiting group and exchange a short series of introductions and polite greetings. Then, Bac Si, my friend and often teacher, asks me to return to Vietnam after taking thirty days of leave to become the only Marine working with the Biet Kichs[53].

Sergeant Baker, the Biet Kich's previous coordinator, has not been replaced since he rotated back to the States several months ago. I am not sure that I understand Bac Si's request. My uncertainty must be evident because Captain Broderick repeats the offer. I thanked everyone and declined the proposal declaring I have a wife anxiously waiting for me to return and begin our life together with our baby daughter born last February during my current tour of duty. Everyone hearing my answer looks disappointed. The Captain, seeing the distress in Bac Si's facial expression, explains that the villagers, especially Bac Si, want me to continue working with or close to the village of Loc Bon. He says, "It's not just the villagers who wish to you to stay; everyone does.

Bac Si's deflated demeanor shows he feels betrayed and abandoned. Because he aided our CAP unit, especially me, his future is forever bound to the U.S. and South Vietnamese Governments. When I asked him for help, he came to my aid. Now he is asking me for help, and I am refusing it. I feel terrible, ashamed, and embarrassed. I also feel the responsibility and love I have for my wife and daughter. With everyone looking at me, I repeat my refusal of their request to return to Lac Bon. Captain Broderick looks at me with a stern expression and replies, "You have earned the confidence of the leadership of this village, and they not only want you to return but feel that they need you to return."

---

[53] **The Biet Kichs were the special, all-Vietnamese force** that used our village as one of its rest stations. Yeah, they would rest up before and after their operations, and some of these operations took weeks to complete.

With a lump in my throat and a tear in my eye, I shake my head and softly respond, "No, I can't." Bac Si is the first to walk away. I am never to see or hear from him again.

Not ever forgetting that awful feeling I experienced the day I left the Village of Loc Bon, I strive never again to disappoint anyone who accepts my leadership or depends on me. To fulfill such a promise, I will need a moral compass and a clear mind.

I am instructed to gather my gear and mount a waiting jeep to transport me to the Marine Combat Base in Phu Bai. No longer the squad leader of Loc Bon, I realize that a five-hundred-pound boulder of responsibility has been removed from my back. The last Marine from Loc Bon I ever see from that day to this is a corporal, one of our best patrol and ambush leaders. He traveled to the Phu Bai Marine Combat Base to return the wallet I left in the village. I am embarrassed for him to see how happy I am.

Yes, I began to realize that I am done with Vietnam. Well, that's what I thought at the time. The truth is you are never done with Vietnam. The overwhelming memory of leaving was when the transport plane's wheels lifted from the tarmac and powered its way through the low-hanging clouds. I then felt relief—no negative thoughts of any kind. Whatever I had to contribute, whatever I could learn, whatever I could withstand, I'd given it all. Flying at hundreds of miles an hour into the first day of the rest of my life, I felt so young; I felt so old. I had transitioned to another me—a man I no longer understood. I felt immensely proud, confident, and a bit frightened by the new me.

After arriving in Okinawa, we are immediately processed through an inspection that checks every item in our possession. Everyone is instructed to surrender all clothing worn or equipment used in Vietnam. The U.S. government is making sure that none of us are bringing back the tools of war. Good idea. No one needs to return with a grenade or claymore mine in their sea bag. But, when a corporal demands that I hand over my Jungle Jacket, the one with a bullet hole in the left sleeve at the heart level, I object. He doubles down with increased intensity, insisting that I hand the jacket to him. I inform him that my battalion commander has permitted any Marine to keep forever any non-lethal government equipment that has been struck by enemy aggression. Our conversation escalates loudly.

The corporal is relentless in his effort to take possession of my only tangible connection to Operation Oregon. Finally, the staff sergeant in charge comes to my rescue, "Corporal, use some common sense before you get your ass kicked. Maybe you would better understand if you had been the one wearing the Jungle Jacket when the bullet went through it." The corporal is visibly moved and utters one word, "Sorry."

Okinawa is one colossal party. We drink and laugh and feel close to everyone around us. No, for the most part, we hadn't known one another previously, but we are all beyond our tours in Vietnam. We are bonded by the experiences of war and the brotherhood of the Marine Corps. At the PX in Okinawa, I purchase a diamond ring for my wife. The ring she never received before our hasty wedding, hoping it would adequately fit her finger.

A day or so later, I sit comfortably in a civilian jet heading for Travis Airbase in California. During the long flight, I begin to think of life with my wife and daughter in complete detail. I form possible plans for the next chapter of our lives. During my time in Vietnam, I occasionally focused on the love and responsibility of the two most important people in my life. However, planning in detail would have been too much of a distraction.

I am full of self-confidence and a bit arrogant. Good. I will need every bit of this self-esteem to deal with my next challenge, the cruel treatment from fellow Americans—the protesters against the Vietnam War.

My first encounter with such anger and open hostility occur during my arrival on U.S. soil. A man sitting on the ground next to the main entrance into the air terminal dressed in strange clothes with long dirty hair asks me if I am proud of the people I killed in Vietnam. I replied, "Excuse me, what did you say"? "You know, all the babies, women, and children you slaughtered."

At first, I am confused, utterly confused, and leave him as I enter the doorway to the air station. In a loud voice, I call out to a group of Marines in the immediate area and ask them to explain what the hell's going on. No one knows, but everyone thinks we should ask him to repeat what he has just said. He is gone. He had, as I later discovered, completed his mission: insult Marines returning from Vietnam. Yes, he made a compelling effort to shame me for my service. I soon forgot the incident, thinking it was just a weirdo, certainly not someone representing a significant movement in my country. I was wrong and soon realize that there was yet another way a Marine could die. Death by civilian!

Meeting my wife at Philadelphia Airport is surreal; I barely recognize her, the driving force of my life. I feel distant and out of place, unable to allow my underlying emotions to surface as though they are a sign of weakness. Arriving at Diana's home, her parents warmly welcome me before presenting my baby daughter. I feel extreme emotion and love for my child, but I can't express my feelings or even touch my baby girl. I am afraid to hold our child. I don't know how to hold a baby. Finally, after a long pause, I utter just a few words; "That's a nice one."

EPILOGUE

Trust me, the mindset of a Marine returning from war is a universe of distance from that of a compassionate, loving, and tender father. Combat requires you to shift into an altered state of mind. However, returning to a non-combat environment, without violence or fear, where you don't carry a rifle or grenades, also requires a mental shift. Regaining a non-combatant mindset that allows you to relax and stop thinking of killing and dying is much more complicated than you may realize. After returning from Vietnam, I had to endure an involuntary distraction. While family and friends spoke to me in everyday conversation, having nothing to do with Vietnam, I would peer into their faces and imagine how they would look dead.

My last military duty station was Marine Corps Base Quantico, located in the state of Virginia. My promotion to the rank of sergeant intitled Diana and me to base housing. After thirty days of leave as a guest in my in-law's home, Diana and I packed our recently purchased used car and a small U-Haul trailer and headed south to our new duty station during a snowstorm.

To my extreme displeasure, I was assigned to work at the base brig, the jail, as "Sergeant of the Guard." Bad news, now I will have to dress in the uniform of the day, every day, with my brass belt buckle and shoes shined to perfection. After a lance corporal handed me my orders, I requested permission to speak with the major who issued my assignment. I explained that I have in-depth experience with counterguerrilla warfare and believe that I will be an asset teaching other Marines the fine points of small unit tactics, especially ambushes. My request was denied.

My new assignment was a blessing, a perfect opportunity to mentally adjust to my new life, one that included my wife and daughter. Guard duty was quite different than serving as a grunt in the infantry. Diana and I enjoyed our military accommodations, a recently built beautiful townhouse. Here at Marine Base Quantico, Diana, our baby, and I became a family preparing ourselves for life after the Marine Corps.

Now, I need a job! Unfortunately, civilian life offered very few employment opportunities for a man with my skill set other than law enforcement. However, a Navy Chief serving as a supervisor at the brig suggested that I study air conditioning and refrigeration because you can always find work in that profession. In addition, the U.S. Government offered an array of home study courses to active armed forces members, making it easy to launch my new career.

Diana and I decided not to accept her parent's generous offer to live with them while attending a technical school in Philadelphia, Pa. We were now a functioning family and thought better about returning to our former neighborhood. With a certificate awarded after completing the refrigeration and air conditioning course, I applied and was hired as an appliance technician at General Electric Company in Northeast Washington, D.C.

After two years of service and turning down an offer to train as a manager, I quit my job at GE and used the GI Bill to attend a two-year, one-hundred-week technical school studying to become an electronic technician. Diana and I both worked while our daughter was in daycare. Yes, our days started early and ended late. I worked every evening after school and every Saturday for three dollars an hour as an appliance technician for a privately owned GE Appliance Store adjacent to the technical school. The job paid poorly but provided me with a van I could use full time. Repairing GE appliances created a daily hands-on lab class for my first semester studying electricity's fundamental principles.

The technical school's two-year program took two and a half years to complete because so many of the original students dropped out, requiring those of us who remained to wait six months for the class behind us to catch up. During my six-month interruption, I used the skills I learned in the first year of school to work as a TV technician for Sears and Roebuck Co.

After returning to school to complete my last year, I continued to work for Sears and Roebuck every weekday evening and every Saturday. The hours were long, but the practical experience was an invaluable extension of my education.

During my final year of technical school, I passed the U.S. Government's First-Class Federal Communication Exam, allowing me to service commercial radio and television high-power transmitters. Upon graduation, I went to work for Motorola Company as a communication technician, and I also taught a night course featuring television technology two nights a week.

After two years of working for Motorola, I was offered an opportunity to open and manage a Motorola Communication Service Center in Lancaster, Pa. The offer was well-received, but it meant that I would be making a career change. So before accepting a new position, I searched the Washington, D.C., area to find high-paying technical employment.

As fate would have it, one of my Motorola Communications clients, NBC News Bureau / NBC Channel 4, needed technicians in NW Washington, DC. The first generation of electronic cameras began replacing film cameras in the mid-1970s, and that meant highly skilled component-level electronic technicians were in demand. That's me with just one small problem. I had no experience working in a TV station, let alone a large network bureau. I was hired with conditions; I must resign from my teaching position, and I had ninety days to prove myself in the job description for which I had been employed. During that time, if declared unacceptable, I could be let go without explanation.

That's when I began studying technology as never before, and I continued to study for the next thirty-five years until I retired. In addition to other assignments, I traveled worldwide as technical support for press crews reporting on U.S Presidents. A career in technology is demanding. You are required to stay current with your rapidly changing profession, or you soon become obsolete.

So, where did I get all the energy to propel myself from a Marine grunt to a highly compensated member of NBC News. I used the residual energy from my war experiences as fuel to comprehend the broadcast industry's ever-changing technology. Real-time technical problems preventing traveling journalists from delivering their news packages through narrow satellite time windows created enormous pressure for those trying to troubleshoot extraordinarily complex electronic equipment and systems. Yes, this job's stress was unavoidable, but not the kind of anxiety created by professional soldiers trying to kill you. My learned ability to focus and perform under stress in combat made a pressure reference point that easily endured my new profession's tension.

Yes, I focused on providing for my family by emerging myself into high-pressure assignments that others wouldn't or couldn't do. That journey had many challenges as the underlying emotions of war often surfaced. Yet, somehow, I used my learned discipline and self-confidence while serving in the Marine Corps to succeed in every endeavor I attempted.

Diana and I have now been married for more than fifty-five years. Born during my Vietnam tour, our first daughter graduated from Georgetown University Law School in Washington, D.C. Born eleven years after our first, our second daughter graduated from the Fashion Institute of Technology in New York City, NY.

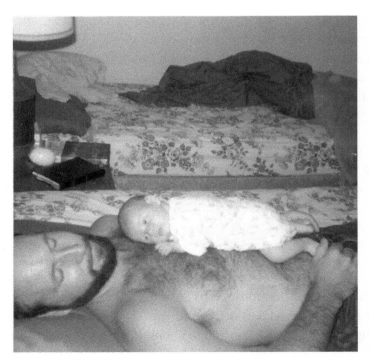

The joy of experiencing the birth of our second daughter
eleven years after Vietnam.

I have found joy in many different activities, from training bird dogs and hunting them in the Dakotas, studying forestry, and volunteering to be the forestry chairman of the Bethesda Chevy Chase Chapter of the Izaak Walton League's Conservation Farm's 491 acres of woodlands. After thirty-five years of continuous service, I continue to volunteer to work with the Maryland Department of Natural Resources, teaching Hunter Safety Courses. In addition, I have provided an "Interpretative Walk In The Woods" for over 1,000 Poolesville High School Global Ecology Students and became a Certified Group Fitness Instructor at 70 and a Certified Personal Trainer at 71. I am a member of the American Legion, the Veterans of Foreign Wars, the CAP Unit Veterans Association, and the First Battalion, Fourth Marines Association.

Never forgetting how blessed we are to be born in the United States of America and how life can end in an instant, I endeavor to live every day as though it is my last. I never want to meet Marines in the life hereafter, who died young, and tell them that I made a mess of my opportunity. Instead, I will share my story of prosperity, how I enjoyed a loving family in a beautiful home surrounded by friends.

BYRON A. MEZICK

Lightning Source UK Ltd.
Milton Keynes UK
UKHW042134301221
396421UK00007B/370/J